Cinema and Desire

Cinema and Desire

Feminist Marxism and Cultural Politics in the Work of Dai Jinhua

◆————————

DAI JINHUA

Edited by
JING WANG and TANI E. BARLOW

VERSO
London · New York

First published by Verso 2002
Collection © Jing Wang and Tani E. Barlow 2002
Translation © the translators
All rights reserved

2 4 6 8 10 9 7 5 3 1

Verso
UK: 6 Meard Street, London W1F 0EG
USA: 180 Varick Street, New York, NY 10014–4606

Verso is the imprint of New Left Books
www.versobooks.com

ISBN 1–85984–743–9
ISBN 1–85984–264–X (pbk)

British Library Cataloguing in Publication Data
A catalogue record for this book is available from the British
Library

British Library Cataloging-in-Publication Data
A catalog record for this book is available from the Library of
Congress

Typeset by M Rules
Printed by Biddles Ltd, Guildford and King's Lynn
www.biddles.co.uk

Contents

Acknowledgments

We are grateful to all of the translators, who worked at a demanding pace, to bring Dai Jinhua's difficult, sometimes tortured, Chinese analytic prose into able, accurate, and meaningful English. To Dai Jinhua herself, we are indebted for her collaboration and her provocative creativity. To Perry Anderson, we would like to express our appreciation of his enthusiastic support for this project. We thank Colin Robinson, his staff at Verso Press, and especially Megan Hiatt, our copy editor, for seeing this volume to fruition.

Our deep affection goes to Donald M. Lowe and Candy Wei for their love and support. Thanks go as well to friends in Durham (Leo Ching, Laura Tran, Benjamin White, Christopher Estes, and as always, Bess Autry) and in Seattle (Resat Kasaba, Tamiko Nimura, Jonathan Lawson, and Carol Langdon) who have contributed to our wellbeing during this book's preparation.

We want particularly to acknowledge the help of Elizabeth Browning, who coordinated the production, Amy Feistel, who compiled the English bibliography, Jonathan Lawson, who made the index, and Tamiko Nimura, who proofed the final galley. All Chinese bibliographical materials were provided by Dai Jinhua herself and her graduate assistants Wang Chang and Yu Hongmei. Our special thanks to Wang Chang for coordinating the Beijing end of the project and translating the list of Dai's published work. Mary J. Saucier helped with a technical problem.

Funds for producing the volume were provided by the Arts and Science Research Council of Duke University and the international studies unit of the Jackson School of International Studies, at the University of Washington in Seattle.

Chapter 6, "Redemption and Consumption: Depicting Culture in the 1990s," first appeared in *positions: east asia cultures critique*, vol. 4, no. 1 (spring 1996), pp. 127–43. The text of chapter 8, "Invisible Writing: The Politics of Mass Culture in the 1990s," first appeared in *Modern Chinese Literature and Culture*, vol. 11, no. 1 (spring 1999), pp. 31–60.

Dai Jinhua would like us to acknowledge Mayfair Mei-hui Yang for first introducing her work to the English-speaking world.

Last but not least, we would each like to thank the other for undertaking this project in such a joyful and wondrous spirit.

Jing Wang
Tani E. Barlow

Introduction

Dai Jinhua has taken contemporary Chinese cultural criticism by storm. In the last decade she has made her mark on several intellectual fronts: as a feminist Marxist, film scholar, and media critic. Having established herself on the domestic and global lecture circuits as a public intellectual and an academician, Dai reaches out to audiences ranging from the students of Peking University to fellow members of the international academic communities of film studies, cultural studies, and women's studies. An extraordinarily rigorous conversationalist, Dai Jinhua captivates a lay audience whenever she appears on TV, be it in Beijing, Hong Kong or Taipei.

This brief introduction locates Dai Jinhua's unique, radical position in Marxism, feminism, and cultural studies. Dai aligns herself with the New Left, which, in 1990s China, consists of a small handful of cultural elites who insist on recalling Mao's Cultural Revolution as an abortive utopia produced by a collective vision and not as simply an episode of arbitrary violence attributable to the whims of one dictator. In its search for this lost ideal, the New Left is critical of both the Chinese state and the new mainstream liberal intellectuals, arguing that they collude to intensify the privatization of the Chinese economy and to depoliticize culture. From within this scissor-hold Dai Jinhua defines her intellectual mission in specific terms: she questions the social legitimacy of consumer culture in China, while problematizing the elitist lineage of Western Marxism and reflecting on Chinese styles of intellectuality during the 1980s. This simultaneous critique of both the discourse of modernity and of the agendas informing China's recent emphasis on globalization requires her to reenvision the history of China in the twentieth century.

Dai also aligns herself with the broad-based Chinese feminist movement, which united briefly and uneasily in 1995, when Beijing and Huairou hosted the United Nations Fourth International Conference of Women. Typical, perhaps, of a line of feminist cultural and literary critics stretching back to the end of the nineteenth century, Dai Jinhua reembodies her own maternal grandmother's livid discontent with the lot of women and belongs to an inheritor generation of feminists. Her intellectual lineage can be traced, in part, to the political theories of the Chinese Enlightenment and, in part, to the great revolutionary transformation of social relations of gender in New China. With other well-known contemporaries such as Li Xiaojiang, Meng Yue, Liu Bohong, Wang Anyi, Liu Huiying, and Zhang Jie, Dai has reconnoitered the pre-Communist conventions of Chinese feminism and helped to initiate and nurture a post-Mao feminist moment that has had a profound impact on the high- and middle-brow female intellectual worlds.

In a culture that habitually employs political name-calling to stigmatize dissenters, critics have indicted Dai Jinhua for a range of conflicting ideological misdemeanors. Ironically, because she and the New Left critics are interested in reinventing the Marxist analytical category of class and calling attention to the social problems arising from capital's uneven accumulation and distribution, Chinese liberals regularly castigate them and accuse Dai of colluding with the Party-State's ruling ideology. To complicate this picture, Dai Jinhua is a feminist whose thought is informed by poststructuralism; she is fully committed not just to the delegitimation of masculinist cultural imaginaries, but also to the eradication of the essentialist woman from feminism. This intersection of neo-Marxism and feminism complicates her political commitments. Dai is a consistently disloyal feminist, telling one reporter that feminism is a broad movement toward female self-consciousness and culture, of which women's movements and civil rights struggles form only one part.[1] (And, she implies, not even a part that requires the agency of women.) Consistently, what engages Dai as feminist praxis is a Sisyphean effort to bring what she calls women's experience and consciousness onto "the horizon of history" (*lishi dibiao*). Wonderfully lacking in optimism, she counsels bluntly that the struggle to tear away the powerful ideological garment of male-dominated cultural discourses will involve difficult and unremitting deconstructive cultural criticism; for the forces of essentialism that are embedded in more institutional forms of feminism, like the seductive forces of consumer culture and political disillusionment, are powerful adversaries.

So a poststructuralist feminist Marxist like Dai finds herself constantly at a crossroads. Rather predictably, the upholders of Chinese Marxist orthodoxy have frowned on her persistent introduction of gender into class analyses of social issues like labor and unemployment; while state feminists find that her anti-essentialist theoretical position subverts their pet projects, which are often supported by the international donor agencies that are currently bankrolling both the middle-brow women's studies movement and some of its social service outreach programs, such as hot lines, advice manuals, and the popular self-help health movements.

This volume is entitled *Cinema and Desire* to emphasize Dai Jinhua's disciplinary commitment to film studies. Dai entered the terrain of cultural criticism as a film critic, and it is through film history that she intends to chart China's cultural geography. But her path has been circuitous. The much acclaimed and frequently reissued book Dai wrote with Meng Yue (a colleague at Peking University, now a historian in California), *Fuchu lishi dibiao* (Emerging on the horizon of history), introduced Lacanian feminist literary criticism to China and set out to reclaim the Chinese tradition of feminist and feminine écriture narratives.[2] This influential book is both a primer of Lacanian feminism and a reiteration and consolidation of the feminist critique of women's fiction in China. In her work with Meng Yue, Dai Jinhua laid down the foundation of her own Lacanian Marxian perspective on literature, history, and female subject-formation.

Dai's academic work situated her as a major force in cinema studies. Her exemplary oeuvre merges film criticism into multiple critiques of modernity and orientalism, examining cinema as a poetics of ambivalence hovering over formalist carnivals and historico-ideological spectacles. This multifarious approach exposes the Fifth Generation's predilection for an imaginary, primeval past of retrograde ideological formations contradictorily cast in modernist aesthetics. In equally iconoclastic vein, Dai also attempts to unsettle the emergent myth of the Sixth Generation by unraveling the dangerous cultural politics of indigenity and internationalism. Her work demonstrates brilliant insights into China's cinema tradition that are inseparable from both the political legacy of Maoism and the current postcolonial order of cultural knowledge. Those early signs of an intertwined formalist and ideological analysis came to blossom later, in the latter half of the 1990s.

Dai Jinhua's profile as a public intellectual is similar to that of Susan Sontag, while her commitment to cinema studies corresponds to that of Laura Mulvey and the Marxist feminists who coalesced around the British journal *Cinema*. But in recent years, Dai's critical framework has expanded even further to allow for a reading of film not simply as a textual signifier in itself, or merely as a commercial or technological industry, but also as a cultural field scored by both elite and popular discourse.

Dai Jinhua dates her entry into cultural studies proper from the moment she realized the limitations of film theory for thinking about film as a cultural product. Leaving behind both the literary Lacanianism that had marked her earlier explorations of the traditions of women's fiction and the political preoccupation with the modernity project that had gripped her and other Chinese intellectuals through-out the eighties,[3] Dai has moved to a more Marxian appreciation of cinema's complexity as technology, practice, imaginary. Her highly personal quest has coincided for the most part with the larger histor-ical transition of the mid 1990s, in which Chinese urban society entered a new era of consumer hedonism. The traumatic memories of 4 June 1989 and all the utopian visions that had leavened the intelli-gentsia's cause of Enlightenment were left behind. Consequently, Dai's awareness of a need to engineer a methodological breakthrough coin-cided with her recognition of the ineluctable challenge that the new, booming popular culture was posing to the elite corps of intellectuals, whose understanding of "culture" has, for the most part, confined itself to the domain of high-brow literary intellectuality, more often than not excluding the cultures of mass consumption.

Significantly, Dai is one of the few humanists willing to wade through a genuine legitimation crisis and emerge, renewed, to pose a fresh agenda, one in which critical engagement with popular culture is a priority. Calling for a Chinese cultural studies that takes into account the anthropological meaning of culture, viewing it as a way of life (the sum total of lifestyle, sociopolitical systems, and symbolic and economic activities of everyday life), Dai pays homage to Raymond Williams's pioneering intervention in cultural criticism, and, in our view, displaces the increasingly reified meaning of cultural studies – a marketing category for university presses – current in Western academic life today. Dai Jinhua seeks to return cultural studies to the lost intellectual moment when agenda and praxis were more valuable than theory. She pushes us forward towards another horizon, by grounding a critical exercise in the local before it inevitably crystallizes into yet another globalized theory.

Dai Jinhua identifies two traps for Chinese cultural studies: the deeply engrained elitist stance of China's cultural workers on the one hand and the alluring image of China's membership in the "global village" on the other. To harbor the fantasy that China is striding alongside the West and to celebrate the total immersion of China in transnationalism is to commit the common fallacy of cultural translation, which disregards the uneven power relations embedded in transcultural negotiation and traveling theories. It also fails to take into account the multiple localities of "China," as well as their multifarious experiences with globalization, and the intricate web of their unequal relations with each other. Because Dai Jinhua is so conscious of the intertwining of the politics of power and the agendas of globalized theory, she is skeptical of the crash-and-burn theory prevalent in Western discourses of China's tumultuous 1980s. In her vision, a Chinese cultural studies must be grounded in genuine historical studies. A first step must be the thorough reassessment of Chinese intellectual traditions and the reconstruction of a history of Chinese problematics.[4] Constantly Dai stresses critical self-reflection and warns against the all-out negation of the immediate historical past, hinting at the huge price that the modern Chinese have paid for the radical breaks advocated by first the May Fourth intellectuals, later, Maoists and now, anti-Maoists. By combining a scholarship grounded in the locale and history of China, positioned to engage meaningfully with theorists of other locales, with a crusader's passion for intransigent social critique, Dai Jinhua is a practising contemporary scholar, public intellectual, and critic all at once.

From her early film studies to her most recent critiques of contemporary pop culture, this volume presents Dai Jinhua's multiple theoretical moves toward writing difference into the Euro-American discourses current in China today; it is an account of both her interrogation of mainstream Western theories and her eventual flight from them. She searches for a theoretical strategy that enables her to narrate critically the intellectual and gendered film history and culture of the post-Mao and post-Deng eras without sacrificing it to the orientalizing gaze of the West.

In chapter 1, Dai Jinhua captures the artistic dilemma of the Fifth Generation of directors in one of her favorite expressions, *taotuo zhong de tuowang* (fleeing from one trap while falling into another). Characterizing the Fifth Generation as Sons escaping from the Name of the tyrannical Father and his ubiquitous discourses, Dai tells how directors like Chen Kaige and Zhang Yimou, in their conflicting attempts at transcendence, represent the ruptures of history and consequently are destined to fall into the aporia of language and representation. Their interrogation of the Cultural Revolution is an act of patricide that casts them outside the Symbolic Order into aphasia. The powerful chanting of the schoolchildren's song, "There once was a mountain, on the mountain was a temple," in *Haiziwang (The King of Children)* best illustrates the tragedy of the Father-Son succession and the circularity of patriarchal historicality. The flight from historical and linguistic cycles describes the real story of the Fifth Generation, which is that of their journey as spiritual (self-)exiles. Chapter 2 demythologizes the international aura surrounding the Fifth Generation. Dai Jinhua situates film production in the 1990s and the work of auteurs such as Zhang Yimou and Chen Kaige in an intense moment of postcolonial cultural politics, played out among the indigenous vanguard filmmakers, European film-festival culture, and Western market logic.

Dai's use of the term "postcolonialism" calls for a note of clarification as it has different nuances from those current in the Anglo-Asian circuit of "Western" theory. "Postcolonialism" in her context has a double reference. It refers to a benign form of Western colonization, a civilized aggression greeted with ambivalence by the local elite. More interestingly, Dai uses this term to describe the peculiar cultural condition of the Fifth Generation from the late 1980s to the mid 1990s. She places the burden of Western cultural imperialism on the "colonized" – in this case, directors such as Zhang Yimou and Chen Kaige – unpacking the complex process of their adoption of Western cinematic aesthetics and their simultaneous entrapment in an orientalism that internalizes the fantasy of the Other/West for an imaginary China that is pre-modern, a splendid spectacle of exoticism and an ancient land ruled by repressed desire. Her assessment of this postcolonial turn in the filmic texts is fraught with ambiguities. She does not downplay the importance of viewing this courtship of cultural colonialism as first and foremost a historical opportunity embraced wholeheartedly by China's avant-gardists in their perilous flight from nineties commercialism.

Chapter 3 extends this reading to the Sixth Generation of directors against the backdrop of the mutually constitutive politics of European film-festival cultures and the Chinese state censors. Tracing the rise of the Sixth Generation as forerunners of the Chinese independent filmmaking industry, Dai maps out the cyclical drama of the birth of a marginal discourse and the reification of its own radicalism through its march toward the center in search of international recognition.

Though it is perhaps less explicit in earlier than in later chapters, the criticism Dai calls postcolonial is saturated with feminist analytics. The conceptual apparatus of the discourse of the Name of the Father and the riddles of the patronym, the bridges that the Sons build over the chasms of historical misogyny are all deeply etched in feminist acid. When Dai turns directly to problems of gendered writing of the film text and latent writing about female subjectivity in the films of women and male directors, this implicit stream of feminist criticism surfaces into a limpid and explicit exegesis. Chapter 4, "Gender and Narration," offers an overview of the female problematic in three historical eras, the Seventeen-Year Era of the "worker, peasant, soldier" policy for cultural work, 1949–66; the post-Cultural Revolution outbreak of 1976–89, which saw a restoration of male dominance; and the contemporary era of bleak and unremitting commercialization, in which the "women's film" is a reinscription of bourgeois gendered norms onto a cinematic terrain where Fifth and Fourth Generation filmmakers inscribe women as tangential, the objects of men, and men as triumphal subjects.

Both here and in chapter 5, an elegant homage to Huang Shuqin's *Ren, gui, qing* (*Human, Woman, Demon*), which Dai calls the only Chinese feminist film ever made, Dai demonstrates how the Maoist ideology of gender equality camouflaged a socialist impasse that did not so much emancipate as masculinize women. Yet she also argues that the contemporary return to gender difference has once again reinstated women as the weaker sex. In "Gender and Narration," Dai shows us how each reiteration of woman – from Hua Mulan's masculinized women to the humanist trope of the post-revolutionary subject to the feminine object under the patriarchal male gaze – is subject to the historical imperative of the reigning era. Throughout her account of the mutually constitutive relationship between gender and politics, Dai gives a nuanced reading of Maoist state feminism, chipping away at both the fetish and the latter-day stigma surrounding the historical problematic, thus returning it to an open-ended sign whose contemporary meaning is highly ambiguous.

Chapter 5's prolonged examination of Huang Shuqin's work provides a critical reading of the alternative available to the formulaic women's films that are congesting contemporary commercial cinema. For modern Chinese women find themselves at a crossroads, in a world where the female desire for self-expression is canceled out by the eventual silence that her social role as an object dictates: a woman (Qiuyun in *Human, Woman, Demon*) can play an ideal man on stage, but the very loss and absence of the male sex in her life offstage dooms her to a life of lack. In the hands of the feminist director Huang Shuqin, the discourse of a modern Chinese woman's predicament is saved from its own fatalism by the self-conscious female perspective within which her own story is told. Perhaps even more significantly, an act of subversion is materialized in Huang Shuqin's use of a classical discourse to deconstruct gendered classical images.

In chapter 6 Dai's focus narrows a bit as she gazes unblinkingly at the problems that "main melody" or propaganda films pose in the disenchanted era of post-Mao commercial culture for a globalizing "socialism with Chinese characteristics." The current de-apotheosis of a decoded and humanized Mao Zedong, whose visage and memory are bathed in the warm commercial wash of nostalgia called Mao fever, is recoded in a wholly transformed landscape. Here gendered subjects are made to seem irrelevant, in a brave new world where consumption and urbanity replace ideology and personal memory. From this dismal cultural scenario Dai extracts a mournful qualification that requires some sense of the sacred in order for a sacerdotal politics to return and animate the call for justice, and a reversal of deepening social inequality, painted over or, using another of her favorite analytic metaphors, bridged, to the mainstream discourse of Mao Zedong fever.

Chapter 7 takes a searching and extended look at the movies of Fifth Generation auteurs whose archaic *mise en scènes* have so delighted Western viewers. Zhang Yimou's *Ju Dou, Hong gaoliang* (*Red Sorghum*), and *Da hong denglong gao gao gua* (*Raise the Red Lantern*) and Chen Kaige's *Bian zou bian chang* (*Life on a String*) are subjected to the same acidic scrutiny as the feminist film *Human, Woman, Demon*. Dai measures the representational code of gendered film relations in Zhang Yimou against the literary texts that he cannibalized for his cinematic compositions and suggests that the doubled mediation "ruptures" the signified, situating the wound of forced modernity in its proper place. If the literary texts enabled Chinese readers and littérateurs to reach over the multiple breaches in the historical Real opened during the twentieth century, the depletion of literature and the rupture of literary signification in the contemporary filmic representations by the Fifth Generation drive history, Dai argues, further into exile.

One of the persistent themes in Dai's work that we have sought to highlight is the effect of corrosive consumerist culture on the tentative, albeit profoundly misogynistic, avant-garde elite culture of the 1980s. In chapter 8, "Invisible Writing: The Politics of Mass Culture in the 1990s," this thematic is delicately worked through the genealogy of a space called the *guangchang* or the plaza. In part a debate with Fredric Jameson over dialectics, in part an effort to transform theoretical Chinese through the tactical use of saturated, peripheral, twisted analytics, the essay also handily shows how the spaces in advertising images are signaling an openness to sharing and cooperation that actually forecloses all possibility of a political culture based in refusal, rights, political vision. Happy shoppers in the placid "shared spaces" of capital are collusive, displacing the space of politics – Tiananmen Square – as the shopping mall – the space of consumption for those who would rise above the mass to dominate and obscure, to pave over material abundance and social inequality with the invisible script of differential. Coded into popular commercial media, then, is not only the stalemate of gender but also the stalemate of class conflict.

On 29 September 1997, Zhou Yaqin, a Ph.D. candidate in the Department of Chinese at Peking University, conducted a wide-ranging interview with Dai Jinhua. Our volume's final chapter presents that interview and with it a sense of Dai Jinhua's vigor and compassion. The questions posed to her in "The Cultural History of Chinese Film" reveal the portentous originality of this remarkable young critic, reclarified and humanized in her own inventive, self-critical, personal voice. Dai Jinhua is a young woman, and yet her powerful, reflexive sense of history, her penchant for auto-critique, and her historical self-positioning hint that she feels compelled to take action. This is the muted yet unavoidable theme of her retrospective glance at the wave of intellectual politics in the heady eighties (when Dai was intensely engaged in translating cinema theory from Europe into Chinese), the crash of the June "event," and the collapse of elite intellectuals' pretensions to preeminence: these episodes appear to have prematurely aged her intellectually and forced her to confront the horrifying speed, the unceasing change, of contemporary history. Her incredible sensitivity to the valences of (non)events, such as the frenzy she calls "periodization fever," is as clear as her persistent, stubborn, and flexible lifelong feminism; and each is available to the reader in a conversational, relaxed tone.

We close the volume with a short biography and a bibliography of Dai Jinhua's published work to date for the reader's information.

For ease of identification, the English-language translations of all titles in the main text (of films, books, television programmes, etc.) are italicized, or styled with quotation marks, to match the Chinese, even when no English-language version has been produced. At each first mention, the English-language title appears in parentheses after the

Chinese original; at second and subsequent mentions the English translation only is used. In the end-notes and the bibliographies, we have endeavored to distinguish those films, books and articles which have been produced in English from those which have not, by using italics or quotation marks only in the case of the former.

Notes

1 Hong Juan, "Yi pingdeng de xintai shuxie xingbie: fang xuezhe Dai Jinhua" (Writing gender with a balanced mentality: interviews with Dai Jinhua), *Zhonghua dushu bao* (Zhonghua readers' newspaper), February 14 1996, p. 2.

2 Dai Jinhua and Meng Yue, *Fuchu lishi dibiao* (Emerging on the horizon of history) (Zhengzhou: Henan renmin chubanshe, 1989).

3 For a detailed discussion of 1980s intellectual history, see Jing Wang's *High Culture Fever: Politics, Aesthetics, and Ideology in Deng's China* (Berkeley, Calif., and Los Angeles: University of California Press, 1996), especially ch. 2; also see Liu Kang, "Subjectivity, Marxism, and Cultural Theory in China" in Liu Kang and Xiaobing Tang, eds, *Politics, Ideology, and Literary Discourse in Modern China* (Durham, N.C., and London: Duke University Press, 1997), pp. 23–55; and Zhang Xudong's "Cultural Discourse" in Zhang Xudong, *Chinese Modernism: In the Era of Reforms* (Durham, N.C., and London: Duke University Press, 1997), pp. 35–99.

4 See Dai Jinhua, "Wenhua dixingtu ji qita" (Cultural geography and miscellaneous notes), *Dushu* (Reading), no. 3, 1997.

Jing Wang
Tani E. Barlow

1
Severed Bridge: The Art of the Sons' Generation

The Fifth Generation was entangled in a hostile historical snare from which they struggled desperately to escape.[1] Their predecessors, the Fourth Generation of filmmakers, had created an art form out of a search for personal memories, wrested from a homogeneous political configuration and the spurious style of officially defined mainstream art. But their attempts only resulted in a recentering of the discourse at the margins.[2] The Fifth Generation, by contrast, sought to transcend the disjuncture of history and culture. Staging symbolic representations of individual trauma in the "shock" of experience invested Chinese history with a different significance and established a novel film language, grammar, and set of aesthetic principles. The Fourth Generation set out to rescue hostages from history, yet in the end their art became a pastiche of outmoded and affected historical metanarratives; while the Fifth Generation, submerged in an evacuated history, in the fissures of culture and language, went astray in the labyrinth of language and representation itself.

The focal point of articulation between Chinese film art and Chinese social life in the 1980s did not rest on economic/productive or reproductive reality. Rather it lay in the recollection of a shared nightmare and a common psychological referent: the historical reality and representation of the "Great Proletarian Cultural Revolution." In Fourth Generation art, the Cultural Revolution appeared absent in its very presence. These artists directly confronted the ten-year Cultural Revolution during the first period of their work (1979–81), but they held a rather fixed psychological approach, adopting an imploring posture of grieving, outworn humanism, to represent the era's "inexorable doom" as if it were a classical romantic tragedy of youth. As they were direct participants in the Cultural Revolution, their object was to cleanse the blood from those unintentionally murderous gangs, using the passions of individual life history and the tears of youthful tragedy. They drew on conventional notions of humanity, human nature, civility, and barbarism to dispel but also to expound on the uniqueness of this phantasmic historical disaster.

In Fifth Generation art, however, the Cultural Revolution is ubiquitously absent. Until the 1980s, the Fifth Generation avoided this topic entirely; however, their films inevitably came to reflect the fact that they (not the Fourth Generation) are the Cultural Revolution's spiritual offspring,[3] heirs to the historical and cultural ruptures it caused. They are the ones who bear an unspeakable historical unconscious. Their generation, following a historic act of Patricide, faces the castrating power of the double weight of ancient Eastern civilization and assaults launched from the West. This generation struggled in despair at the margins of the Imaginary but failed to enter the Symbolic Order. The art of the Fifth Generation is the art of the Sons. The history of the Cultural Revolution determined that their struggle would painfully negotiate an abiding Father-Son symbolic and a Fatherless reality. Thus, in the 1980s, the Fifth Generation's films traversed the rift between history and culture, only to collapse in the form of a severed bridge. The novel film language and innovative mode of historical narration they struggled so hard to create became a biography of a generation's spiritual exile.

Outside the Carnival

The sum total of every absurd image in the history of China, the Cultural Revolution turned itself into a disastrous spectacle. The performance of this tragedy as farce or, shall we say, the unfolding of its original intention as a solemn squaring with the detritus of history resulted in one of the darkest acts in the cyclical drama of Chinese history.

Authoritarian state power (or feudal fascist autocracy) paradoxically used a spectacular form of Patricide as a precursor to establishing an absolute patriarchy. The onset of the Cultural Revolution witnessed Patricide in the name of the Father: it destroyed the existing order, by way of a control beyond every control. Perhaps most absurdly, the Cultural Revolution, which generated a culture of murderer-Sons, began unexpectedly with a Sons' carnival: the Red Guard movement that shocked the world. People prostrated themselves before the three loyalties – loyalty to Chairman Mao, loyalty to Mao Zedong thought, loyalty to Chairman Mao's revolutionary line – and the four infinities – boundless love, absolute devotion, firm belief, and infinite adoration (for Chairman Mao). They also justified mass destruction and tyranny under the slogan "to rebel is justified." ("There are a thousand truths in Marxism but fundamentally, those are but one: to rebel is justi-fied." *Quotations from Chairman Mao.*) So on one hand lies a transcendent image of authority beyond question (doing one's utmost to establish the absolute authority of Mao Zedong and Mao Zedong thought); on the other, a profanation of powerholders, authorities, and elders – the "mortal" Fathers. The powerholders equal the capi-talist roaders equal the enemies in the new historical circumstances. The authorities equal the mouthpieces of the capitalist class equal the garbage of history. The elders equal backward elements equal the obstruction of revolution. Seemingly overnight, then, China entered a revolution against order, a disorderly chaos mobilized and approved by patriarchal authority, that formal order beyond all order.

The Cultural Revolution was an exuberant and uninhibited carnival of the Sons compared to the genuine, social, political, cultural, and lin-guistic Patricide of the May Fourth Movement. The Sons of the newly born, delicate Young China shouldered the unbearably heavy burden of teleological condemnation as a consequence of May Fourth. Initially they registered elation. Eventually elation gave way to a hyper-rationalist, historicist reflection and a guilty, despairing grief. That is the stricken cry of Lu Xun's *Kuangren riji* (*Diary of a Madman*), the ambivalence of Bing Xin's *Siren du qiaocui* (*Alone and Weak*).[4] The Patricide of the Cultural Revolution, by contrast, received prior for-giveness and affirmation in the transcendental Father's name. Moreover, it used an anti-rationalistic fervor and ecstasy as its emo-tional register. As phantasmic historical spectacle, the Cultural Revolution's first scene looked like this: the carnival of killing Fathers and Sons, an officially sanctioned activity, reenacting the preexisting dominant ideology, which was a narrativized myth of revolutionary war. Most of the Red Guard Movement's members completed (or failed to complete) their education and their process of interpellation precisely within this ideological formation. In this historical narrative mode, revolutionary battle (that is, rebellion) was the only way to affirm that they had "entered the gates."[5] The Cultural Revolution offered them this providential opportunity.

However, to reenact this historical myth, they had to complete the inversion of the myth's subject, which is to say they had to reverse the myth of the Father's generation. The Father was precisely the exalted, valiant hero of revolutionary historical myth; thus the Red Guard Movement, through permanent revolution, had to reinscribe the Hero/Father as the enemy. As they performed once again the myth of the Hero/Father, the Sons' generation witnessed the ideal Father's collapse. This turned out to be more about blasphemy and disillusionment than brutal heroism. If the May Fourth Movement was a death and rebirth à la Guo Moruo's "Phoenix Nirvana," a reconstitution of cultural essence even in the process of reinterpreting history and culture, the Cultural Revolution was cultural destruction, pure and simple.[6] The carnival of Sons simply lacked the capacity to establish a fraternal alliance or order after killing the Father, because no means existed to surpass the transcendental signifier – the Name of the Father.

This signifier's extraordinary castrating force lay in its coexistence with the deconstructive and dehistoricizing power of the Cultural Revolution. Thus, when this seemingly endless but ultimately short-lived carnival was over, the Red Guard Movement, that grand power, was sent to the countryside and border areas, subsequently metamorphosing into the equally formidable "up to the mountains, down to the countryside youth movement." For the core Red Guards, this was far from a forced exile or demotion. Rather they took it as a continuation of the festival. They completed their coming-of-age ritual in this "vast and open wilderness."[7] But the harsh reality was that this expedition turned into the carnival's final scene. Their coming-of-age ritual was continually deferred. In the existential reality of China, they became conscious of a rigidity in the Father-Son political order. They came to an awareness of the cultural and psychic reality of Fatherless Sons, which is that of exile from the Symbolic Order.[8] The Sons were doomed to experience an endless spiritual exile.

To comprehend Chinese society in the 1980s and the Fifth Generation, however, by making the Cultural Revolution their main psychoanalytic referent and discursive context, a critical reality must be kept in mind: most Fifth Generation filmmakers were not part of the nucleus of the Red Guard Movement. The Red Guard Movement was certainly not a revel for all sons. Sons did not comprise a unified subjectivity. An extremely rigid Father-Son order divided their collective subjectivity into the "five red categories."[9] Indeed, the inversion of the subject of revolutionary war mythology meant that most Fifth Generation filmmakers (who grew up in elite families) lost their position at the heart of the inner circle. In the generation of the Sons they represented class difference and were stigmatized as belonging to one of the "five black categories." They, too, "drew a clear class line" against Fathers, taking up the rights and duties of Patricide. But this action could not alter their categorical position, since the stigma resulted from their fathers' high social status. Dominant ideology, having designated them as "educable children," offered them a promise of interpellation, but forever deferred its fulfillment (like waiting for Godot). If the first stirrings of the youth movement comprised the final act in the carnival of Sons, for most Fifth Generation filmmakers it was an exile in the real sense of the term. It was a dismal April Fools' for the five black categories – that is, those Sons in the categories of difference. The Fifth Generation felt the Cultural Revolution as one immense shock, one deep internal wound, an interminable descent where fervor met humiliation.

The Red Guard Movement generally misrecognized the Cultural Revolution as a historic rite of passage into adulthood ("All Under Heaven Is Ours, All of Society Is Ours").[10] The experience of those in the black categories was, by contrast, regression to a prediscursive stage. They were forced to stand outside the carnival and watch, from an outsider's position, the performance of this historic, fantastical play. This generation was destined to undergo an endless spiritual wandering, as a consequence of the inability of the preexisting Symbolic Order to produce an imaginary relationship between them and the existential Real, a relationship that might organize and communicate their experiential shock. Their spiritual exile began, then, almost at the same moment as the carnival.[11] Onlookers marked by their category of difference, eternal quasi-subjects in a social sense, they could not help but extend some sympathy toward the Fathers.

Even more lucidly and painfully than the Red Guards, they witnessed the humiliating collapse of the myth's heroic Father image. They became fearfully conscious that this collapse signified the end of an era. Their internal psychic world – legitimate, transcendent, existential – disintegrated in the shock of experience encountered in cruel reality. This shock determined the contradiction they encountered between cognition and emotion. On one hand, they subjected themselves to the mainstream discourse, in the hope of resolving their spiritual wandering and entering the Symbolic Order. This meant they had to resort to mainstream discourse. In the social context of the years 1976 through 1979, they had to reinvent the inverted historical myth. They had to rehabilitate the Name of the Father, to renarrate the historical myth of revolutionary war. This became their enduring passion.

On the other hand, they found the rational reflection that comes of being the carnival's displaced spectators. This lonely exilic form of reflection determined their interrogatory posture toward the transcendental Father, the Father-Son order, and the myths recounted through history. It determined their pained but sober self-reflexive realization of history's circularity, culture's disjunctures, and the aporia in language. It necessitated their desire to create a new language, to struggle free from this linguistic vacancy and nameless condition in order to seek a symbolic vehicle for their inner experience of shock. They had to withdraw their investment in self-pity and acknowledge the reality that they were Sons without the Father, and finally to seek a way to name themselves. The social-discursive world after 1979 offered them this distinct possibility.

Thus, the fact that Fifth Generation filmmakers consider *Yige he bage* (*One and Eight*) their inaugural undertaking should not completely surprise us.[12] In narrative terms, the film is a classic revolutionary war myth. Written by sixties mainstream poet Guo Xiaochuan, it draws on mythic plot devices, such as "the hero meets misfortune" and "pure gold proves its worth." The film has a wronged, misunderstood hero, Wang Jin, who faces humiliation and even death as a test of his boundless loyalty. He is the inspiring Communist Party member who steps forward bravely at the key moment of imminent peril. The film swells with enduring heroic passion. *One and Eight* was a renarration of the classic hero myth. It reflected the structural emergence in the late 1970s and early 1980s of a reconstituted order and the return of the Father's collective subjectivity. Simultaneously, it was a self-referential declaration, a self-defense, by a Fifth Generation which had once borne a class stigma. It demonstrates a posture of subjection.

The film was also a "deconstructive iterability" (to borrow from Derrida). It used new concepts and new formal aesthetics to rip aside the familiar screen representation of the mythic world. Jump cuts, stationary camera work, high- and low-angle master shots, non-diegetic camera movement, extreme stylization, and rejection of classical composition by placing characters at the margins of the frame – these techniques completed the defamiliarization of historical myth. Further, the film used an excess or overflow of expressions and devices to push history into a temporal depth of field, out of which an objective narrative distance emerged. This excess exposed an a priori subject as well as the very presence of the camera; this discloses both the ideological effects of historical myth and the desire in the film narrative to transcend ideology. In renarration, the auteurs of the Fifth Generation hoped to rectify the hero/Father's Name (and simultaneously, for themselves, the name of the legitimate hero's Son). At the same time, through the self-deconstruction of the narrative, they wanted to return the myth of the Father to the Father, to the era and history that had indeed subsided.

What displacement wrought through of excess of representation was the projection of the creative subject (rather than the character in the film) through camera work itself. Using high- and low-angle shots – techniques that dispense with illusion – displacement brought to a close the farewell ceremonies of the generation of Sons. It directly structured the grammar of the last narrative sequence in *One and Eight*. In it, another bandit hero, Thick Eyebrows, finally emerges from the Valley of Death, a survivor. In an overhead shot, at the lower left margin of the frame, we see him kneel down hurriedly and raise his gun to indicate his determination to leave. The scene then shifts to a close-up of Wang Jin's benign face, positioned in a matching low-angle shot in the middle left of the frame. This maneuver overlaps the Son's farewell to history with the gaze of the hero/father. But then Thick Eyebrows unexpectedly appears in a low-angle extreme close-up. Raising the rifle in farewell, his hands divide the frame into two symmetrical triangles. In this moment, the subject's and the narrative's points of view are reversed. Thick Eyebrows assumes a posture of subjection when proclaiming his intention to desert, thereby appearing to affirm the image of authority and to share the burden of history's fate.

But the dislocation reveals that Thick Eyebrows does not accept authority's rules. Cutting to a long shot, we see Wang Jin accepting the rifle. Thick Eyebrows then lifts his face, decisively raises himself, and walks off toward the horizon. In repeated shot/reverse shots, Wang Jin and Commander Xu (the figure of official authority in the text), in extreme close-up, watch Thick Eyebrows leave, alternating with a long shot of Thick Eyebrows as he is walking away. Suddenly, the film cuts to an extreme close-up of Thick Eyebrows's rapidly disappearing back. He slowly turns his head, as the film cuts to a full frame of Wang Jin and Commander Xu supporting one another. The camera tracks up slightly, then stops. This leaves the hero out of focus, but fills the screen with a spacious, empty horizon, a cloudless backdrop and dazzling sunlight. The out-of-focus hero transforms into a hazy mirage on the horizon. This characteristic reversal of scenes and points of view marks the shift of discursive power. It reveals the heart of Fifth Generation art: resistance from within subjection, self-determination within redemption.

Indeed, tales of subjects who are misunderstood, unjustly treated, and expelled from society but who then undergo a test and are reaffirmed, together with a filmic structure based on an excess of representation and freedom from diegetic space, are hallmarks of the creative work of the Fifth Generation. In *Daoma zei* (*Horse Thief*), this trope of loyalty is personified by the thief who is eventually exiled precisely because he articulates loyalty.[13] The characteristic structure of the narrative is repeated in temporal experience ruptured and constrained by ritual space and in imposing spatial imagery, each of which is an effect of "autonomous" camera action. It is there as well in the endless journey between revolt and belief. *Horse Thief* ends with a funerary pyre at the Sky Burial Dais (a signifier of how power has been shaken and destroyed), after a sacrificial goat has been slaughtered (symbolizing a type of self-destructive rebellion as well as a symbolic patricide). But Luo Erbu never completes this journey: he dies midway up the path toward the pyre.

In *Heipao shijian* (*The Black Cannon Incident*) and *Juexiang* (*The Last Sound*):[14] we notice a different narrative form if we view the structured presentation diachronically, it is easy to see how, in the myth's renarration and in the off-center narrative form, the subject in descent drifts away from the present progressive tense. In *One and Eight* and *Horse Thief*, the subject is still the main actant, realizing the Fifth Generation's hopes for "negotiation" and "participation." He exhibits and explicates their hopeless loyalty; he is truly the text's subject and hero. In *The Black Cannon Incident* and *The Last Sound*, by contrast, the now prosaic subject is merely the formless, absurd, and passive bearer of unjust fate. He has no way even to establish reciprocal relations with other actants in the text. Also, he mediates a harmonious complementarity that gradually surfaces between his own doubled symbolism as sacrifice and sacrificer (that is, between order and authority). In *One and Eight* and *Horse Thief*, passion and loyalty comprise the content of what is narrated, while narrativity arises out of symbolic excess, thus creating a dangerous tension in the text. In *The Black Cannon Incident* and *The Last Sound*, however, a tolerant, ironic narrative tone and a compassionate yet detached rhetorical structure replace that tension. The Father's tale is being returned to the Father's world. In the text, rectified Fathers have already lost their idealized Father halo.

In *The Last Sound*, a father, never highly honored, takes the musical score to which he has devoted his entire life, burns it and then dies quietly. His son Guanzai subsequently decides to abandon his career and uses the surviving remnants of the musical score as wallpaper, thus turning it into a silent element, a spatial figure. His step-sister, Yun Zhi, then rips apart and destroys that old musical soul for a second time when she plays her piano concerto. The abrupt jarring noise of Guanzai scraping wood to the sound of the piano concerto deepens the mood of thorough destruction and silencing. There is nothing left but the lonely and deserted alleyway, a symbolic scene that recurs throughout the film. Only the vicissitudes of the human world, the mad laughter of the wandering idiot linger in the alley. Culture has already been ruptured. Historical sensibility emerges from the dissipation of historical ambience.

History and the Severed Bridge

A generation of Sons without Fathers, the Fifth Generation's predicament, its historical paradox, does not really lie midway between seeking and interrogating the Father, conversion and rebellion, sentiment and reason. These represent mere signifieds in this generation's psychic reserves. Their major historical predicament is the search to represent an individual experience of shock as legitimate historical experience. Yet they encountered shock precisely in the ruptures and dissipation of discourse about historical experience. They had to transcend History (more exactly, the discourse of History) before they could organize their experiences of trauma and represent these as organic to History. The problem was that their desire to transcend History destined them instead to fall back into the aporia of language and representation. Their efforts to vault historical discourse and touch the essence of History led not only to their inscription of History as the lasting absence of the Other in the text, but also displaced the inscribers themselves outside of the Symbolic Order. Consequently, their coming into manhood was continually deferred.

The Fifth Generation's art practice and their historical predicament both disclose deficiencies in post-May Fourth intellectuals as subjects. When they abandoned Chinese culture – historical metanarratives (or feudal culture) – they created an aporia in the linguistic/Symbolic Order. In the effort to touch the historical Real they repeatedly lost themselves in a certain aphasic fabrication. Representing historical reality, or rather the historical unconscious, is in its essence still a way of using language to narrate non-linguistic phenomena, an expression of the ineffable. But to yield to the linguistic/Symbolic Order means giving in to the cyclical tragedy enacted throughout Chinese history through the order that links Father to

Son. The struggle of the Fifth Generation was another spiritual flight from a trap, undertaken by the new generation of Sons in the pale light of yet another Young China's dawn. Those Sons were compelled to reclaim a whole new world from five thousand years of historical discourse crammed with the silent spirits of the dead, so that a generation of Sons could live, create, and freely express themselves. Like Thick Eyebrows, they had to turn and leave once they had paid a pious tribute to History, despite having to face the empty and barren horizon that was opening up in front of them. Only in this kind of temporal space could they properly place a memorial wreath in their own visual territory.

Huang tudi (*Yellow Earth*) repeats this same visual intention in the character of Hanhan.[15] Three times, Hanhan rushes against the human tide and runs straight out of the frame. Indeed, this could almost be seen as an allegory of the Fifth Generation's spiritual breakthrough, a breakthrough that contains an explosive force which might always spiral out of control. And it still cannot cure Hanhan's aphasia: between the playful and profane "Bed-Wetting Song" and the empty, rousing "Revolutionary Song," Hanhan never attains his – that is, the Sons' generation's – own language. Chen Kaige's film is precisely the inscription of this attempt to achieve such a sublime spiritual breakthrough.

In their elaboration, respectively, of the film's direction and cinematography, Chen Kaige and Zhang Yimou (who revolutionized Fifth Generation film language) drew on Laozi's aphorism, "A massacre makes no noise, a grand image has no form."[16] They thus directly avowed that, in their representation and counter-representation (to historical discourse), they were attempting to convey the inexpressible. The subject of *Yellow Earth* is not the story of how the Eighth Route Army soldier, Gu Qing, collected folk songs; nor is it the story of how the peasant girl, Cuiqiao, resisted the feudal system of marriage; nor even that of the tragedy of ancient history itself. Rather the film's true subject is a historical discourse about history, a meta-history, a meta-language. Thus, "looking afar from the Yellow River," "the vast sky" and "deep earth," the yellow earth, yellow river, cave dwellings, and oil lamps, Cuiqiao's father, Cuiqiao, and Hanhan are all composed architechtonically through the use of stationary shots, deep focus, decentered perspective, postmodern shot composition, and monochromatic color schema. In its entirety (including the people living on the yellow earth) the film creates a spatial, non-linguistic, non-temporal existence. Only in the traces and ruins of spatial images (for example, the close-up of Cuiqiao's father's face under the oil lamp) can the passage of time be conveyed.

The antinomy of space and time is a dissonance between visual image and language. The weightiness of the historical unconscious and alternation in historical representation are distinguished in this antinomy. The sole moving figure in the film is Gu Qing, who comes and goes. He is a temporal image and he possesses language, but he is still unable to alter in the least a largely spatial existence. He is motivated linguistically to collect folk songs. When his hope of turning folk ditties into revolutionary songs is dashed, his project becomes a self-reference to the Fifth Generation (especially to Chen Kaige). Language (Gu Qing's "revolutionary songs" and filmically the ubiquitous, self-revelatory camera) is suspended before the yellow earth. If the realization of language means bracketing "true reality," then language operates as an inverted yearning in the creative work of the Fifth Generation, especially that of Chen Kaige and Tian Zhuangzhuang. They make reality present, even though the desire to place language – its legibility and connection to the experiential world – in the Symbolic Order is then lost. Nonetheless the paradox of a Chen Kaige style is that its screen world is wedged between two layers: a series of viscerally realistic cinematic images new to Chinese cinema, on the one hand, and the fact that this "real" image appears inside an unprecedentedly conspicuous frame, on the other. Between the frames and the symbols the self-referentiality of the film's diegesis opens up. In other words, the emergence of an anti-language has as its outcome an overwhelming presencing of language. "Reality" and "history," in contrast, are lost.

In *Haizi wang* (*The King of Children*), Chen Kaige confronted this predicament head on. He finally told his (the Fifth Generation's) own story. With a reasoned, self-reflexive consciousness, he narrated his experience of a long, lonely spiritual wandering. This is a tale of the red earth, of an educated youth. In *The King of Children*, the Fifth Generation stepped out naked onto the stage. It is, according to

Zheng Dongtian, "the testimony" of the Fifth Generation.[17] However, even in *The King of Children,* the Cultural Revolution appears as an absent presence. The film's protagonist is actually the director, Chen Kaige, rather than the educated youth, Lao Gan. The events narrated in the film are best understood as representations of the Fifth Generation's artistic predicament, rather than as the mundane, if intriguing, experiences of an educated youth during the Cultural Revolution. Lao Gan's short career as a teacher provides the readily available signifier. Its signifieds are history and language, the linguistic and the anti-linguistic, the expressible and the ineffable. This is a truly self-referential film: four times in the movie a framing, stationary frontal shot embedded in the middle of the screen – Lao Gan (that is, Chen Kaige) in the window – reiterates this aspect of its thematics.

In *One and Eight,* the narrator, in the position of Wang Jin, explains the Fifth Generation's traumatic experience of shock, which came at them from two directions. On one side was the shock arising from humanity's savagery and brutality: the burned villages that the Japanese left behind, a killing field strewn with the bodies of old people, women, and children. The other shock came from the unwarranted but authoritative accusation the capitalized Other/Subject/Masses lodged: "You had the nerve to watch!" "You're the ones who helped the Japanese devils do it!" Wang Jin and the bandits were blamed for this act of brutality.

In *The King of Children,* the forces that perplex and imperceptibly restrain Lao Gan also come from different sides. One is the clear and resounding voice of the woman who lives next door to the classroom, reading aloud a text ("Old Workers Teaching Others").[18] This is the discourse of politics/power/history, the persistent and expressive form of language. The other is the ceaseless sound of the cowbell ringing across the landscape of blue sky and red earth and the white-clad shepherd whistling and bounding forth. These noises are non-linguistic images, bearing reality or rather the historical unconscious: the persistence of that which cannot be expressed and refuses expression. The same leitmotif appears again even more forcefully: after a close-up of Lao Gan under a lamp framed in a window, the film cuts to a bright moon in the night sky (a symbol of eternal, wordless nature, of things non-linguistic); simultaneously, a jumble of voices surges in from outside the frame, a recitation of *The Book of Family Names* and the multiplication table in various voices and dialects. The voices mix with the sounds of temple bells and drums and the peasants' unrestrained singing. The camera cuts to a close-up of Lao Gan's illuminated hands leafing through the dictionary (signifier of the source of language and the Symbolic Order). The reverberating sounds grow stronger, mixed with the sound of labored breathing. This is a linguistic space, a space filled with the discourse of language and History. It is a moment when the repressive and castrating force of History is realized. Suddenly, the sounds stop. All is calm. The film cuts to Lao Gan holding a lamp, walking toward the right and out of the frame.

Outside the frame, a door is pushed open a crack. In a close-up, with the camera rising in sync with the hand holding the lamp, we see Lao Gan's indifferent and exhausted expression. In a reverse shot, the beautiful figure of a calf appears in the doorway. The calf runs out of the frame toward the left (film language). What we then confront is Lao Gan (that is, Chen Kaige himself), who is so pressed between the discourse of language and history and that of the eternal and silent Being that he has no way to breathe.[19] The true motivation behind the cultural reflection unfolding in the Fifth Generation, and in all of 1980s Chinese culture, lies in revealing the deep structure of the tragedy of the Father-to-Son succession, as well as history's circularity. Moreover, the Fifth Generation explored the pragmatic possibilities of ending the circularity and breaking through to the deep structure. However, this History's existence and continuity is far from *The King of Children*'s ability to budge or change it. The film uses a literal millstone as a metaphor for History: in the course of the film Lao Gan makes numerous efforts to force the millstone to turn. Except for bursts of piercing shrieks from its wooden axles, however, it remains immobile. Lao Gan can only, as he finally leaves, leap playfully and self-mockingly onto the millstone and slide down it to the ground.

Yet the tragedy of the Lao Gans of China does not lie in their inability to impact history, but in their inability to change historical discourse; that is, the discourse of and about Fathers. Their yearning to terminate circularity immediately collides with historical discourse's circularity of expression, captured symbolically in the song that the adults and children merrily sing in the film: "There once was a mountain. On the mountain was a temple. In the temple there was a monk telling a story. What was he saying? There once was a mountain."

As Lao Gan (Chen Kaige) knows very well, the Real historical unconscious is neither on his side nor in the transcendent Father's powerful discourse as propagated in a classroom text such as "Hundreds of Millions of People, Hundreds of Millions of Red Hearts." Nor was the Real evoked in the ideological fabrication of class struggle reiterated in a text such as "Disquietude within Quiescence." Historical reality exists between the yellow earth and the long and unbroken, silent and eternally steadfast red earth. (In *The King of Children*, Chen Kaige twice uses frame-by-frame shots to display the red earth from dawn to dusk.) Historical reality exists on the side of Wang Fu's illiterate father, Wang Qitong, in the crisp sound of the cowbell, in the creaking of the millstone, in the annual ring of the tree stump. The shepherd boy is merely the allegorical icon of this non-linguistic reality. In *The King of Children* (the Fifth Generation) self-referentiality is self-veneration. It is also self-loathing. The Fifth Generation wants to light a lamp to see into historical reality/the historical unconscious. For instance, in Lao Gan's hallucination, he raises up an oil lamp as he is teaching, and each student is shown writing under an oil lamp. The scene enacts the proverb, "If Confucius were not born, eternity would be one long night," and casts the light of knowledge into the world.[20] But in the sequence following the fantasy, Lao Gan is holding up an oil lamp and looking perplexedly at his reflection in the mirror on the wall, which has been split into two asymmetrical images. Lao Gan then spits at his own mirror image: it is a broken figure, a psychically split self. On one side is creative expression, revealing a true sense of mission and yearning. On the other, however, is the reality of the loss of language.

In the dark-red light of dusk, Lao Gan and the little shepherd boy are shown together in a medium close-up. Lao Gan moves into teaching mode, hoping to pass on language/voice to the boy ("I know how to read. Let me teach you, all right?"). But the shepherd boy merely turns around and walks off. The extreme close-up of the boy cuts to a long shot of Lao Gan. The camera is slowly lowered, so that the red earth gradually rises, causing Lao Gan to disappear behind the silent earth. The Fifth Generation gazed intently at this earth and at its history. And yet the earth blocked the real historical field of vision. The Medusa's gaze of history that has filled China's entire world paralyzed, swallowed, and buried them in its silent circularity. All their efforts to represent the historical Real resulted in nothing more than self-representation and, ultimately, they were engulfed by this inexpressible reality. A counterpoint image to Lao Gan and the shepherd boy is the text's representation of the written character for *son*, Wang Fu. Wang Fu is tenaciously determined to learn how to read, and thus to speak for his father (signifier of a non-linguistic historical Real, that which is ineffable): "Father is unable to speak," he says, "I should study hard so I can speak for father." Yet all he can really do is reiterate things and copy from the dictionary, thereby entering the circularity of historical discourse. In a frontal stationary shot, Wang Fu supplants Lao Gan's position as the frame within the frame; together, the pair repeatedly describe a circuit, a heart-wrenching and hopeless circularity. In the end, it persists amid their efforts to articulate the circularity and thereby to transcend it.

The brilliance of the Fifth Generation lies in both the creation of a new cinematic language and in their revelation of the enigma inhabiting archaic Chinese history. They attempt to eventually dispel the discourse of historical circularity. However, just like Lao Gan, the result was the creation of a new word, a made-up unreadable character combining *cow* and *water*. It is a pictographic representation of the shepherd boy's true condition. But it is only a slip of the pen, an image that no one would recognize or accept. Lao Gan writes his last words – "Wang Fu, from now on don't copy anything, even the dictionary" – on a large tree stump. Like the dense tree rings and the dark cracks in the earth, the words, too, are merely decorative patterns representing a silent, non-linguistic reality.

The Fifth Generation were, in the end, rejected by the Symbolic Order, incapable of changing the subject-position of Son. Their art remained the art of the Sons' generation. Their struggles to transcend the rift in the valley merely created a severed bridge, a self-referential image that looked towards historical reality but could never reach it. At the film's conclusion, after an extreme close-up of the shepherd boy, we see an eighteen-shot montage sequence framing distorted human-like charred tree-trunks and Lao Gan. After cutting to an extreme close-up of Lao Gan, we see a distant shot of an embankment. A surging flame and dense smoke rise to cover the mountain ridge. Like the phoenix, Chen Kaige repeatedly places his hopes in destruction. Destruction is approaching. But it will not take the shape the Fifth Generation anticipates. They will meet in shock once again.

Hero on Stage and Woman as Background

I have argued to this point that *The King of Children* accomplishes the portrayal of the renegade Son in its filmic inscription of anti-Hero/anti-Father/anti-History. In the process of this inscription the historical and linguistic dilemma that the Fifth Generation experienced is enacted as historical tragedy. *Hong gaoliang* (*Red Sorghum*) actually brings this submissive posture to completion when it reintroduces onto the stage the Hero/Father/History.[21] In a melodramatic deconstruction of the historical and linguistic dilemma of the Fifth Generation, the film achieves the Son's long-deferred coming of age. Thus ends the heroic age of the Fifth Generation:[22] *Red Sorghum* signals the fall of the Fifth Generation, though it is indeed a glorious fall.

As *Yellow Earth* and *The King of Children* may be termed failures of salvation, *Red Sorghum* certainly represents the salvation of failure. If *Yellow Earth* and *The King of Children* employ the allegory of the disappearance and fragmentation of history and entrust the heavy legacy of this earth to an empty future, *Red Sorghum* employs narrative signification to demonstrate the totality and continuation of false history. *Yellow Earth* and *The King of Children* try to restate and redefine the Son's identity via the deconstruction of the myth of the Hero/Father. *Red Sorghum*, in contrast, seeks to erase the mark of Cain from the unfilial Son's forehead in the process of narration (not repetition) of the story of the Hero/Father. This is, in other words, a historical return to the social. *Red Sorghum* successfully uses imaginary relation to achieve ritual absolution and a rite of passage to adulthood. So not only does it narrate an individual's life story, revealing a consciousness in retreat and submission, it is itself also a successful ideological sacrifice, an ideological practice in terms of a social, symbolic act.

In *The King of Children*, director Chen Kaige exhibits the self-consciousness typical of a lone rambler, one who hopelessly tries to save himself by salvaging historical representation, and attempts to open up a linguistic space for the Son's generation in the space crowded with the words of the Father. Thus Chen's expression is a metadiscourse on expression itself; his language is the longing for language itself. This longing for history and language becomes a struggle reminiscent of the interminable wait for Godot. In *Red Sorghum*, however, director Zhang Yimou adopts a "mischievous attitude toward this extraordinarily heavy material."[23] He shuffles the fragments of history's marginalized language and substitutes the language about desire for a desire for language. The film introduces History/the Other through historicized representation, thus acknowledging the Father's "rules." This is a reversal of the attitude Chen Kaige represented through the character of Thick Eyebrows. *The King of Children* and *Red Sorghum* therefore constitute the polar opposites of the Fifth Generation's treatment of History.

In fact, the Fifth Generation broadly defined – spiritual sons of the Cultural Revolution – are the initiators and participants of the movement for reflecting on culture and History. Yet this cultural reflection, a signifier with infinitely expanding explanatory power, must still traverse the cultural wilderness of those revolutionary years and free itself of the amorphous condition of being the Son. Even more important, this cultural reflection must build a bridge over the post–May Fourth gap while simultaneously widening it. In addition to its ambiguity and diffusion, cultural reflection exists in the narrow space between war, national salvation, and social transformation. Like all cultural movements after May Fourth, it is built on a dilemma. On the one hand, it conducts a "root-searching movement" in order to revive national culture, national tradition, and national spirit. On the other hand, it issues a call for enlightenment, a call to critique and negate national culture and tradition, to excavate "the ills of national character," and to portray the silent spirit of the citizenry. To state it more plainly, on one side of the gap is the slow and difficult task of building the bridge, while on the other side is the similarly painful and torturous task of dismantling the freshly built bricks and tiles of Qin and Han.

The cultural-reflection movement turned out to resemble all post–May Fourth cultural movements, its glorious creation just like the winding sheet of Laertes, woven by Penelope during the day only to be unwoven at night. It is as though the bridge were destined to be a broken one, and its construction a legacy eternally entrusted to the future. On a smaller scale, the dilemma of the Fifth Generation is precisely the dilemma of recent Chinese history and cultural movements. Because the other shore of Chinese history and culture is forever out of reach, intellectuals are forever facing a no-man's-land in history and the singular enormity of historical discourse. They must continue the circular dance between the namelessness of the Sons and the name of the Father; they must choose between silence and fabrication. Either they are like Chen Kaige, coining unintelligible words on the wrinkled and blurry parchment of history, or they are like Zhang Yimou, fabricating mythical stories about history, thus smearing a few false but colorful and lively pictures on the yellowed pages of that ancient and brittle volume.

The Fifth Generation's prehistory and social context then is the memory of the Cultural Revolution and the era after Cultural Revolution. They recall the act of killing the Father, the carnival of the Sons, the revolution within the Order against order, the castration of History inherent in the order of Father-Son, and the death and resurrection of the Father of experience. If this is indeed the case, then in *Red Sorghum* Zhang Yimou is actually positing an era of pre-history with the line "I will tell you the story of My Grandpa and My Grandma." The setting of this film is a place within Order but outside Law: the world of Eighteen-Mile Hill and Qingshakou. It locates the act of patricide within the narrative environment: "My Grandpa" kills Li Datou, the only elder male in the text and the sole signifier of power (the de facto Old Boss at the distillery), and takes his woman. *Red Sorghum* thus becomes an acclaimed, triumphant legend and an exquisite myth about Chinese men and Chinese history.

In 1987, *The King of Children* and *Red Sorghum*, polar opposites of Fifth Generation film production and both of them important artifacts in contemporary Chinese film history, appeared at the same time and competed for international film awards simultaneously. *The King of Children* lost out at Cannes, but *Red Sorghum* won the Best Picture award at the Berlin Film Festival. Although coincidence or serendipity may have had a hand in this, the result appears to have been inevitable, when viewed in the open-ended grand narrative of contemporary Chinese history. This is especially true of *Red Sorghum*. A mythical story about history, it brings to a close the historical suspense of the Fifth Generation as Chen Kaige and Tian Zhuangzhuang had portrayed it. With its imaginary killing of the Father and the eventual submission of the Son, *Red Sorghum* completed the infinitely deferred coming of age of the Fifth Generation. Precisely because it is a historical myth, the most important aspect of the film is also about the era of mythmaking; precisely because it is a story of the Son, the film is about desire, rebellion, order, and submission.

In terms of mythmaking, the year that produced the film, 1987, is indeed a crucial moment in the history of New China, a moment rich with historical events and rare historical opportunity. After ten years of accumulation and preparation, the New Era of reform was accelerating rapidly. In an unusually open posture, China was stepping into the world economy. With increased urbanization and industrialization, a wave of commercialization washed over the populace before they were really aware of it. The abrupt presence of the West/the Other/ commercial civilization inflicted a tremendous shock on the Chinese, who found themselves thrown into a brave new world. This new presence revealed itself to be a brand new historical castration, unfamiliar but nonetheless powerful. National culture was once again facing a total onslaught from commercial culture. And with the disappearance of historical awareness, national history once again faced a pending crisis. At the very moment the central bureau of the Communist Party proposed the exact steps of systemic economic reform, it also proposed initial plans for political reform: The Chinese nation must seize this rare historical opportunity; it must step over the narrow threshold and "march to the world." In the face of commercialization, the historical lock through which the Fifth Generation navigated with difficulty appeared extremely narrow. *The King of Children* was "exiled to the distant future – [Was Chen Kaige] filming for the 21st century?"[24] Yet *Red Sorghum* sneaked through ingeniously. Thus Chinese/Fifth Generation films gloriously stepped onto the podium of international cinema. An apt metaphor for Chinese history/reality in the year 1987.

As "a mythmaking era" and *Red Sorghum*'s social context, the crucial features of the year 1987 are as follows: the reestablishment of concentric circles of power; the multi-centeredness of social life; the tremendous shock of the onslaught of Western/Other culture; and the enormous power of commodity ideology to deconstruct and castrate history. One important achievement of the past decade of the New Era [the 1980s] has been the continuing negation of the Cultural Revolution, which completed the return of the Fathers' generation, the interrogation of the transcendental Father, and the reestablishment of a new order. As a spiritual biography of the Fifth Generation, *The King of Children*, in all its subtlety and complexity, gives vent to the Sisyphean condition of the generation of Sons struggling under the yoke of history and culture. The film demonstrates, in spite of itself, that the Fifth Generation must acquire the Father's image. They must turn away from the empty horizon. They must end "the anxiety of expression" and achieve self-expression through the acquisition of a new narrative.

However, this onslaught of reform has produced a new order. Commercial economy and foreign culture have powerfully destabilized the ancient and fragile forms of Chinese spiritual existence. And not just for the Fifth Generation: the whole of China has been thrust under the castrating power of the complacent Other. All at once, it seemed, there was "only one sun" (the title of Zhang Jie's novel). To the movement for cultural reflection, this registered as another earthquake rippling under the ruined bridge, another rupture of history and culture. But this time, the chasm appeared not only to reveal the futility of cultural and historical reflection; it seemed to be indicating the very disappearance of history itself. National history had to be salvaged; national culture, revived (even if only in the Imaginary). Once again, China became the nation in need of a hero, and we faced yet again an era requiring a hero. Thus, *Red Sorghum* was born.

Perhaps it was a coincidence. Yet *Red Sorghum* presented a perfect answer to what this country "needed," indeed to everything the era was demanding. With its son-cum-father nationalist hero and the insolent and violent story of patricide, the film completes the coming of age for the Fifth Generation as well as the ritual of entering the symbolic realm. By castrating the castrator/foreign invader, the film consoles a nation that is leaden with anxiety and in danger of losing its memory. *Red Sorghum* announces to the people the continuation of history. So it not only traverses the latest rupture of history/culture; it also effortlessly passes over the wasteland of Cultural Revolution, and the cultural rupture of the May Fourth era as well. *Red Sorghum* thus pushes back into a "prehistorical" era the coming of age of the Fifth Generation and that of the whole nation. This prehistorical era, ambiguous in time, exists in a wilderness outside Ur-society itself.

Fifth Generation art is the art of the generation of Sons, and as such one of its basic characteristics is to elevate prohibition over desire. In the classic films of the Fifth Generation, more than the object of desire, the figure of the woman functions as the object of prohibition. The only woman in *One and Eight* is a young nurse, a skinny, adolescent girl. (In an earlier version of the script, she is Wang Jin's girlfriend.) According to the logic of the text, only bandits, the Japanese invaders, or animals could possibly harbor desire for such a girl. She will lie down on the noble and pure altar of the national spirit, clothed in pure white and pierced by a clean bullet. In *Yellow Earth*, Cuiqiao is tightly bound by the rules of the Party and the rules of peasants, so that only the black hand, the blackened hand of her old peasant-husband, whose face is not shown, can sully her. When her song finally stops short, she will be swallowed up by the silty water of the Yellow River, which stretches virtually the entire width of the screen as she becomes yet another bride of the river spirit/history. In *Horse Thief*, as punishment for his "crime," Luo Erbu loses his son. In the end, he returns his wife and son to the tribe (Ur-society) and dies a lonely death in atonement. In *The Last Sound*'s final grand sequence, Guanzai and Yunzhi are at one point mistaken for a couple, though Yunzhi, Guanzai's half-sister, could never become "woman" on the horizon of male desire. Female as a sign of forbidden desire and lack-in-desire points not only to the Name of the Son in which the Fifth Generation embodies itself, but also to their dilemma and anxiety as they struggled outside the Symbolic Order.

In a gesture of reversal, *Red Sorghum*'s very first grand sequence places the woman in the field of vision of male desire: at the beginning of the film, immediately following the fade-out of the credits, there is a close-up of Jiu'er's face. The camera frame, like the gaze of desire, steadily and greedily fixes itself on this woman's face. A set of five detail shots follow, reiterating the first close-up: flowers are put in her hair, facial hair twisted off with a silk thread, bracelets clasped on, buttons fastened, earrings dangled, until a red silk veil descends over the young woman's face. Shots inside the bridal sedan add still more close-ups of Jiu'er's face, as well as incorporating the classic signifier of desire, the color red: red sedan curtains, red jacket, red pants, red shoes. These shots present a woman amongst macho men, framed by the vision of desire. The reverse shot represents the transference of desire as Jiu'er peeks through the sedan curtain at a man's (My Grandpa's) naked, muscular back. This naming female desire foreshadows her tacit consent to and even encouragement of his later act of patricide. It is precisely after the four shifting sequences of shot/reverse shot of the close-up on Jiu'er's face (her eyes expectant, encouraging, and acquiescent) and My Grandpa's medium to close-ups (moving from pity for Jiu'er to uncertainty to determination that My Grandpa and the other sedan carriers overpower and kill the highway man. This is the first scene of violence that is motivated by desire; it is also a rehearsal for the act of patricide. Although the victim this time is a mere robber, he is the one who dares to use the name of authority (at least with the potential castrating power) of Crack-shot Sanpao, the bandit. Indeed, it is precisely this act, and not the real act of patricide (the murder of Li Datou) that wins over the woman of the village (who occupies the position of the Mother) for My Grandpa.

The second grand sequence, the illicit union, creates an intoxicating ceremony for the Sons' generation with a series of shots: dazzling sunlight; rapid shot/reverse shot; a round altar made of trampled-down red sorghums; a high-angle panoramic shot of the woman in red lying on her back, the man kneeling by her side. All this is accompanied by the sonorous twang of the trumpet and images of the red sorghum blown about wildly as though possessed. The whole scene is carnivalesque with a tinge of the tragic. This is both the coming of age and the christening of the Fifth Generation. This scene signals the satisfaction of desire and the fulfillment of self-expression. However, this rare sequence in the film history of the New China, though about the personal and the real, is not yet the spectacle of an individual life. Rather than a ceremony of the Sons, it is in fact the ritual expression of an ideology. The illicit union of Jiu'er and My Grandpa in the red sorghum field at Qingshakou – a world outside the Law – does not represent iconoclastic individualism à la romanticism. Rather, it represents the Chinese Adam and Eve in the act of reconstructing the national myth. If we say that it is a spectacular scene, then it is a spectacle of national culture (Chinese folk rituals and customs). The story it tells is not only about desire or even the satisfaction of desire; rather, it is a story about the grandeur of heroism and the power of national, primitive life force. What it provides for the audience is not only the pleasure of voyeurism, but also the consoling fantasy of the whole. Thus, in the third and fourth grand sequences, the story of desire between the man and woman will no longer be that of illicit union, an action that is outside order. Instead, it becomes a history of My Grandpa's actions against the order: killing the Father/Li Datou, taking the name of the Father, legally taking possession of Jiu'er, and finally becoming the real owner of Eighteen-Mile Hill. The eventual confrontation with Crack-shot Sanpao (not his imitator this time), in a scene that is reminiscent of the classical novel *Shuihu zhuan* (*The Water Margin*), confirms My Grandpa's sole ownership of Jiu'er (the Father's woman): "You defiled my woman." Finally it is through an act of primitive sacrilege – urinating into the wine vat – that he announces his legal ownership of Jiu'er to the workers at the distillery (an Ur-society outside Society). According to the narrative logic, this act of sacrilege represents an exhibition of phallic power to the people of this Ur-society. He is not only a Son who kills the Father, he must acquire the Father's Name and reestablish the Father's Law. This act is not only an announcement and a confirmation, it is also an ancient threat: a Father-like threat of castration.

A coming of age ritual by itself is not enough, however, for he must now make sure that society as a whole acknowledges it. For this reason, three times My Grandpa must grasp Jiu'er by the waist in front of everyone and throw her over his shoulder, as though pulling up a green onion straight from the field (surely a meaningful signifier). He then must march imperially into her bedchamber carrying her over his back. The appearance of the son Douguan in the fifth grand sequence and the authoritative tone of his narration of My Grandpa and Grandma's legend further dispels any question that My Grandpa is the legitimate possessor of the Name of the Father. The film's narrative thus describes a perfect chain of events: it starts from non-order and moves first to anti-order and then to the reestablishment of a new order. By doing so, it thus revises the historical situation of the Fifth Generation and resolves in the Imaginary their historical and linguistic predicament. More important, the forever-absent History makes its appearance in this film and grandly becomes the center of attention, the center of the Symbolic Order. At the same time, the film symbolically signifies the social reality of the decade-long reform era, signifying the "historical act of patricide."[25]

As the art of the generation of Sons (thus also signaling the end of the Sons' identity and their art), what is most interesting about the central narrative event in *Red Sorghum* is that the act of patricide itself is but a linguistic act, unrepresented and unconfirmed. It appears as a puzzling, unintelligible code. "Just when My Grandma was cursing her father, something happened in Eighteen-Mile Hill. Li Datou was murdered. Just who did it was never known. I've always felt that My Grandpa might have done it. But until he passed away, I never asked him about it." Furthermore, there is another textual trick: the father in the narrative, Li Datou, is forever an absence in the visual/auditory world, the textualized world. In the bridal chamber scene, he does not even make an appearance as the black hand did in *Yellow Earth*. Instead, his existence is like an echo, confirmed only through Jiu'er's frightened flinch and her sharp cry in a voice-over. Thus, in the textual structure of *Red Sorghum*, Father/Li Datou is without question an absence, an empty seat waiting for its signified, for My Grandpa/the Name of the Son to occupy. The fact that, in reality, Li Datou is never able to own Jiu'er implicitly absolves the Son's transgression on the Law of the Father. Thus the act that is explicitly represented in the text – the illicit union or the taking possession of the Father's woman (the Name of the Mother) – is absolved of its crime and punishment.

The film tells a story of patricide, a story of anti-order. At the same time, it also tells a story of paternal heritage through the order of language and address: a story told by My Grandpa, My Grandma, My Dad. My Grandma is also known as Jiu'er; My Dad as Douguan. Only My Grandpa is nameless (though he is called Yu Zhan'ao in the original novel). Thus from "my" perspective, the perspective of the narrator, Grandpa is confirmed as the only natural and legitimate father, the only owner of the Name of the Father. This is precisely where the subtle power of the text lies, for it represents the act of patricide as an act of transgression already textually absolved. It is an act of anti-order (against the old order) that is already acknowledged by order (the new order). As no more than a fact of narrative context, the act effectively absolves the Father's threat of castration and the Son's anxiety about his own namelessness. Herein lies the mysterious power of *Red Sorghum*, the power of a successful ideological practice.

Furthermore, in the narrative structure of *Red Sorghum*, the substitution of My Grandpa for Li Datou does not destroy the existing order itself. In the context of the narrative, what is being substituted for is an old and useless father ("Li Datou's oozing white and yellow pus. He's about to kick off") and what is substituted is a young and virile father (My Grandpa). In contrast to the original novel, in the film after My Grandpa presumably kills Li Datou, he does not become a bandit brandishing a shotgun, the image of a thorough outlaw. Instead, he inherits Li Datou/the Father's legacy: the distillery on Eighteen-Mile Hill. Even his primitive act of sacrilege and threat, his urinating into the wine vat, is magically efficacious in terms of production. That particular vat of wine, known as "Eighteen-Mile Red," brought an unusually high price and therefore unprecedented prosperity to the distillery (the Father's legacy). Eighteen-Mile Hill, the dissolute corner of the world forgotten by most people, henceforth becomes an amazingly prosperous town, as demonstrated by the fifth grand sequence of the film, which begins with the image of a wine flag fluttering above the castlelike gate. Giant letters on the flag read: "Eighteen-Mile Red." In the subsequent panoramic shot, we see piles of giant wine vats in the foreground; in the background are streams of busy carts, big and small, customers conversing familiarly, distillery hired hands rushing to and fro. Among the vats are Douguan and My Grandma, playing hide and seek. The hitherto desolate world outside law and order – Eighteen-Mile Hill – now appears surprisingly orderly in its harmony, prosperity, and festivity.

The narrative role of My Grandpa has, as a result, also changed from that of a criminal, patricidal Son to a young and productive Father, filling and reinforcing an empty position and thus becoming the upholder, even creator, of law and order. It is he who has transformed Eighteen-Mile Hill from a place cut off by fear and evil, tarnished by Li Datou's disease and filth, to a lively example of the Ur-society, throbbing with life. As a textual performance, *Red Sorghum* accomplishes an ideological strategy and experimentation. Using the order of Father-Son as a reference system, the text acts out a covert ritual of absolution, thus recognizing the death of the old Father and the appearance of the new Father. Even though the film presents an imaginary picture of a particular historical situation of the Fifth Generation, in the narrative context it nonetheless must employ the language of desire to narrate the life history of an imaginary hero/individual. He therefore can only be a pseudo-subject, interpellated by another ideological ritual so that his individual heroic legend can be perfectly fitted into the social imaginary as a whole. The film cannot but use history as its ultimate horizon, its final reference point, so as to realize this prehistorical story about the imaginary relationship between the individual/subject and his existing conditions.

There is, then, a clear disjuncture in the narrative body of *Red Sorghum*. Within the film, there are two mutually independent narrative sequences, each narrating a separate event with a different context in its textual performance. One is "the story of My Grandpa and My Grandma," in which each grand sequence follows the classic Greimasian narrative grammar: conflict, victory, and transfer. Each time, it is My Grandpa (the hero) who triumphs over his enemy and consequently wins the valued object (My Grandma), thus completing the transfer of the object. As a complete narrative sequence, what is interesting is that each time My Grandpa battles against an imaginary enemy. The first time, the battle is against the highwayman at Eighteen-Mile Hill; but the highwayman is a fake. The second time, it is against Li Datou, whose absence is represented by the empty seat. During the scene of lovemaking amidst the sorghums, the role of the enemy is actually performed by My Grandma's Dad. Yet once again, there is no real conflict. (As an act of amnesty, the scene reinterprets My Grandpa's possession of My Grandma, turning the act of taking the Father's woman into the act of acquiring the Daughter from the Father.) The third time, the conflict is not so much getting Jiu'er back from the kidnapper Crack-shot Sanpao, but rather ascertaining that he "hadn't defiled my woman." The fourth conflict is not against the masses in the distillery, for they do not pose a real threat or opposition. The implicit opponent is only Luohan, a sort of protector of law and order for the Ur-society, the respected head of hired hands in the distillery. My Grandpa's victory then is nothing but an open acknowledgment of his right to possession. The scenario ends with Luohan's departure.

Red Sorghum's fifth grand sequence takes place after nine years have elapsed. The image of Douguan (the son) has erased all traces of the story of patricide. At the first sight of the returning Luohan emerging from the far end of the bridge, My Grandma runs toward him, and My Grandpa chases after her. This episode connects two narratives by bringing us back to the Qingsha Bridge once again, where My Grandpa saved My Grandma the bride from the bandit-hijacker. The merging of these two narratives is achieved through the return of Luohan (the only enemy from the previous sequence whom My Grandpa failed to conquer, the protector of the old order). A panoramic shot of My Grandpa squatting at the head of the bridge, his expression ambiguous, cuts to a medium-long shot of My Grandma. Exhausted but smiling, she says apologetically, "It is Big Brother Luohan."

All of a sudden, in the panoramic shot, My Grandpa freezes in midstride, as though in response to a great shock. The camera cuts to a close-up of his dazed and confused face, his eyes gazing over the sorghum fields. This is followed by an omniscient low-angle panoramic shot of the bridge, accompanied by the voice-over: "Suddenly, the Japanese were here. In July that year, the Japanese started building a road right to the Qingsha Bridge." In the panoramic shot, from the depth of My Grandpa's field of vision, a Japanese armored personnel carrier appears to be driving straight onto the Qingsha Bridge, its national flag fluttering. Thus My Grandpa's gaze allows the filmic text to weave together two separate narrative events. And this is when "real" history manifests itself in the film. The previous time-frame, set in an indistinct prehistoric period, is suddenly suspended, and the story is thrust into a specific historical era with a specific historical event. At the same time, the isolation of Eighteen-Mile Hill from the rest of the world dissolves. The sudden appearance of hundreds of thousands of people, driven along by the Japanese troops to trample down the sorghum stalks, signals the existence of a national Ur-society.

Red Sorghum thus relies on a textual strategy to push back the Sons' coming of age into a prehistoric time zone. For as soon as this rite of passage is completed, real history breaks in. The violent rupture between the two different narrative events symbolically hints at the sudden invasion of commercialism and alien cultures in 1987, which generated a tremendous sense of shock and confusion among the Chinese people. Immediately afterward, the film presents a gory scene of someone being skinned alive (and castrated), thus hinting at the violent arrival of a new history's castrating power.

With this bloody narrative sequence, the film delivers a new value system, represented by the loyal and brave national hero: the triumph of the national spirit. All this is achieved through the relationship between the unwilling butcher-executioner Hu Er and Crack-shot Sanpao; through Hu Er swinging his bloodied butcher knife and shouting curses at the Japanese; and particularly through Luohan's fearless and defiant expression as he is skinned alive, during which time he hurls curses at the Japanese until his last breath. In this same sequence, we are told in a voice-over that Luohan is a Communist Party member. Thus, the protector of an ancient order is transformed into the protector of a new order. Through his brave and horrible death, his body is sublimated into a transcendental signifier, the new possessor of the Father's name, an authoritative figure with the symbolic power of ideology. This is again an absent position, an absent presence with tremendous power to deter as well as to inspire. The scenes following Luohan's death depict the oath of revenge, the ambush under the moon, the wait at the bridge for the Japanese, and the final fight to the death against the Japanese/foreign invaders. On the narrative surface, this is a folk story about kinship revenge. In the deep structure of the narrative, it is a paean to the national spirit, an imaginary ritual of castrating the castrator.

At the same time, the narrative is also a social coming of age after the personal coming of age of the Son – the story of desire. It is an ideological ritual of the individual being interpellated and subjugated by the signifier of authority, a ritual whereby the Son returns the Father's woman to the transcendental Father. If the first half of the filmic narrative is a de-centered story, in which a heroic legend of the Son/Father is composed of history's marginal discourse, then the second narrative event is a process through which the center is reestablished, where a nationalist, political myth is constituted through classic history's mainstream discourse. In comparison with the first narrative event, the basic relationship between the characters is fundamentally reversed in the second narrative event.

In the sixth grand sequence – the ritual sacrifice for Luohan – a large bowl of Eighteen-Mile Red on the altar table signifies Luohan, the transcendental and idealized Father. Jiu'er, after kowtowing solemnly and taking a deep draught from the bowl, takes her position beside the altar table. As the one presiding over the ceremony, Jiu'er becomes the physical manifestation of Luohan's absent presence: this is a Mother substituting for the authority of the Father. From her burning gaze, the camera cuts to My Grandpa, Douguan, and the hired hands standing in front of the altar. Following her commands to her son Douguan – "Kneel down!" "Kowtow!" and "Drink up!" – are cross-cuts of the flashing eyes of My Grandma and My Grandpa. She issues the authoritative command: "If you are men enough, drink up this wine and go blow up the Japanese tanks in the morning. Avenge Brother Luohan's death!" This command in effect transforms her into the role of a sender. What is especially interesting is that the response to this command comes from My Grandpa, who sets fire to the bowl of wine that signifies Luohan, leads the hired hands in kneeling in front of the altar table, and starts the "Song to the Wine God," holding the wine bowl in his hands. Thus, not only does he respond to the command My Grandma issues to her son Douguan, he also visually assumes Douguan's position.

If in the first narrative event Douguan as the Son signifies My Grandpa's possession of the Father's name, then in the second narrative event, Douguan as the Son signifies My Grandpa's state of submission. This is the second time in the film that the "Song to the Wine God" is sung. The first time is when the new wine emerges from the distiller under Luohan's general command. A dilapidated, rather unauthoritative statue of the wine god appears in a reverse crane shot. What really fills the entire screen are the hired hands standing in front of the altar table, on the same horizontal level with the camera.

By the end of the song, the screen is saturated with humanity, accompanied by a hearty venting of the primitive life force. The second time, however, the bowl of burning sorghum wine appears in a close-up at a low angle, while My Grandpa and the hired hands, kneeling beneath it, appear in a posture of submission. This time, the "Song to the Wine God" represents a promise, a blood pledge, for it shows My Grandpa in submission to a different value system, a subject as social being, thus completing the ideological and social coming of age for the Sons' generation.

But this is not enough. In order to fully complete the rite of social passage, in order also to stitch up the suture between the first and second narrative events, he must return the Father's woman. He must sacrifice this woman/Woman on the altar of History, thus demonstrating his total submission and self-sacrifice. Thus, in the fight against the Japanese, in the imaginary ritual of castrating the castrator/foreign invader, Jiu'er must be the first to be sacrificed, the one sacrifice visually represented and in the most resplendent manner. She must, for the second time, fall on her back in the blinding light. In the first instance, dressed in red (signifier of desire), she lay down on the altar table of male desire, her eyes brimming with hot tears. It was a glorious stage in the individual male subject's coming of age. In the second instance, now dressed in white (signifier of sacrifice), in an elevating medium shot, slowly waving her arms up and down as though in an elegant dance, she falls down on the altar table of history, once again becoming a beautiful object of sacrifice for the collective male society's coming of age.

The final grand sequence fully exemplifies all the basic characteristics of an ideological ritual and an imaginary castration. When the Japanese tanks start to roll in, to the whistle of automatic machine guns, Wangsao, Jiu'er, and Wang Wenyi fall in rapid succession. Following My Grandpa's screamed command, Dazhuang and Erzhuang fire the cannon; yet the bursting cannon itself leaves Dazhuang and Erzhuang nowhere to be found. Close to madness at this point, My Grandpa pulls the fuse of the land mine; at the other end, no blast appears. Yet in the elevating shot that follows, holding in their hands smoking homemade bombs and waving broadswords, My Grandpa and the hired hands rush the Japanese tanks. A great blast,

and smoke blackens the entire screen. As the smoke slowly clears,
except for a broken Japanese vehicle, all we can glimpse are the
corpses of the hired hands. In an elevated shot, My Grandpa stands
alone, like the statue of a national hero, his whole body covered with
mud, gilded bronze by the setting sun. After this symbolic eclipse,
only the wildly dancing sorghum remains, the color of deep crimson.

Then, resonating with Liu Dahao's screeching trumpet, an almost
festive ethnic drum music emerges in the background. At the same
time, the whistle of the machine guns, the noise of the engines, all suddenly disappear. Rather than a bloody battle to the death, this is
instead a contest between national spirit/culture and an alien culture.
It is a ritual of cultural combat. Through the representation of the castration of the castrator, the film symbolically assuages the collective
anxiety and shock of the present-day Chinese, again faced with an
onslaught from alien cultures. Like a cadenza to the productions of
the Fifth Generation, this film presents the hero/subject in unusually
high range, at the same time pronouncing the final defeat of the desperate spiritual charge by the Fifth Generation. It is still the Sons' art,
but now the Sons are in submission. No longer a broken bridge, it now
seems like an ancient, albeit marginal, rainbow of discourse. But this
rainbow cannot bring us to the other shore. The Fifth Generation
faces a historical ending.

Conclusion: Confusion, Salvation, and Sacrifice

Four other important films were produced by the Fifth Generation in
1987: Sun Zhou's *Gei Kafei jia dian tang* (*Add a Little Sugar to the Coffee*);
Zhang Zemings's *Taiyang yu* (*Sunny Rain*); Wu Ziniu's *Wanzhong*
(*Evening Bell*); and Zhou Xiaowen's *Zuihou de feng kuang* (*The Last
Madness*). As representatives of the Sons' art, these films share some
common characteristics: that sense of the lonely rambler by the side of
the broken bridge, as well as that weak and desperate backward glance
from the bridge's far side. *Add a Little Sugar to the Coffee* and *Sunny Rain*
are the first Fifth Generation films to focus on urban life, and as such
they depict the surface signs of a modern metropolis and express the
experience of shock from the lonely rambler's perspective. At the

same time, these films show that both the economic reform and the process of industrialization have already blocked the generation of Sons from history and traditional culture. It is still the Sons' generation. However, it is no longer a generation that lost its Father, but a generation that does not have a Father. Even the Father-Son hierarchy seems to give way to a new order led by someone else. As another chapter in the fragmented spiritual autobiography of the Fifth Generation, these films are again filled with signifiers that are excessively representational, over-saturated and infinitely self-exposing.

This is no longer a rebellion against a historically cyclical discourse; rather, it is an expression of wordlessness, experienced in a new, perhaps even greater and more profound, shock. No longer an attempt at capturing the imagery of national history and the space for national survival, it is rather about the sense of confusion when faced with a radically new experience of time and space. We see waves of humanity swarming in the metropolis, pressed flat in a long shot, children stomping to a break-dance rhythm, old men following the slow and gentle forms of t'ai chi; we see people appear like ants against the background of a gigantic commercial billboard, and the tears of an even younger generation, shed for a fallen spaceship on the other side of the ocean. As the spiritual sons of the Cultural Revolution, the Fifth Generation cannot make themselves part of the crowd through their urban films. They are forever looking for a way home. It is as though, through the story of a woman cobbler from the country, a "woman from a century back," they are trying to find a "grand and tragic" classic romance, a real gateway to enter history (*Add a Little Sugar to the Coffee*). Yet all they can do is take a lonely ramble along the evening streets amidst the hazy waves of blinking lights from the shop windows, like the female protagonist of *Sunny Rain*. At the right-hand corner of the screen, the word *home* formed by neon lights registers the fact that they can never go home again.

Once again, history is made discontinuous and fragmentary. An era – perhaps the era of the Fifth Generation – is at an end. At a time when the dead are not yet dead and the newborn are just being delivered, the Fifth Generation is again turning its gaze toward salvation, not for themselves, but for memory, history, national culture, and survival. The basic narrative event in *Evening Bell* is the burial of a war: the corpses left over from a battle already finished, and perhaps an entire tragic era. It is really a reiteration of *Red Sorghum*, purging the threat of alien cultures in the Imaginary, castrating the castrator with a superior ancient civilization. Yet in *Evening Bell*, in the face of castration anxiety, the excessive expressiveness characteristic of the Fifth Generation is more than ever shown to be empty, weak, and fragmented. Only when it is injected into the filmic image of the invaders does it regain its dynamic force. Even the imaginary ritual of castration is left uncompleted. The savior, in the process of salvation, has fallen further than ever.

And yet, the first successful commercial film of the Fifth Generation, *The Last Madness*, succeeds in amply illuminating the historical fortune of the Fifth Generation in a strikingly mature and carefree manner. In the final grand sequence of *The Last Madness*, the camera renders an even, cross-cut shot of the hero and the villain (both cast in the image of the Son in the filmic context). In the midst of an intense fight, together they tumble down a sharp slope by some railroad tracks. Following the blast from the bomb tied to the villain's waist, it suddenly becomes very quiet; the screen fills with slowly dispersing smoke. Cut to a screen filled with a soft white fog; a train rolls in. Cut to the same train pulling out. A sad tune is piped in. On the white background of rolling credits drops of blood begin to spatter, until the whole screen is stained red. Perhaps this can be understood as a symbolic gesture of farewell from the Fifth Generation to its own historical existence, a gesture that is both sad and also carefree. It is as though the generation of Sons must use itself as a sacrifice in exchange for the peace and salvation of the Ur-society, in exchange for the trouble-free ignition of the historical engine. Perhaps, the broken bridge is still a monument of Fifth Generation art, a monument never to be built on human strength.

Notes

1 The Fifth Generation refers to a group of young directors, all of whom graduated from the Beijing Film Academy after 1982, except Zhang Zeming. They include Chen Kaige, Zhang Yimou, Tian Zhuangzhuang, Wu Ziniu, Huang Jianxin, Zhang Junzhao, Hu Mei, Li Shaohong, Sun Zhou, Zhou Xiaowen, and Zhang Zeming.

2 The Fourth Generation refers to a group of outstanding film directors who graduated from the Beijing Film Academy before and during the Cultural Revolution and began to direct movies independently after 1979. They include Ding Yinnan, Wu Yigong, Teng Wenji, Huang Jianzhong, Xie Fei, Zheng Dongtian, Zhang Nuanxin, Yang Yanjin, Huang Shuqin, and Wu Tianming.

3 In his 1992 film *Lan fengzheng* (*Blue Kite*), Tian Zhuangzhuang became the first filmmaker to directly present a Cultural Revolution scene. The following year Chen Kaige also represented the Cultural Revolution in *Bawang bieji* (*Farewell, My Concubine*) In contrast, Zhang Yimou presented the Cultural Revolution as a tragicomedy in his 1994 film, *Huozhe* (*To Live*).

4 Lu Xun, *Kuangren riji* (Diary of madman) in *Lu Xun quanji* (The complete works of Lu Xun) (Beijing: Renmen wenxue chubanshe, 1956); Bing Xin, *Siren du qiaocui* (Alone and weak) in *Zhongguo xiandai zuojia wenji, Bing Xin* (The collected works of modern Chinese writers: Bing Xin) (Beijing: Renmin wenxue chubanshe, 1985).

5 In other words, they had access to the pre–Cultural Revolution ideological formation.—TRANS.

6 This is a poem by Guo Moruo (1892–1978) that uses the Indian myth of the phoenix burning to ashes every five hundred years and then being reborn again.

7 This phrase was used by Mao to exhort the youth.—TRANS.

8 See Guo Xiaodong, *Zhongguo zhinqing buluo* (The tribes of China's youth) (Guangzhou: Huacheng chubanshe, 1990); Deng Xian, *Zhongguo Zhiqing meng* (The dreams of China's youth) (Beijing: Wenhua yishu chubanshe, 1997); Du Honglin, *Fengchao dangluo 1955–1979 nian: zhongguo zhishi qingnian shangshan xiaxiang yundong shi* (Through storm and stress 1955–1979: a history of China's youth movement) (Shenzhen: Haitian chubanshe, 1993).

9 See "Xuetong lun" (Theory of class inheritance) in *Wenge zhong de guaishi guaiyu* (Strange occurrences in the Cultural Revolution), ed. Jin Chunming, Huang Yuchong, Chang Huimin (Beijing: Qiushi chubanshe, 1989).

10 This was a prevalent phrase during the Cultural Revolution.—TRANS.

11 See Chen Kaige, "Qinguo ren" (The people of the kingdom of qin) in *Dangdai dianying* (Contemporary cinema), no. 5, 1985, pp. 101–7; *Yijiu liuliu: wode hongweibing shidai* (1966: My time as a Red Guard) (Tokyo: Jiantanshe, 1989); and the interview with Tian Zhuangzhuang in Wu Wenguang's documentary *1966: My Time as a Red Guard.*

12 The film *Yige he bage* (*One and Eight*) was completed in 1983. The director was Zhang Junzhao, the cinematographers, Zhang Yimou and Xiaofeng; it was produced by the Guangxi Film Studio. But after the 1984 release of *Yellow Earth, One and Eight* was subjected to over one hundred revisions before being released in 1985.

13 *Daoma zei* (*Horse Thief*) (1985) is the second work by the Fifth Generation director Tian Zhuangzhuang.

14 *Heipao shijian* (*The Black Cannon Incident*) is Fifth Generation director Huang Jianxin's first film. *Juexiang* (*The Last Sound*) is Fifth Generation director Zhang Zeming's first work.

15 *Huang tudi* (*Yellow Earth*) is the second work (after *One and Eight*) by the Youth Film Group of the Guangxi Film Studio. It was directed by Chen Kaige; the cinematographer was Zhang Yimou. The film won the prize for best cinematography at the Nanterre Film Festival in France, and both the Best Cinematography prize and the Special Jury Prize at the Hawaii International Film Festival, among other international awards. Soon after, Chinese film, represented by the work of Fifth Generation directors, began to gain international attention. For a time, Chen Kaige's *Yellow Earth* was the signature Chinese art film.

16 For the filmmakers' remarks, see *Beijing dianying xueyuan xuebao* (Journal of the Beijing Film Academy), vol. 2, 1985. [Laozi, often transliterated as Lao Tze, is the founding philosopher of Taoism.—TRANS.]

17 Zheng Dongtian, "Congqian youkuai hong tudi" ("Once there was a piece of red earth"), *Dangdai dianying* (Contemporary cinema), no. 1, 1988, p. 69.

18 A popular Maoist exhortation and practice.—TRANS.

19 See Xie Yuan, "Ta jiao Chen Kaige" (His name is Chen Kaige), *Dangdai diangying* (Contemporary cinema), no. 1, 1993, pp. 84–90. [Xie is the actor who played Lao Gan. –TRANS.]

20 That is, there would be no knowledge to illuminate the world.—TRANS.

21 After acting as cinematographer for *One and Eight* (1985), *Yellow Earth* (1984), and *The Great Parade* (1985), Zhang Yimou starred in *Old Well* (1986), directed by Wu Tianming. In 1987, Zhang directed his first feature film, *Hong gaoliang* (*Red Sorghum*), which won the Golden Bear award at the Berlin International Film Festival, the first Chinese film to win a major European film award.

22 Zhang Xudong, "Yinmu shang de yuyan zhi wu he lishi zhi wu – dui zhongguo xindianying de changshixing bawa" (Filmic language and the historical object: on the new Chinese films,) *Dianying yishu*, (Film art), vol. 5, 1989.

23 Mo Yan, "Yingpian 'Honggaoliang' guanhou zagan" (Reflections on the film *Red Sorghum*,) *Dangdai dianying* (Contemporary cinema), vol. 2, 1988, p. 53.

24 Yang Ping, "Yige shitu gaozao guanzhong de daoyan – yu qinnian daoyan Tian Zhuangzhuang yixitan" (A Director Who Wanted to Change the Audience: An Interview with Young Director Tian Zhuangzhuang), *Dazhong dianying* (People's film), vol. 9, 1986, p. 4.

25 Li Yiming, "After the Act of Patricide," *Dianying yishu* (Film art), vol. 6, 1989, p. 10.

Translated by Lisa Rofel and Hu Ying

2

Postcolonialism and Chinese Cinema of the Nineties

Between Preindustrial Society and Postmodernist Culture

Films of the early 1990s exhibit complex meanings when their social context is considered. Mainstream films reemerged then, presenting a historical monologue of the preindustrial social order while simultaneously reproducing orthodox discourse.[1] But art films also entered production during the noiseless infiltration of postmodernism, under the interpellating gaze of privileged Western culture, providing an awkward foil to a relatively delayed modernization process. Chinese art film of the nineties, primarily the work of Fifth Generation directors, was caught between preindustrial society and postmodern culture, mired in a dilemma that was heightened by the crushing economic reality and the ruptured national culture.

In 1987, Fifth Generation filmmaking was noted for its historical and cultural retrospective drive, its construction of meta-history and meta-language, and its typically modernist attempt to express the inexpressible. Its full spectrum of aesthetic and cultural narration was most completely represented in *The King of Children* and *Red Sorghum*. But Fifth Generation directors started producing film texts about Chinese history again in the nineties. These texts no longer presented the nation's survival as a cultural allegory that hinged on introspection or self-critique. Nor did they conduct an organic, polyphonic dialogue between reality and history. In China, the 1980s had ended in social upheaval, leaving behind a traumatic memory. Panicked, the epochal historical retrospection, all prepped for the arrival of a whirlwind new civilization, lost its foothold in reality. The

Real, a primary horizon where historical allegories are supposedly constructed, lost its clarity and its anchor. The Real seemed to be simply an episode in the circular dance of history; perhaps merely a familiar link in a shattered chain found among the ruins. In the Fifth Generation's filmic texts reality and history tend to head in opposite directions whenever they seem about to overlap. Moreover, since film is an artifact connecting art, commerce, industry, and ideology, the Fifth Generation directors had an even harder time trying to survive the social and economic reality of the nineties. Indulging in a pure artistic narcissism was no escape, since film is an excessively expensive discourse.

Rather, escape required them to perforate another market, the Western, especially European, market for art films. Winning awards at important international film festivals appeared to be the only way to reach that market. Initially an indicator of the success of Chinese art films, winning awards soon also became a means of survival, providing a chance to secure foreign investment, coproduction, or other forms of assistance. Ironically, this narrow gateway became the sole opening for directors who wanted to keep a cultural foothold in art, evade the commercial tide, and thus avoid the mainstream model.

Even while fleeing through it, however, the directors fell into a different trap. Since securing foreign investment for future projects through successful appearances at European film festivals had become the focus, the prerequisite for filmmaking became the representation of an Orient that was palatable and intelligible for Western viewers. The resulting internalization of this Western cultural perspective – the aesthetic preference of film-festival judges – induced Chinese/Fifth Generation filmmakers to reconstruct their narrative subjects according to projected Western expectations. Fifth Generation films that managed to squeeze through these narrow gateways to become self-conscious, marginal representations of an Other in Eurocentric culture simply fell under the yoke of one discursive power in their attempts to escape from another. Moving between these two poles, the text of Chinese art films gradually filled with breaches. For when the narrative of history ceased to be a deconstructive retelling based on a (Chinese) reality, it became a (Western) postmodernist replication. It became a field of meanings that might appear to be different yet not at all alien to Western eyes, putting on display the spectacle of an imagined preindustrial China.

In this book's first chapter, "The Severed Bridge," I mentioned that the movement for historical and cultural retrospection, begun in the mid 1980s, contained a self-contradiction and presented various mutually exclusive cultural and political agendas. On the one hand, this so-called enlightenment intended to complete a deeper cultural introspection and a historical critique, to bury the 5000-year-old spectre of history forever, and to open a passage for the impending modernization. It sought to resume the May Fourth Movement of the 1920s, which the war effort against Japan had interrupted. On the other hand, the search for roots sought to bridge over the rift of May Fourth culture, to return to the source of national culture, and to reconstitute the nation's cultural subjectivity. The root-searching movement was both a deeper and more internalized demand of the search for enlightenment. Returning to history – to "ancient Chinese medicine and archaic books" – proved the sole route to rewriting this history; only by piercing the mist obscuring the rift that May Fourth culture represents for language, time, and space could one complete a profound, unhurried retrospective examination. In actuality, of course, this alleged retrospection and search for roots would be the last such effort undertaken before the whirlwind of civilization completely blocked history from view. It was perhaps the most desperate effort since the May Fourth Movement to end the internal exile of Chinese culture and Chinese intellectuals.

As a cultural revolution, the May Fourth event's most profound effect was its replacement of the classical language (*wenyan*) with the vernacular (*baihua*). If the linguistic order, that core representation of social order and language structure,[2] is, though seemingly different, structurally in fact the same as that of power,[3] then the May Fourth revolution in language and writing surely opened a cultural and historical rift. A surge of foreign words and the introduction and internalization of Western culture accompanied the establishment of the vernacular. Since the May Fourth Movement, though not during it, generations of Chinese intellectuals have been alienated from their national culture. This is a cultural and spiritual process of internal exile. Antitraditionalism and the critique of history (breaking completely with traditional values) have become the sole mainstream ideology, constantly reactivating the memory of the bloody hundred years to fortify this process. As an outcome of the newborn language order, replete with newly introduced cultural models and newly ideologized cultural positions, internal exile transformed Chinese national experiences and necessarily estranged Chinese intellectuals. (This is what I will call the lay-out of an emptied-out history.) The movements of cultural retrospection and the root searching in the mid 1980s also attempted, in a certain sense, to end this internal exile, and organically relocate the nation's cultural experiences and memories in contemporary culture.

Yet, while the processes of accelerating modernization and impending commercialization interrupted cultural retrospection, a new chasm was also opening up. In the early nineties, an ambiguous yet enchanting visual text of Chinese history reemerged to showcase the very same internal exile in yet another new process of estrangement and alienation, a newly distorted version of postcolonial culture. Internalizing the gaze of Western culture, Chinese national culture and national experiences were even more profoundly alienated, frozen in the language and representation of the Other.

History and Discourse

Of those who successfully navigated the bottleneck of that era, Zhang Yimou seemed best able to elude the gazes of both cultures and the threat of their discourses of power. An architect of Fifth Generation film language and one of the group's initial groundbreakers, he made his first film, *Red Sorghum*, a landmark at the edge of the cultural chasm. Zhang Yimou created an elaborate and expressive national mythology aimed at superseding the cultural dilemma of allegorical self-entanglement facing the Fifth Generation. In a filmic and symbolic coming-of-age ritual, with the Fifth Generation itself as the supposedly absent hero, Zhang showcased himself to the Western world as a sign of the oriental/Chinese cultural subject. Unusually for art films of the 1990s, his *Ju Dou* and *Raise the Red Lantern* successfully cut into European, and even American, cultural perspectives on the strength of Zhang's award-winning momentum. Incidentally, each film was nominated for the Best Foreign Film Oscar in successive years, establishing Chinese films as contenders for Oscar recognition. *Ju Dou* was not favored at Cannes. But *Raise the Red Lantern* won the Silver Medal in Venice. Both films have proved popular in the Western film market. So, while marginalized in China, Zhang Yimou's films served as representatives of mainstream Chinese films in Western culture.

Zhang Yimou succeeded, or fell into the trap (more accurately, he leaped into it), because he cleverly avoided the Sisyphean spiritual journey of historical and cultural retrospection. Gracefully leaping the double barrier of the Fifth Generation's root-searching return to culture and their concomitant critique of history, Zhang thus avoided the quagmire of conflicting missions. The collective internal exile – or emptied-out history – piled up detritus sufficient to block the retrospective view. This refuse heap provided Zhang Yimou with a sanitized, convenient playground. In it he found a space for turning history into discourse, the narrative of history into the repetition of historical stories. And there his retrospective mission turned toward re(producing) the surface of an oriental culture within the scope of the cultural expectations of the West. *Ju Dou* depends on the concept of cyclical history for its narrative circuit, irony, and build-up. It takes form as a narrative model of cultural retrospection. A strict hierarchical relation of Father and Son, a woman who belongs to the Other, and the descendant of the Other who destroys history, all help construct a Western – and Freudian – visual theme of voyeurism and a narrative about desire. The dregs of history, its lingering ghosts and shadows, make up the marvelous spectacle of colorful hanging cloth in an archaic dye mill. An oriental historical discourse about the slaying of the Son is successfully superimposed by Zhang Yimou onto the Western patricide complex.

Ju Dou's story of lust and violence is thus set in an archaic *mise en scène*. In most of the film's daytime sequences, a misty golden light illuminates the dye mill. Plummeting like waterfalls, the colorful pieces of cloth animate the mill's ancient, heavy machines with a sense of motion. Even the prisonlike courtyard, captured in repeated aerial shots, takes on the coquettishness suggested by the swing and fall of bright red and yellow cloth. In the film narrative every element of the plot and *mise en scène* presents itself in circulation and destruction, suggesting a contemplative view of history as cycle. The father–son relationship, desire and prohibition, fatalism and the castrating power of History comprise not only the film's representation of the Symbolic Order, but the very core of what is being narrated. If the prototypical narrative of the root-searching artists ("the wife of a good man is never good enough, though the beasts secure the beauties") is read as a critique of history, an allegory of the Father and Son structure of power, the castrating power of History itself, then Zhang Yimou codes the narrative in *Ju Dou* to suggest ossified forms of history and power. The Father and patriarchal power rule over the historical space in the name of the Father. In the narrative context of *Ju Dou*, patriarchal power is always an empty but indestructible signifier of sanctity. The place of the Father in this story is undoubtedly occupied by the owner of the dye mill, Yang Jinshan (played by Li Wei). Yang's social status and money form the basis for the prototype and enable him to *own* Ju Dou (played by Gong Li) just as he owns the dye mill and the mule. But ownership exists in name only for Yang, though even the Father's impotence does not vitiate his patriarchal power. On the contrary. The Father's legal ownership of the woman in the narrative oppresses Ju Dou, and it denies her to the Other or Son's generation, demonstrating history's power to castrate. Yang Jinshan is not actually an embodiment of patriarchal power or order. As one of the successors to own the ancestral tablet of the Yang family, he is simply one among countless Sons who form the family chain. Desire in its entirety is a desperate and, for him, entirely futile mission of producing another son to continue the family.

The most important circuit in the film's plot is the rectification of patriarchal power – off-kilter, slanted, and damaged – in the generation of the Son. In *Red Sorghum*, the son Douguan, who idles away his time by playing hide-and-seek with his parents among the wine vats, confirms the head sedan-chair carrier as the lawful occupant of the Father's position rather than as a usurper. In *Ju Dou*, however, the fact that little Tianbai calls Yang Jinshan "Father" signifies the return of a lawful title and the reaffirmation of the order. It is not the actual patriarch (the pedantic and senile head of the Yang tribe in *Ju Dou*) or his power to terrorize that obstructed Tianqing (played by Li Baotian) and Ju Dou's arrogant desires, and drives them out of order, into an underground cell. It is the Father order, by which I mean the naming of and recognition between a Father and a Son who are not actually related by blood. In the rather ironic and comic sequence of stopping the coffin, seven shots of Tianqing and Ju Dou wailing and falling into the dust are matched with six reversed low-angle shots of Tianbai, who, in the dazzling sunlight, sits atop the coffin, holding the memorial tablet for the dead. This contrast lends the sequence a tragic sense that history is a cycle. Condemnation seems to come from both Father and Son. When the power of the Father becomes the empty Name of the Father, its authenticity and terror increase, since the only enforcement it has is the younger, stronger, Son-generation. The nursery song, "Ding-dong Bell," heard twice in the film, testifies in its cyclical occurrence to the eventual victory of the patriarchal power and order. It first appears when the usurpers seem to have won a victory: their baby Tianbai cradled in the brightly dyed cloths, Tianqing and Ju Dou cheerfully sing the song to the rhythmic beat of the machine. The second time, however, it is sung by Yang Jinshan as he sits in a wooden bucket hanging from the roof. Ju Dou's contraceptive attempts are torturing her. The stubborn little Tianbai keeps throwing stones at the "licentious" room where Ju Dou and Tianqing meet. In a tilt shot of the empty, gruesome house, the rafters echo with the same melody in an ancient, venomous, and happy register.

Ju Dou is based on *Fu xi fu xi* (*Obsession*), a cultural retrospection and roots-searching fiction by Liu Heng.[4] Doubtless it is an Eastern story of Son murder, the silent murder in which no blood is ever shed. By contrast, in *Ju Dou* the Father is murdered twice. The first murder is an accident: little Tianbai topples the wooden bucket that contains Yang Jinshan, drowning him in the blood-red dye basin. The second is a conscious patricide. The adult Tianbai carries the unconscious Tianqing up from the cellar, where Tianqing and Ju Dou have been cloistered for their tryst, and casts him into the blood-red dye vat. Then Tianbai ignores Ju Dou's desperate begging and viciously clubs Tianqing's hands loose from the rope. This is in fact one of the most important changes in the transition from prose to film. In the original, Tianqing finds it impossible to endure Tianbai's wintry gaze day after day and drowns himself, naked, in a vat of water. This death is a humble apology. In the film, a bloodless suicide is turned into a sanguinary and heinous murder. It is still, nevertheless, the murder of the Son. Tianbai is only carrying out what Yang Jinshan is no longer able to do. "I'll tell the absolute truth now," Ju Dou screams in the film. "Your real father is Tianqing." And this said, the murder can then be viewed under the Western gaze as an expression of the Oedipus complex. In a visual repetition, brightly dyed cloths pour from the rafters. For when Tianqing and Ju Dou initially consummated their love, red cloth fell against Ju Dou's face and hair, echoing the wildly dancing red sorghum of another Zhang film.

When Tianbai knocks Tianqing's hands loose from the rope, red cloths cascade into the vat, covering and entombing Tianqing. Here lies another of Zhang Yimou's changes from the original. In the novel, after Tianqing's modest suicide, Ju Dou returns to her village with a new baby named Tianhuang, a name that places him in the same generation as Tianqing and Tianbai. In a reference to Lu Xun's famous parable of cultural suffocation, the mother and baby are said to live in an "iron house" of endless suffering. In the film, a panoramic low-angle shot of the mill building is superimposed over a shot of a deluge of red cloth. Then, in a longish sequence accompanied by a sound-track of a violent fire, the hysterical Ju Dou burns the mill down. This fiery devastation tragically repeats in the conclusion Yang Jinshan's earlier comic attempt to set the place on fire. Besides forming a visual climax, it also encloses the narrative and blocks the extension of any historical perspective. Historical retrospection terminates with the end of the narrative.

Although the closing-in and internalization of the Western gaze in *Ju Dou* plays out for us the restoration of ancient objects and a poeticization of the surface text, complete with the representation of a Freudian cave and the classical scene of voyeurism narrated in a language of desire and set in an Oedipal situation, all this does not completely account for the Fifth Generation's excessive filmic mode or the historical as well as cultural retrospection contained in *Obsession. Ju Dou*, after all, provides an allegorical text. In a certain way, it relates the heavy and painful emotions associated with the Tiananmen Square crackdown to the China of the nineties.

In *Raise the Red Lantern*, however, Zhang Yimou found a cleverer narrative mode for representing history as discourse and façade for the Western gaze. Here, the myth and allegory of Chinese history is canceled out. Replacing it is a mirror image of China, captured in the Western gaze as the Other. In a typically enclosed Chinese space, in a writing style à la Su Tong, author of the story, "Qiqie chengqun" ("Wives and Concubines"), on which the film is based, Zhang Yimou cancels time and consequently the extension of history, and produces a mirror image of Chinese culture frozen into a façade. Zhang has fabricated a discourse of Chinese history saturated with the Western discourse of power, desire (the desire to desire), and repression; and because it focuses on women, his story about "the mad woman in the attic" makes the mirror image even more attractive.

Most interestingly, Zhang Yimou selected a museum as the setting for the historic story to which Su Tong has contributed a nice post-modern twist. But the Chen residence in *Raise the Red Lantern* is not just a space for exhibiting cultural relics as an ancient building, it is itself a cultural relic. A museum is a bridge between reality and its representations. It does not lead one to any truth, essence, or origin, because the museum can only display objects metonymically, at least twice removed from that which they are originally supposed to represent or signify.[5] For Zhang Yimou, the choice of a museum for the *mise en scène* (the most important element of visual language) is meaningful in and of itself. The museum succeeds in turning the noumenon of Chinese history into a filmic discourse of history. In Su Tong's writing, a fictitious narrative signifies ruptured time and space in language that, on the one hand, alienates and estranges Chinese history and its specific politics and discourses, and on the other, deconstructs the discourses of power in history.

In Zhang Yimou's film, the selection of this *mise en scène* sends into exile all historical retrospection and seals it into the façade of history; it reorganizes an oriental cultural order under a Western gaze. The estrangements in *Raise the Red Lantern* are not intended to be viewed by a Chinese audience, but are exhibited for the delectation and inspection of the West. As one American film commentator admitted with a tinge of embarrassment, "I may be expressing a sense of superiority, but what attracts us to the film, I have to admit, is its exoticism."[6] The film's narrative hinges on this *mise en scène*, shot in full from a fixed high-angle camera, to convey a classical Chinese sense of enclosure. The narrative provides an authentic historical sense and lends it the themes of imprisonment and alienation. Song Lian (played by Gong Li) says at one point, "I don't understand what is meant by a human being in this courtyard. The humans act like dogs or cats or whatever. But never like human beings." Her line resonates with Western contemporary culture's most striking spatial metaphors: the blueprints of the prison and the panopticon as allegories of human society. And herein lies the cultural heroics of the Fifth Generation. *Raise the Red Lantern* serves as an exemplary effort to express the inexpressible in Chinese history and culture. Fifth Generation films are consequently twice-removed museum representations. *Raise the Red Lantern* turns Chinese history first into an allegorical representation of a historical façade, and then into an exotic object for the Western gaze. The Fifth Generation's common visual theme of space's victory over time becomes an empty but alluring form for grounding this narrative.

The film's use of red lanterns, another crucial element of its *mise en scène*, adds a coquettish touch of color to this typical Chinese museum. But the lanterns are not there just for their oriental appeal, they also construct the major part of the filmic narrative. In such sequences as the women's struggle for favor, the fight over ordering vegetable or meat dishes (a privilege that travels from house to house with the lanterns), the tragedy of the servant Yan-er, and the haunting of the third wife's house, lanterns lead the way. At the same time, the lanterns also internalize the Western gaze. They signify the centrality of the ceremonial in the history of old Chinese life: lanterns being lit, extinguished, or sealed; lanterns left on overnight; wives waiting to be selected in the courtyard at dusk; the fabricated ritual of "feet drumming." All this, plus the ironic rhythm of Peking opera and the pathetic wordless female humming bereft of instrumental accompaniment, the lively nursery rhyme about bloody or bloodless killings, and the rhythmic sounds of "feet drumming" in the dusk are all included to signify the deathly dance and hollow ceremony of old China.

This struggle for favor that breaks out in a "women's kingdom" is more a story of power than of desire. What rules this closed space, what is deciding to light or to extinguish the lanterns – the Name of the Father – is not necessarily attached to a human being; it may simply be the "rules of the courtyard." With its medium-specific way of negating and dislocating its subject, the film keeps the object of five women's desires – powerful Master Chen, who controls their collective destiny – always in silhouette, absent in his presence, an offscreen voice. This effectively makes him into a puppet who carries out rules. Struggles, hatred, and grievances among the five women in *Raise the Red Lantern* provide an empty signifier that deters either contemplation of history or the predicaments of reality, and turns this story of power into a narrative of desire for a Western audience's consumption. The frequently used frontal close-ups of Song Lian in balanced frames feed the Western male gaze and its expectation of oriental beauty, making her image fundamental to this panorama of the orient.

As in *Ju Dou*, the temporal cycles in *Raise the Red Lantern* (a four-season year stretching from summer to summer) are clearly marked with the vermilion word *xia* (summer), written in cursive hand and punctuating the arrivals of the fourth and the fifth wives; this device transforms a contemplation about circularity in Chinese history into a structurally enclosed filmic narrative. The Eastern story of oppression, murder, and "cannibalism" is a romance for the Westerner. Indeed, Western film critics have highly praised the chilling and suffocating quality of the narrative, calling it "beautiful" and "enchanting." And so *Raise the Red Lantern* transcends China to become a "global" artifact. Chinese history and culture are turned into a dead butterfly: colorful and delicate but pinned down under the Western gaze. With this film, Zhang Yimou offers us a typical postcolonial cultural text.

Ruptures in the Signified

Among the Fifth Generation filmic texts, Chen Kaige's *Bian zou bian chang* (*Life on a String*) presents another interesting example of this syndrome of "fleeing from one trap while falling into another." Like *Yellow Earth*, *Life on a String* tells a story about Chinese history and culture. The difference, however, is that here history no longer bears even the mark of temporality. A few dilapidated scenes of generalized eternal space convey the evacuation of time. Nor is history here a narration except in the sense that the Chinese agrarian existence is bound to earth, dependent on heavenly waters. One feels the omnipresent heaviness of history and is painfully helpless in the encounter. It is like watching Hanhan run in *Yellow Earth*, against the crowd and toward a final, balanced, brightly lit but empty horizon.

In *Life on a String*, Chinese history, its gaze of retrospection and critique, no longer forms a context. Indeed, the film does not even include in the representational order the presence of an influential absence that might condition how the filmic signifiers present themselves. In comparison to *Yellow Earth* and *The King of Children*, *Life on a String* is actually more tightly focused on the narrative object of Chinese history and culture. It is distinctive in that it is not an introspective, spiritual journey through the chasm of national culture. Rather, its narrative of history targets the West, tries to locate the entry point into Western culture. History, that long, strangely compelling history of China in the Western gaze, is merely an empty signifier in *Life on a String*. The film is nothing more than a broad and random space for situating meaning.

Based on Shi Tiesheng's novel, *Life on a String*, the film tells the story of a blind minstrel who plays the *qin*, a guitarlike musical instrument. His master told him that, when he had broken a thousand strings playing his *qin*, he would find a remedy that would restore his sight hidden inside it. The minstrel spends his entire life playing the *qin*, but when he breaks his thousandth string and opens it up, he finds only a blank piece of paper. The film, nonetheless, turns what had been a critical allegory of history and culture into a text filled with, fractured by, events and marvels, redundant and contradictory contexts, cultural judgments and spiritual redemption, meanings and non-meanings. For when he abandoned his sense of reality, Chen Kaige also lost his historical perspective. Consequently, this narrative space is crisscrossed by fissures and multiple meanings. Caught in a double discourse of Chinese/Western, national/global, Chen oscillates from culture to counter-culture, pulled by his conflicting desire to reestablish a cultural center and also to orient himself outward toward the world.

Life on a String is not, as Chen Kaige claims, "a very simple film." It is not about the theme that "a person lives only once."[7] On the contrary, it is an overly complex and over-coded text. Compared with Zhang Yimou, Chen Kaige is in a certain sense more affectionate and faithful to Chinese history, culture, and reality. Or, to put it another way, Chen has a more pronounced cultural rather than a cinematic sense of mission. His faithfulness to Eastern and national culture; his contemplation of the dilemma of reality; his direct encounter with reality while escaping from it; his effort to turn estrangement and detachment into anxiety about submitting to the Western gaze, as shown in *The King of Children*; his defiance as a member of the Chinese cultural elite; and his sense of inferiority due to his admiration for Hollywood films: all this overloads the text of *Life on a String*, giving it a two-fold perspective, Eastern and Western, and themes that contradict and cancel each other out.

Life on a String has basically kept intact the plot of the original tale. Hence, it is built on the latter's themes: cultural retrospection, the tragedy of human life, and a critique as well as a redemption of history. An embodiment of darkened despair braced by cultural heroism, the film unfolds the theme of civilization versus ignorance. This is a staple theme underlying China's advance towards modernization. Blindness, besides its special allegorical meaning of hardship, is no doubt also an allegory of ignorance and the castrating power of History. That blank paper, passed down from a master three generations earlier, represents hope in the hopeless journey of human life. It is a promise of light that is continually delayed, as Beckett's *Waiting for Godot* has also shown. Yet Chen Kaige adds a new perspective to this classical Fifth Generation/root-searching theme when he makes the blind old minstrel an allegorical messenger of ancient Eastern culture. The *qin* strings no longer signify the delicate lives others have fiddled; fiddling now conjures up the inspirational and cohesive power of cultural tradition. Strings no longer serve as metaphors of fate or hostages of history; they now represent the redemptive power of Chinese/Eastern culture.

Again and again in the film the Ur-society names the blind man Shen Shen, or "Utmost Holy Master." The film opens on a stagelike space where hanging strips of white cloth mark out in dim blue lights an emphatic square. The dying old master gives his last instruction in a hoarse voice: "The recipe is in the *qin*. Remember, a thousand strings!" A frontal low-angle shot records the scene: in the foreground, a holy *qin* on its stand; in the midground, the master in his eternal sleep; in the background, the disciple chanting, "A thousand strings broken, *qin* will open; / *qin* will open, to reveal medicine; / To reveal medicine, for seeing the world, of its glistening." Still chanting, the disciple stands up slowly and raises his arms toward the evening sky. The camera, meanwhile, cranes up to the booming sounds of a sudden tempest that sends the white strips dancing wildly. The old man's image fades into a long-range shot of mountains and valleys. Without a doubt, this is not the time when a historical lie is passed down but rather the moment when a cultural mission is inherited. The new Shen Shen is born and succeeds the old. When the camera cranes down once again, sixty years have passed. Clad in white, the gray-haired Shen Shen sits playing his *qin* in front of his master's tomb. Then, as he sets off rapidly on his crutch to the market in search of his own disciple, Stone, a high-angle shot shows rows of hands, hands moving in respect and awe, moving dexterously one by one to clear the rice baskets out of his way. "Who is this old guy?" a stranger asks. "Don't you know him?" the locals along the way say, bewildered by the stranger. "Are you that ignorant?"

His lofty sense of mission drives Shen Shen from place to place, singing about the hard life of people living on a barren land. His songs nourish and irrigate the dry, yellow earth. Following the film's opening sequence is a panoramic shot of master and disciple marching along the horizon of yellow earth and blue sky, the Gobi desert in burning sunshine. Their heads and legs are wrapped; they resemble pilgrims in Western art. At night the desert looks barren and mysterious, like a moonscape. In such a space as this, master and disciple proceed with their philosophical inquiry, asking, "What is the blue ocean?" and "Is blank space really white?" This is followed by another stagelike scene: a small noodle shop, on the banks of one of the nine bends in the Yellow River, overlooks the surging water that sends wave upon wave. This image is a far cry from all other literary and filmic tributes to the Yellow River: it corresponds to neither the yellow earth nor the Yellow River.

Here, a single sound from Shen Shen's *qin* immediately halts a mob in combat, his melody putting an end to the people's fighting. When stubborn old Shen Shen induces the boatman to take him across the Yellow River by saying, "I have to go across. People at Goat Col Village are waiting for me," ten athletic topless young men appear out of nowhere in response to a single wave from the boatman's beckoning hand and deftly launch the ferry into the water. Singing a robust ferry song, master and disciple march onto the ferry as if embarking for battle. A little girl clothed in red jumps onto the ferry holding a torch in her hand. Water in the river surges. When they arrive at the other side of the river, one person asks the boatman if the old fellow is insane. The boatman answers with certainty, "No, he is an utter deity."

By now the film has established an epic or allegorical style. It is not a story about a victim of history but a story about a prophet, or at least a story told by a prophet. Nor is it exactly an episode of history but more like a new episode in the national mythology. When the people of Goat Col Village raise up Shen Shen above their heads and walk him onto the altarlike stage circled by torches, he does not sing folk songs from primeval stories, like "Filial Son Dong Yong Buries His Father,"[8] "Qin Xianglian,"[9] "Woman of Meng-Jiang Family,"[10] or "Little Luocheng."[11] Instead, he sings rhythmic songs about national genesis and deliverance: in ancient times, there was a hero named Kuafu; he pursued ten suns for five hundred years and shot down nine, one by one. In ancient times, there was a woman named Nüwa; she created the Universe with her five-colored stones in five hundred years. In ancient times, there was an ancestor of ours named Big Yu; he tamed the waters for five hundred years.

Life on a String is not just a myth about a nation and a culture, but also a myth about this culture's savior or messenger. When the primitive villagers thoughtlessly begin an internecine battle, the only person who can stop the absurd public massacre is Shen Shen, who, ignoring his illness, throws on his jacket, grabs his *qin*, and resolutely sets off on his way. His disciple kneels in front of him sobbing. "If you become ill again, you will never be able to play enough to break all the strings!" In a panoramic response shot, the old man hesitates only for an instant. "So be it," he says; the call to deliver the people has overruled even his desire to see.

The next sequence shows Shen Shen from the back, clad in white, sitting on the top of a hill holding his *qin*. In the background, down in the valley, masses of people swarm like ants; the high-angle panoramic shot shows the clouds of dust kicked up by the warring factions in a scene redolent of an ancient battleground. Shen Shen strikes the *qin* and sings: "You are human. They are human. We are human. When can a person be human? Human, human!" The song echoes louder through the valleys. A frontal shot closes in on the saintly Shen Shen, who continues singing loudly as he gropes toward the scene of battle. Back-lit, he seems clothed in radiance. The crowd is shaken and capitulates. One by one, people stop madly fighting, throw down their clubs, and run toward Shen Shen. They gather around him, sunflowers turning towards the sun, birds calling the phoenix, to create a human flow of love and energy. The camera catches wild geese streaking across the sky, in a pattern forming a huge Chinese character *ren*, or "human." The reconciled crowd cheers in unison, "Shen Shen! Shen Shen! Shen Shen!" Their voices shake the sky. Just then the old man's final string, the thousandth one, breaks by itself; the mountains echo with the sound. Blindness no longer signifies hardship and ignorance, but a cross borne by believers, the very fire of purgatory that allows their ascent to heaven.

This is one of the film's most important messages. According to the old man's story,

> Once, as the Jade Emperor of Heaven's two sons were bathing in the heavenly river, they accidentally fell through the clouds. So the Jade Emperor deployed his soldiers to blind them, saying, "It's such a filthy world down there. It's best they do not see it."

In this sense, blindness protects innocence and confers sacred status on Shen Shen, making him a sort of Jesus Christ of the East. When this implication is sutured to the mythical and magnificent *mise en scène* of the torrential Yellow River and the image of the sailors lightly raising the ferry boat with their hands, the film takes on the allegorical meaning of the primitive life force and the redemptive power inherent to an ancient culture. Undoubtedly, this is a specific posture that Chen Kaige adopts in facing Western civilization. Surely this is a rebellion of national culture under the gaze of the superior Western culture, and a struggle to re-center that tradition.

Yet, in his pell-mell flight, Chen fell into another trap. His national myth offers precisely the redemption that Western culture is searching for in its Other. The film's conclusion differs from that of the original story, which leaves the old man a blank sheet of paper and a broken-stringed *qin*. In the concluding scene of the film, the old man again starts to play his *qin* as if resurrected. He sits up straight on an altar, torches surrounding and illuminating him, and sings in his loud, antique voice: "Let's sing together. Be merry!" This so far exceeds the diegesis that it becomes a pure intrusion, perpetrated by the film-maker: the world is now the stage. On it sits Chen Kaige, who sings the ancient myth of China. Chinese history and reality fade into the shadow of the emergent myth. But an unfamiliar myth about Chinese nationality and culture can hardly contain or cancel the tragedy of life as a string. The meanings of introspection/demonstration, retrospec-tion/celebration, and death/eternity mock and deconstruct each other throughout the text of *Life on a String*. One cannot be certain whether this national myth has intercepted the tragedy of a cyclical his-tory and a cultural lie, or if it is itself deconstructed by a reinvented discourse of history.

An important change from the fiction is the film's elevation of Stone and Lanxiu's love story (another indication of Chen Kaige's desire for commercial success). Unlike the novel, the film no longer showcases how the tragedies of the two generations repeat each other and how the lives of the blind minstrels are doomed to despair. On the contrary, because of Lanxiu's suicide, it becomes a wondrous love song. The stories of Stone and Shen Shen, a contrast between taking part in society and escaping from it, open up a textual rupture that contains within it a structural contradiction. The two stories surface to form yet another set of meanings and to cancel each other out. That is to say, while Shen Shen represents transcendence and the mission-ary drive for cultural redemption, the worship and pursuit of vision, Stone stands for love, desire, and acceptance of this world and its reality.

While Shen Shen sings of Kuafu, Nüwa, and Big Yu, Stone sounds a different tune: "to become immortal is . . . to have nobody look after you when you grow old." The lonely journey of the blind minstrel is no longer seen as tragic, an unfair fate, to be accepted with no option. It is for Stone a choice between taking part in or escaping from society. The film is not about deprivation by fate or castration by history but about active renunciation à la existentialism. With the emergence of the individual, universal fate and the idea of the option – all of which transcend history – as well as the meanings of history, nationality, and culture are consequently canceled out. If fate were optional, if the hostages of history could always raise a Sartrean banner and write "no" upon it, there could be no possible way to transcend history, cultural difference, or divergent perspectives between East and West. The mountains, the long river, Kuafu, and Nüwa (nationality and national culture) would also have lost their appeal.

None of this, however, appears to reflect Chen Kaige's initial intention in selecting the story of *Life on a String*. Shen Shen gets up at midnight and asks himself: "Sixty years just for this one look. Is it worth it? I have nothing left. Everything is lost but this prescription. Is it worth it?" He then determines, "It's worth it." After finding out that the prescription is only a blank piece of paper, Shen Shen smashes his master's tombstone. A dark green screen presents his dream: two brides dressed in green, a green sedan chair abandoned in the sand, green lamps. Here Shen Shen is once more shown to be a victim suffering at the hands of a historical lie.

A moment before, Lanxiu and Stone, innocents just awakening to sexual love, are sitting side by side in front of the dilapidated temple. Lanxiu playfully breaks a sunflower, showering Stone with its seeds. Then she dissolves into tears and sits disconsolately gazing at the flower's empty husk. The scene changes to a field of golden haystacks. Lanxiu holds in her hands the dry skeleton of a fish. While both a sunflower and a fish visually and semantically symbolize fertility and prosperity, the empty husk of the flower and the skeleton of the fish undoubtedly signify denied desire and a castrated life. In this sense, Stone's personal tragedy becomes an inescapable historical fate.

Precisely this contradiction between Shen Shen's and Stone's stories means the film has internally canceled out not only the original literary tale but its own added emphasis on historical cycles, a constant thematic for Chen Kaige and the Fifth Generation generally. One may argue that Shen Shen's fate repeats that of his master. However, one cannot maintain the same about Stone. From the very beginning

Stone has a different attitude towards life and behaves as an independent and inquiring individual. "I am different," he says to Lanxiu. "I will break only as many strings as I can." He is concerned about the "blue ocean" and "if blank space is really white." When the death of Lanxiu intercepts his desire to be worldly, however, he does not capitulate by following the role model of his master. The repetition of the stagelike space of dim blue light marked out by falling strips of white cloth is, this time, not real but one of old Shen Shen's nightmares. Although his master bequeaths to him the will to break one thousand and two hundred strings, what Stone places in the *qin* is not the same paper passed down for generations but the letter that Lanxiu wrote before her suicide.

Stone seals up his own intentionality rather than an ideal that is both historically imaginary and a lie. Stone's is a dream that is named as a dream out of completely self-conscious conviction. After Stone buries Shen Shen in the water and is ready to take to the road, the *qin* on his back, a close-up focuses on Shen Shen's prescription. It is now merely a bit of paper tossed about by the wind in front of an idol in a decimated temple. Even when people seize his *qin*, which contains Lanxiu's letter, and offer to carry him on their shoulders as the new Shen Shen, he declines resolutely and leaves of his own accord. If Stone is still destined for a tragic fate, he won't repeat Shen Shen's. Stone will never be the idealist who sticks to his beautiful illusion, sacrificing himself to it only, eventually, to lose the ideal in the very process of the quest. He is going to be a Sisyphean hero who fights for a cause doomed to failure. Unlike the Eastern, historical, social tragedy of Shen Shen, Stone's tragedy is about the individual. More to the point, it is the story of the individual's fate under a Western gaze.

It is in this sense that, by the end of the film, Stone's story has canceled out the cultural connotations of Shen Shen's fate as a national myth. *Life on a String* is thus a fractured terrace. It is torn between a self-reflexive Eastern belief in repetitious history and the representation of a Western belief in linear history. Even more interestingly, Chen Kaige is himself a split character. He is both a victim of Chinese historical tragedy and a messenger of the glorious Eastern culture; both a critic of the repetitious history and a midwife for Sisyphean heroes, and thus a prophet of progress in history. Chen himself is a

believer in elite culture and an image-producer within the commer-
cialized mass culture; himself an accuser of the "nameless butchers" in
China's historical past and a descendant of the adherents of humanism. Chen Kaige, the ultimate incarnation of our mask for his filmic
narrators, transcends this array of chaotic meanings.

To obtain an omniscient or even transcendental point of view, in
Life on a String Chen Kaige creates a character who represents but
transcends all human beings: the mysterious owner of the noodle shop
on the Yellow River and the clay idol (played by the same actor) which
appears in the film's most important *mise en scène*, the temple where
Shen Shen and Stone stay. The idol – a fictional device – is supposed
to be an Eastern deity. It resembles three figures: an arhat, the Big
Dipper or god of literature, and the judge of the underworld. The
character also corresponds to Western gods of fate and death. As the
most important element of the *mise en scène* and meaning, this character struggles to raise the film's, and Chen Kaige's, story to an
archetype. When old Shen Shen's whole life is revealed to be a lie,
back at the Yellow River, the mysterious noodle shop owner opens his
mouth: "It doesn't matter who you are," he says. "Coming to this world,
you have to perform the play. Some do better, some do worse."
Surprised, the dispirited Shen Shen asks: "Who are you?" The
response is not an answer: "How can you judge a play if you don't stay
to the end?" "What will happen today?" Shen Shen asks again. "You are
a lucky person" – is the smiling rejoinder. Their stylized dialogue,
resembling with its meditative inquiries Buddhist texts such as *Wudeng
huiyuan* (*The Collated Essentials of the Five Lamps*), elevates the film from
an Eastern mythical story to a performance of human lives in "the Big
Void." Shen Shen then takes his leave. "When are you coming back
again, blind grandpa?" asks a little girl clothed in red. The idiot waiter
at the noodle shop shouts a response mixed in with loud sound effects:
"A boarder comes and goes!"

The suggestion here is that, like a boarder's, human life is a matter
of checking in and out. When Shen Shen mounts the altarlike stage
one more time to sing an Eastern version of *Ode to Joy*, the mysterious
noodle shop owner sits in the audience. Seeing that the old man is
singing again, the shop owner gives a satisfied (or perhaps it is a deri-
sive) grin and turns to leave. If this vantage point of transcendence is

meaningful within the narrative, then all of us might just as well glide through life like leisurely clouds or wild geese, or stay put like an old horse in its stable, never bothering about issues like retrospection and myth, history and reality, massacre and universal love, or East and West. In this light, *Life on a String* is an over-coded and vague text. Indeed, it is a visual representation of China's contemporary cultural dilemma, a deformed fetus in the age of postcolonial culture.

Similar filmic texts of the nineties are *Xuese qingchen* (*A Bloody Morning*) by Li Shaohong; Sun Zhou's *Xin xiang* (*Fragrance of the Heart*); and *Mama* (*Mother*) by the even younger director, Zhang Yuan. But if these films only have a marginal status in China during the nineties, they represented mainstream Chinese filmmaking under the gaze of West, anticipating the new and archetypal cultural dilemmas faced by Chinese filmmakers. The renewed modernization process will surely enlarge the historical rupture in culture, driving history into exile. The unavoidable process of globalization that brings China and the world together will further postcolonial syndromes and fracture Chinese culture even more. Are we encountering a historical chance to disseminate "the iron house" of culture? Or is this a tragic collapse of a national culture? As an intellectual sharing with Chen Kaige and Zhang Yimou not only the same global cultural market, but also a history that is still shaping itself – an open-ended plot – I find myself at a loss as to how to answer these questions.

Notes

1 The early 1990s witnessed the production of mainstream films based on the subjects of revolution and history, such as *Da juezhan* (A deciding battle), directed by Li Jun, 1990; *Zhou enlai*, directed by Ding Yinnan, 1991; *Jiao yulu*, directed by Wang Jixing, 1990.

2 Roland Barthes talks about this concept in *The Pleasure of the Text*, trans. Richard Miller (New York: Hill and Wang, 1975).

3 Michel Foucault talks about this in *The Archaeology of Knowledge*, trans. A.M. Sheridan Smith (New York: Pantheon Books, 1972).

4 Liu Heng, "Fu xi fu xi" (Obsession), *Beijing wenxue* (Beijing literature), no. 3, 1988.

5 I am referring to Eugenio Donato's work as analyzed in Meng Yue and Li Yijian, *Benwen de celüe* (Textual strategies) (Guangzhou: Huacheng chubanshe, 1988), pp. 97–8.

6 Quoted in Li Xiao, "Shanguang de jinshi: Weinisi dianyingjie jianjie" ("Shining golden lion: an introduction to the Venice Film Festival"), *Film World*, no. 3, 1994. Also see Zhang Ling, "Waiguoren yanzhong de Zhang Yimou" ("A foreign perspective of Zhang Yimou"), *Film Review*, no. 3, 1993, pp. 9–10.

7 Interview with Chen Kaige, March 21, 1992, aired on Hong Kong's Chinese Satellite TV Station.

8 Stories about Dong Yong circulated in southern drama. Dong was a very poor peasant, a filial son, and very kind by nature. A beautiful fairy fell in love with him. They got married and had several children, but the fairy's mother eventually found them. She took her daughter back to heaven. In desperation, Dong Yong followed his wife with their young children. Blocked by the Milky Way, they were all turned into stars.

9 Qin Xianglian is a famous character in Beijing Opera. Born under the rule of the Song Dynasty (960–1279), she was a dutiful wife, mother, and a model daughter-in-law. Her husband, Chen Shimei, went to the capital to take the civil-service examination. He passed it with high honors, became an official, married the emperor's daughter, and never returned home. Qin Xianglian finally took her children to the capital looking for her husband. Chen Shimei did not want to acknowledge them. Instead, he sent assassins to kill them. After she pleaded her case to the fair-minded Judge Bao, the judge was infuriated with Chen's cruelty. Despite the protests of the imperial family, he had Chen Shimei executed.

10 The story of Meng Jiangnü comes from a famous folk legend. During the Qin dynasty (221–207 B.C.), the emperor enlisted laborers by force to build the Great Wall. The beautiful woman from the Meng-Jiang family lost her husband on their wedding day. She went looking for him at the Great Wall. The husband by then had already died of exhaustion and was buried in the wall. His beautiful bride cried day and night beside the wall until it collapsed to reveal her husband's bones. She reburied him and later died there too.

11 Luo Cheng is a famous young hero who lived during the Sui Dynasty (581–618).

Translated by Harry H. Kuoshu

3

A Scene in the Fog: Reading the Sixth Generation Films

A Smooth Sailing

A variety of cultural signifiers have appeared on the complicated cultural horizon of the 1990s. Once again, hindsight periodization informs us that the ecstasy at the birth of postmodern nineties culture put an end to the decade of the eighties. There is no remorse or reflection. There is no threshold hesitancy, not even "a farewell party" or "a memorial to forgetting." In an intensity paralleling the crisis consciousness of the eighties, the nineties have announced a rupture and the end of history, amid China's frantic knocking at the door of the new century, its epoch-making "march toward the world." In the nineties, the postmodern landscape rests on an entirely new terminology. We smoothly sail through the imagery of the "cultural desert," the "isolated cultural island" and the "decadence of art" like an optimistic boat, conjuring up an alluring vision of "China synchronous with the world."

If the cultural landscape of the eighties in flux signaled China's grand march toward the world, kept aloft in optimistic discourse, the constituents of the nineties cultural landscape – a far more complicated synergy of motive, fantasy, desire, and lack – have bypassed and betrayed the intellectuals' wish to go global. Nineties Chinese culture is still struggling under the yoke of power, but this power comes from various centers. Complex as eighties Chinese culture is, it is still subject to integration into "modernity," on the basis of a common desire for progress, social democracy, and national prosperity, and by virtue of its resistance to historical inertia and the stronghold of mainstream ideology. In the nineties, however, the following elements feed a different sociocultural situation: the ambiguous ideology of the post–Cold War era; the implosion and diffusion of mainstream ideology; global capitalism's tidal force and the resistance of nationalisms and nativisms; the penetration and impact of global capital on local cultural industries; cultures' increasing commercialization in global and local culture markets; and the active role local intellectuals, besieged by postmodern and postcolonial discourse, have undertaken in their writing. Nineties Chinese culture is in fact becoming a unique space, open to crisscrossing perspectives: it is a city of mirrors. Contemporary Chinese culture resembles a scene in the fog, transfixed between orientalism and occidentalism, interpellated by different, diametrically opposed power centers, existing in a proliferating, multiple, overlapping cultural space. The light optimistic boat is destined to be overloaded with the heritages of premodernity, modernity, Cold War–era and eighties culture. In the 1980s, the birth of various cultural currents and the discourse on "generations" not only satisfied an internal lack and need for certain grand narratives, it suggested the cultural fact of established order and newly emerging generations as well. In the 1990s, cultural signing and naming are more like a deft yet desperate linguistic tourism, a seeking of a signified for the signifier. Perhaps even more aptly, they resemble the strategic or gaming demonstration of a certain cultural, discursive desire, vamping and performing for a certain audience.

I am not claiming that the nineties are a wasteland in a fictional paradise. On the contrary, in the wake of the dawning silence there emerges an uncanny, crisis-ridden, yet vibrant cultural landscape. It could be the realization of the marginal culture hidden beneath eighties elitism. More pertinently, the "playful generation" Liu Xiaofeng predicted at the end of the eighties is not materializing in playful gestures and civilities.[1] Its drama – enacted in various guises in the city of mirrors and on double or multiple stages, torn asunder by crossed gazes and reconstructed in discourses of power – is, in the end, a cultural Real. The drama is too weighty and complex to be carried by the optimistic naming that the metaphor of smooth sailing entails. So-called Sixth Generation film is precisely such a 1990s scene in the fog.

A Certain Narration

Film periodization is itself a characteristic discourse. Beginning in the mid eighties various discourses on "generations" have become the labyrinthine map of the new era. In one short decade, periodizing has commenced with proclamations of beginnings and endings, ruptures and beginnings. Each seeks to predict the birth of an entirely new culture and social structure. Yet each "generation" steps onto the historical stage to play its part, only to step right down again. More to the point, the discourse on "generations" is not configuring contemporary China's cultural map; it is in and of itself an important cultural scene. Chronologically, we witnessed first the emergence of the literature of the "Third Generation." Its self-indulgent yet self-deprecating narration of bitter, romantic heroism[2] presaged the immediate rise of a swashbuckling, restless "Fourth Generation" also demanding historical space and an audience.[3] We hear at the same time about the need to move the Red Guard ("the old three generations") cohort into the Third Generation slot, and to relegate reeducated youths to the Fourth. Meanwhile, to navigate this labyrinth, serious young scholars have chosen to periodize intellectuals beginning with the May Fourth generation, the generation of liberation, the generation of April Fifth, and the playful generation,[4] thus sketching out yet another map of twentieth-century Chinese culture.

Virtually the same thing has occurred in the field of poetry. Barely had the "Misty Poetry" gained a steady footing, when "a new era" of poetry arrived under the slogan "surpassing Bei Dao." The modern (*xiandai pai*) literature had only just appeared before avant-garde fiction began its attack on "pseudo-modernism" and triggered, in turn, the debate over Chinese postmodernism. After a temporary silence at the turn of the nineties, literature of "the new human condition" and "the late generation" poetry signaled increasing attempts at an escape from the city of mirrors.[5] In the field of pop music even more turbulence prevails. Barely had Cui Jian emerged with his cry, "I have nothing whatsoever," than the "post–Cui Jian" rock star replaced him. In film production, the post-thirty-something "young directors" came to prominence in 1979, after great tribulations, only to be upstaged in 1982 by a group of new graduates from the Beijing Film Academy who, after a ten-year hiatus, would catch the world's attention.

It is still not known who invented the label "Fifth Generation." But under this name for a group of young directors, Chen Kaige and Tian Zhuangzhuang are the leading representatives, though Zhang Yimou topped them in 1987 with his *Red Sorghum*. Since the 1979 group was called the Fourth Generation, in hindsight their predecessors (the founders and promoters of Chinese film) were presumed to be the Third Generation. Nobody questioned the rationale underlying this periodization. Nor did anyone take the trouble to designate a First or a Second Generation.[6] Five years after the birth of the Fifth Generation, 1987 yielded two important works: Chen Kaige's *The King of Children* and Zhang Yimou's *Red Sorghum*. Instantaneously, some were already declaring "the demise of the Fifth Generation."[7] "Post–Fifth Generation" became the term used to describe yet another, subsequent group of directors who are, in fact, contemporaries of the Fifth Generation.[8]

Interestingly, the Sixth Generation, unlike its predecessors (the Third, Fourth, and Fifth Generations), does not refer to a specific group of creators, aesthetics, or even a sequence of works. Even before its appearance, the Sixth Generation was already predicted and outlined in various cultural yearnings and lacks. Not only did the naming of the Sixth Generation precede its praxis, its discourse up to now remains a pastiche of linguistic journeys in search of the signified or the signifier. Consequently, the Sixth Generation is an entangled cultural phenomenon tucked away under various names, discourses, cultures, and ideologies.

The following are terms either referring to the Sixth Generation or overlapping with it. "Chinese underground films" and even "Chinese dissident films" are two signifiers popular in Euro-America; on mainland China the catchwords are "independent filmmakers," "independent filmmaking," "new documentary movement." Beijing Film Academy classes of 1985 and 1987 use the labels "new imagist movement," "situation film" (as an illustration of the culture of the "new human condition"), and "new urban film." Hong Kong and Taiwan discourse refers to "mainland underground films," even simply to "the seven gentlemen," which is derived from the Ministry of Broadcasting, Film, and Television's censorship of seven filmmakers. These include veteran Fifth Generation and Sixth Generation feature-film directors, documentary producers who issue their works in the form of videos, and amateur videographers.

Chinese intellectuals are accustomed to sweeping all these complex cultural phenomena under the umbrella of the "Sixth Generation." For them the term covers at least three types of films and praxes (at times connected, even overlapping, at other times completely differentiated from one another). They include the following categories: first, independent filmmakers of the nineties who are either self-financed or have European Cultural Fund underwriting, and who make low-budget features that are separate from the official film production and censorship system. Typical works are Zhang Yuan's *Beijing zazhong* (*Beijing Bastards*) and Wang Xiaoshuai's *Dongchun de rizi* (*The Day in Winter-Spring*). Into a second category fall popular young directors graduating from 1989 through 1991, who work within the filmmaking system: Hu Xueyang's *Liushou nüshi* (*The Woman Who Remains*) and Lou Ye's *Zhoumo qingren* (*Weekend Sweetheart*), for instance. A third refers to turn-of-the-nineties documentary-makers closely connected with the group of nomadic Beijing artists widely known for their "painters" village at the Yuanmingyuan Summer Palace. These documentary-makers, a tight-knit artistic group, sought to launch a Chinese documentary movement that reverberated with television's desire for innovative art and expression in its very praxis and approach. Their praxes, as signified by Wu Wenguang's *Liulang Beijing – zuihou de mengxiangzhe* (*Roaming in Beijing – The Last Dreamer*) and Shi Jian's *Wo biye le* (*I've Graduated*), combined the makers of documentaries and television programs into a creative group around their particular cultural positioning and experiences.

Independent filmmakers and new documentary-makers coalesced because their common mode of production fell outside the usual operations of the system. Or perhaps more importantly, their bonding responded to certain post–Cold War projects regarding Western cultural needs. This was an act of involuntary self-fictionalization under the Western gaze, a wishful thinking about the smooth sailing of a native culture. As a result, various discourses on Chinese independent filmmakers have proliferated under the terms of PRC "underground film," "cultural dissidents' resistance," the materialization of the mainland "civic society" and "public sphere," the praxis of postmodernism, and so on. These architectural discourses are the surplus signifier. It gestures toward, but always bypasses the Sixth Generation. This turns the new, inchoate cultural praxis into a sort of fantastical nineties Chinese culture: yet another spectacle in the city of mirrors.

Generations in Film

A certain periodization seems necessary in response to a multiplying and multifarious new period of culture. Ever since the decline of China in the last century, quasi-modern and contemporary Chinese histories have always been described as "grand periods," rendering Chinese intellectuals in a sense "the sons and daughters of the grand periods." Isolated social and cultural structures, and since 1949 inescapable waves of political movements, have repeatedly forced people into a historical turmoil that actually yielded no common experiences. During this historical process of the simultaneous building and disintegrating of power and will, different generations of Chinese people experienced their trauma and the collapse of reality in different ways. We could almost designate generational labels for specific groups of Chinese intellectuals on the basis of their participation in certain historical events, their responses to particular icons and certain discourses, or even according to the sacred aura or specific interpretations they attach to certain books, paintings, and songs. The swarming influx of "twentieth-century Western culture after the national gates were flung open" forms an infinitely complex cultural formation precisely because different cultural demands, choices, and capacities for reception were so specific to each age group. The designation of a cultural generation depends not simply on a physiological age range, but on a specific cultural "feeling," some particular historical experience or deeply felt historical event. The new era's cultural generations are more like spiritual communities than representations of sociocultural fact. They have found spiritual allies on the basis of a common resistance to one particular mode of mainstream culture and power structure, "not because they are contemporaneous, but because they are consanguineous."[9]

Consequently, the implications of the various discourses on generations in the new era are not obvious to laymen. For example, since

1979, in an intensive effort to break away from mainstream cultural discourse, literature and art have struggled desperately to achieve individual artistic expression. But their individual attempts at depoliticizing in the early and mid eighties only succeeded in producing a clear picture of generational distribution in cluster form. The effort to break out of concentric structures only proved the homogeneous Ur-society's stubborn resistance to change. "A new generation" may occasionally differ from its predecessors (the old generations?), but their similarities are more conspicuous. The whole new era is simultaneously informed both by new names and by a rejection of and resistance to the abusive act of naming. Although affiliation with a generation guarantees a certain artistic status, it also doubtlessly drowns once again the already shaky "individuality" and "self." What concerns me then is not simply the fact of periodization, but rather the mechanism producing such discourses in the new era. For film, at least, the discourses on "generations" do refer to artists of different age groups. But more importantly, name becomes a criterion (perhaps even the most important criterion in the mid and late eighties) for evaluation of artistic worth. Not all artists of a certain age group will bask in the aura of his or her alleged generation.

In my 1994 conversations with Chen Xiaoming, Zhang Yiwu, and Zhu Wei, published in *Zhongshan* under the title "Xin shi pipan shu" (The ten new critiques), I decisively denied the existence of the Sixth Generation.[10] One of my reasons for doing so was that I was still committed to the worth of art and its objective artistic value. The Sixth Generation had only produced a handful of original creative works at that time, in my view. Though they occasionally manifested a new social perspective or cultural rewriting, they failed as a new generation of filmmakers to challenge the existing Chinese film art. At a 1995 film festival I attended in the US, one of the organizers, a blonde, blue-eyed American lady, enthusiastically introduced a new Sixth Generation feature, *Youchai* (*Postman*), directed by Jianjun, as "an important mainland Chinese film whose inclusion is a special honor to the film festival." She exhibited no such enthusiasm for the Fifth Generation features – Huang Jianxin's *Bei dui bei, lian dui lian* (*Back to Back, Face to Face*) and Li Shaohong's *Hongfen* (*Flush*) – that were also exhibited and which are artistically far superior. A *New York Times* review published shortly before her description of *Postman* echoed the same note. Except for hollow, flamboyant praise and a plot précis, the only comment on *Postman*'s value was that "it was completely different from the Fifth Generation works." Naturally the "Sixth Generation" will differ from the "Fifth Generation." But being different does not in itself say anything about the Sixth Generation. This is precisely the cultural absurdity of the "Sixth Generation."

My other reason for denying the existence of the Sixth Generation was a hidden, optimistic expectation. For me, the clear succession of generations in Chinese culture, or in Chinese film at least, is a profound sorrow rather than one of the glories of contemporary culture. This is another example of fleeing from one trap while falling into another, the desperate performance of breaking out. "Rewriting literary history," allegedly the most important cultural phenomenon of the eighties, was, in a sense, nothing more complex than casting a spotlight on personal, marginal writing lying outside mainstream literary groups. On the one hand, it constituted a powerful resistance to hegemonic discourse. But on the other, it also revealed contemporary culture's internal lack and its desire for marginal writing, for "individualization." Therefore, I harbored the optimistic, perhaps chimeric, expectation that when social transformations shattered cultural heroism, a new generation of filmmakers might be able to appear in their own names, rather than in the name of any new "generation." The increasing presence of a Sixth Generation has made it more and more clear that this new generation is not yet able to shake off or challenge the Fifth Generation. Its work is still, socially and culturally, that of a new group of youths attempting once again to break away from mainstream discourse and to emerge from the shadow of the preceding (in this case the Fifth) generation.

Just as the refugee always subconsciously refers back to the persecutor, the breakaway's history always begins with imitation. In 1979, the Fourth Generation took the stage when they accurately copied young Russian directors who were active in the Thaw years. Likewise, in the early nineties, the Sixth Generation made its brief, abortive appearance as imitators of the Fifth Generation. In fact, when the first New Era group of Beijing Film Academy graduates – the class of 1978 – entered film production in 1982, the Fifth Generation's journey of glory and conquest began. The Class of 1978 formed the mainstay of the Fifth Generation, and was therefore synonymous with that generation in film circles.

They originally formed "youth production teams" in collaboration with their classmates, and won great attention at home and abroad.[11] The five short years from 1979 to 1983 saw the successive replacement of no less than three generations of filmmakers. This undoubtedly produced the interesting illusion among filmmakers in China, and among those interested in China, that chronic replacement was becoming a principle of Chinese film culture. The question constantly popping up at international film conferences that I attended was "Which generation is it now? The Seventh?" When I responded, "Still the Fifth Generation," they always greeted the news with disappointed expressions. Ever since the Fifth Generation appeared, expectations of the appearance of a Sixth Generation have been simmering in Chinese film circles. Obviously, since the Beijing Film Academy's Department of Direction is the only national film academy, such an expectation was pinned on the next graduating class.

Three years later, after the institution resumed general admission and when that expectation had become entrenched, the classes of 1985 and 1987, who did indeed seem to constitute a Sixth Generation, obviously internalized this attitude. They developed an intense sense of mission and confidence in their film careers. With the appearance of the inaugural work by Zhang Yuan (class of 1985, on the heels of Zhang Yimou), *Mother*, latent anticipation regarding the long-awaited birth of the Sixth Generation began to pervade the quiescent film scene of the nineties. Finally Hu Xueyang, the only lucky one, released his first work, *The Woman Who Remains*, in 1992, for the Shanghai Film Studio. He proclaimed his manifesto immediately: "the five classes of the '85 class are the Sixth Generation of filmmakers." As the de facto representative of the Sixth Generation, Zhang Yuan was more clear-minded in his subtle response. "'Generation' is a beneficial appellation," he said.

> We've seen the success to be achieved by being called a "generation"; to the Chinese people it means a remarkable quantity with irresistible force. Many

of my partners are my classmates. We're about the same age, and know each other well. Yet I still believe that filmmaking is personal. I try to be different from my predecessors and different from my contemporaries. When something is another's, it's no longer yours.

Still, Zhang Yuan went on to express a sense of "generation" when he could not resist saying, "our generation is more passionate."[12] There is an interesting anecdote regarding Guan Hu, one of the Sixth Generation directors, also from the '87 class, who designed a calligraphic 87 in the credits of his inaugural work, *Toufa luan le* (*Disheveled Hair*) originally titled *Zang ren* (*The Dirty Person*) – for the Inner Mongolia Film Studio, 1994. Only those who empathize with him can decode this meticulous effort and distinct sign of generational consciousness.

Breaking Out of Their Predicament

Despite high expectations and lavish nourishing, the new generation stepped onto the stage at a disadvantageous moment. The tremendous turmoil at the beginning of the nineties cast optimistic, idealistic Chinese cultural workers into bottomless disenchantment. With the exception of Wang Shuo's unbridled waywardness, the literary circle was abruptly paralyzed and silenced. The booming popular culture's commercialization towed in its wake both besieged elitism and art. Quasi-film phenomena (TV and video) that are irrelevant to film per se intensified the crisis of cinema in the planned economy. Increasingly, art films (even some film-festival prizewinners) came to be regarded as box-office poison. Meanwhile, global capital's cultural operations showed special interest in Fifth Generation directors and poured astronomical sums of capital into Chinese film production. Riding high on the crest of the wave of orientalism, the Fifth Generation undoubtedly produced a China fever, or a hunger for Chinese film in European and American art film festivals. But it also hindered and forestalled the "resurgence" of a subsequent new generation. The artistic talent, cultural preparation, and life experiences of the Sixth Generation were not the problem here. The problem was that they were not born under the same lucky star as their predecessors.

The emergence of the Fifth Generation had coincided with the beginning of the grand march of the eighties toward innovative experimentation. Therefore, as one of the pioneers of Chinese cinema, the Fifth Generation filmmakers became the crucial pillars of film departments and quickly found the means to bring their work into the world. Most '85 and '87 graduates, however, had difficulty getting assignments via the national plan to the integrated, isolated film industry. The few lucky ones who did squeeze in had to go through a lengthy apprenticeship, lasting from six to ten years, climbing the ladder from member of the producing staff to associate director, even when their studios remained solvent. Afterwards, the chances of getting national funding for an individual project were still slim to none. Unwilling to accept abandonment by the film industry, and failing to take off from marginal studios (which was typical of Fifth Generation experience),[13] they ended up in various venues, joining the nomadic Beijing artist groups, or making their living with TV programs, advertisements, and MTV, or doing temporary work on various film-production teams, yet still committed to their dream. They began to roam around Beijing as marginal film artists burdened with unnameable anxieties.

The first glimmer of light in their desperation came from Zhang Yuan, an excellent Sixth Generation filmmaker. At the outset of his journey, the young graduate decided to give up the current lifestyle and creative modality. Of Sixth Generation feature filmmakers, Zhang Yuan was most involved with Beijing nomad artists. He and Wang Xiaoshuai, his classmate and Sixth Generation director-to-be, prepared a screenplay and tried in vain to purchase a film quota number from a studio. The quota as yet ungranted, without having had the screenplay inspected, he shot the first Sixth Generation work, *Mother*, with the tiny budget he was able to obtain from a private enterprise. Not until the whole production was finished did they succeed in getting the quota from Xi'an Film Studio; through this studio, they sent the film for inspection. With only a few color video segments, *Mother* was the first black-and-white feature since color films had replaced black and white in China in the sixties. Indeed, it could perhaps be seen as the "first" Chinese black-and-white feature, in terms of the diffuse richness and subtle, bitter, poetic melancholy of its extreme documentary style. It rehearsed virtually the entire course of the avant-garde movement in Chinese film history. Due to the limited budget and its unique artistic vision, the film was produced completely on location; all of the actors and actresses were amateurs. *Mother* is dedicated to "the international organization of handicapped people" and relates the miserable experiences of a mother of a mentally retarded son. On another level, it also serves as a cultural, artistic manifesto for a new generation. The subtext of *Mother* lies with the son, who can be read as the real protagonist.

As the art of the Son, the Fifth Generation authors based cultural resistance and betrayal on the acknowledgment of the Father's Name/authority/order. Their art consequently fell prey to the dilemma of disowning or identifying with the Father. On the one hand, late-eighties urban films typically replaced the old nuclear family with the family image of brothers and sisters. On the other hand, they materialized the cultural and psychological fact that the Father's authority had become internalized. This is seen in the image of the dead parents' pictures hung high on the wall in *Fengkuang de daijia* (*The Price of Frenzy*) and *Benming nian* (*Black Snow*); in the long-distance news about the mothers in *Taiyang yu* (*Sunny Rain*); in the elder brothers and sisters stepping in as the surrogate father in *Gei kafei jia dian tang* (*Add a Little Sugar to the Coffee*) and *The Price of Frenzy*; and in the monogamous romance that grows out of promiscuity in both *Lun hui* (*Samsara*) and *Add a Little Sugar to the Coffee.*

In this light, the hidden story of the "son" in *Mother* becomes a new generation's cultural parable narrated through an aphasiac, retarded boy. His idiocy can be interpreted as the Son's rejection of the Father and fixation with the pre-Oedipal stage, his aphasia as the rejection of the Symbolic stage, and thus the Father's Name, language, and culture. In frame after frame, scenes of the son alone were shot in a style redolent of religious iconography portraying the newborn Jesus surrounded by an aura. A sourceless light bathes the sick child from above. The image of the child, swathed in white fabric, curled in the fetal posture, far exceeded the film's documentary style and narrative context to suggest an anti-cultural gesture secreted in the narrative of maternal love, or a new generation's cultural parable.

Mother's appearance undoubtedly brought new hope and direction to struggling contemporary filmmakers. Zhang Yuan followed up *Mother* with another splashy gesture that transcended the system that had so compromised people's imagination, and thereby pointed to an entirely new way out. Following his failed release in the domestic market (at first only six copies were ordered), Zhang exhibited *Mother* at a film festival in France that was showing films from three continents, where the Fifth Generation masterpiece *Yellow Earth* had first received recognition. With no official permit or prior arrangement, he won the Committee Prize as well as the public grand prize. Thus began *Mother*'s fascinating journey in and out of twenty film festivals. With incredible courage, Zhang Yuan simply stepped onto the cinematic stage and walked toward the public in the most direct, "simple" way.

As another Chinese director known to the West, Zhang was following Chen Kaige and Zhang Yimou. According to Tony Rayns, a European authority on Chinese film, "*Mother* is still an astounding film in today's Chinese film circles. Coming from the hand of a very young Film Institute graduate, it is no less than a courageous achievement." Rayns went on to predict, "If a Sixth Generation is on its way in China, it will definitely differ from the Fifth Generation in terms of interest and taste. *Mother* may as well be the cornerstone of this new generation."[14] After this success, Zhang Yuan undertook a second feature, *Beijing Bastards*, this time in color, collaborating with the uncrowned king of rock and roll, Cui Jian. This film, based almost exclusively on the collaboration of colleagues and friends, was never intended either to enter the system or to make any concessions to it. Zhang Yuan went on with self-financing and independent production work, interspersed with work on MTV, in advertising, and on documentaries. His MTV work was broadcast overseas. Cui Jian's *Kuai rangwo zai xuedi shang sadianye* (*Let Me Run Wild in Snow*) even won American MTV's grand prize. *Beijing Bastards* was finished in 1993 and began its circumambulation of the world's film festivals. Wang Xiaoshuai shot his standard-length black-and-white feature *The Day in Winter-Spring* in the same year, with CNY 10,000 he had raised himself. If *Mother* was Zhang Yuan's leap in the dark, *The Day in Winter-Spring* was a grand performance. At that time on the mainland, feature films cost a minimum of CNY 1 million. Zhang Yimou's "standard budget" was CNY 6 million, and Chen Kaige's *Farewell My Concubine* that same year cost HKO 12 million. *The Day in Winter-Spring* was also a difficult avant-garde experiment. Another young director, He Jian Jun, was just producing *Xuanlia* (*Suspended Love*) in black and white and a similar manner, at around the same budget. Following on its heels came the color feature *Postman*. Wu Di, the cinematographer of *The Day in Winter-Spring*, and his colleagues had produced *Huangjin yu* (*Golden Rain*). Independent filmmaking was becoming an undercurrent in Chinese film circles.

Paralleling this trend was the work of Hu Xueyang, an excellent and very lucky director who had come out of the Beijing Film Academy. His graduate work, *Tongnian wangshi* (*Memories of Childhood*), reflecting on the protagonist's childhood during the Cultural Revolution, won a prize at the American students' Oscar film festival. Son of the famous dramatist, Hu Weimin, Hu Xueyang got an opportunity to direct a film independently at the Shanghai Film Studio and finished his first film, *The Woman Who Remains*, in 1992. It was entered at the Cairo Film Festival that year, winning in the Pyramid Best Film and Best Actress categories. In other words, Hu emerged as the first Sixth Generation director to win a grand prize at a Third-World film festival. After this, he finished *Yanmo de qingchun* (*Buried Youth*) in 1994 and his long-envisioned inaugural work, *Qianniu hua* (*Morning Glory*), in 1995. Other Sixth Generation directors had their share of repeated frustrations trying to release their films. Those titles that finally entered the market in 1994 include Lou Ye's *Weekend Sweetheart* for the Fujian Film Studio, *Weiqing shaonü* (*Bewitching Girl*) for the Shanghai Film Studio, and Guan Hu's *Disheveled Hair* for the Inner Mongolian Film Studio. Analogous to the Fifth Generation's frustrations between 1983 and 1986, the first half of the nineties witnessed the difficult entry of the Sixth Generation.

On the Solitary Stage

The appearance of Sixth Generation films suggested a break away from commercial culture's ambush of art film. Their avant-garde style also constituted a subversion of the official system of film production. More precisely, the Sixth Generation feature directors' cultural pose and the creative style they selected were more or less an enforced choice. Documentarists working in video did not experience this productive pressure. In a sense, the new documentaries that appeared under the labels "Sixth Generation" or "China's underground film" were actually the works of those who had been eclipsed by eighties mainstream culture. In other words, marginal cultural forces banished during the social turmoil of the eighties and nineties now gathered strength along with other exiles and began the march toward the center.

The mid and late eighties saw the formation of unique nomadic artists' groups along the edge of urban Beijing. These artists mostly did not have Beijing household certificates or steady jobs, and therefore lacked a steady income or place of residence. They formed an unprecedentedly footloose group, and they had to pay for this freedom: they were not allowed (or were refused) to enjoy the security and safety that society can provide ordinary citizens. They included painters (popular "political pop" of the nineties originated from this group), rock stars, avant-garde poets, art photographers, unknown writers, experimental theater directors, and dedicated yet scantily financed would-be film directors. They picked up whatever work they could find in TV, film, advertising, and art design, earning a difficult living and continuing their arduous creation. They also shared an appellation with refugee peasants, forced off their land by natural or human disasters during the fifties and sixties, namely "a blind flux." Under constant threat that their exhibitions would be closed or their performances forbidden, they were driven from their temporary dwelling places, and frequently went hungry. Obviously, what drove them to their lives on the run was more a sacred than a physical satisfaction, a certain vague dream. In a sense, they were the genuine new people of the new era. Although they occasionally edged into the fragmenting mainstream scene, generally speaking, in the eighties they formed an invisible margin. Wu Wenguang, who made new video documentaries and who originated this new style, was one of them. At the end of the eighties, he began to intermittently and arduously record the daily life of his friends and roaming artists. Like his subjects, his intuitive work had no connection with any contemporary fashions. He did not project his work into the future or seek its exposure one way or another. Perhaps this was a passionate love affair unfolding on the contemporary Chinese stage. The cultural toppling and upheaval at the beginning of the nineties stimulated the appearance of marginal groups. In Wu Wenguang's frank admission, "I felt a sudden silence on the Beijing stage after 1989. Suddenly I felt elated. Perhaps I wanted to achieve something while everyone else was doing nothing." Excited at the silence and exaltation, Wu finished *Liulang Beijing* (*Roaming Beijing*) with the subtitle "The Last Dreamer". Wu conceived this as a slight oblation to the eighties. "I was thinking that after the eighties, the age of dreaming had come to an end. The nineties is probably an action. The dream must be put into action."[15]

Another cornerstone of the new documentary work, *Tiananmen* (*Tiananmen Square*), served in another manner as a floating bridge over the abrupt precipice at the end of the eighties, a vibrato on the final note. Written by the young scriptwriter Shi Jian, shot by Chen Jue, this long special serial was actually an extension of an eighties style, the culmination of a long series of documentaries mixing discussion of topical issues with documentation, interviews, and parables that included *Xiao muwu* (*A Small Log Cabin*), *Heshang* (*River Elegy*), *Gongheguo zhi lian* (*For Love of the Republic*), and *Wang Changcheng* (*Looking to the Great Wall*). This series constituted the most prominent cultural/ideological praxis of the eighties. It could even be said that the series was itself part of the state ideological apparatus.

Like *Roaming Beijing*, the production of *Tiananmen Square* "accidentally" bridged 1989 and 1990. Shooting transpired between 1988 and 1990, production wrapped up between 1990 and 1991. Due perhaps to the transformation of the discourse, or to the presence of the generation born in the sixties, or even to the special moment it was completed, *Tiananmen Square* displayed an obvious deviation in meaning and structure from its predecessors, although they were all sponsored by CCTV. It is possible to still read the grotesque scene of the changing of the Chairman's portrait on the rostrum in Tiananmen Square as an attempt to construct a parable, and to read a grand narrative of twentieth-century China's history into the documentary. Nevertheless, the documentary elements transcended political commentary and parable, unleashing a force unknown in similar works. Using a clear descending shot, the camera gave up the grand yet hollow imaginary panorama, to approach the ordinary people. Of course, by the time of completed postproduction, it was no longer possible to release *Tiananmen Square* through official channels. Although it had once been a carrier of mainstream production and discourse, it now exiled itself to a new margin. In 1991 two young scriptwriters and directors launched a "structure-wave-youth-film group," and initiated a "Chinese new documentary movement"; in December they organized the Seminar on Beijing New Documentaries.[16] *Tiananmen Square* was entered in the Asian film category at the Hong Kong Film Festival as an independent work in 1992. By then, the marginal group had completed its break away from the center and a new margin made up of exiles began to come together. The ten or so young people embarked on their new video documentaries as independent producers in a specific cultural space that emerged from the context of the nineties.

In 1992 Shi Jian finished *I've Graduated*, a powerful work unique both in style and in content. It documented the last seven days of the 1992 graduating classes at Qinghua and Beijing Universities, and was made up of interviews with the graduates, footage of the campuses, and some performance pieces. Just like the perfect fiction torn open to reveal real waste, like heaven's enclosure being pried open, the almost ruthless, witnessing documentary style, which originated with *Roaming Beijing*, revealed not only certain (types of) facts and events, but also the dazzlingly naked psychological landscape. Instead of exposing the scar left by abusive power, it revealed an unexpected spiritual legacy and explored the psychological world of the immediate sufferers. It marked the first time an ordinary person's view was introduced into the narration of a finished historical social event.

Nineteen ninety-three saw the birth of Wu Wenguang's new work, *1966 – wode hongweibing shidai* (*1966 – My Red Guard Year*). Different from the direct, intuitive style of *Roaming Beijing*, this documentary had a delicate structure. Its main body was composed of interviews with five old Red Guards, interlaced with official documentary episodes about Red Guards during the Cultural Revolution and supplemented by a rehearsal and performance by Cobra, an all-female rock troupe, of a song entitled "My 1966." Also woven intermittently into this work, producing a certain rhythmic effect, are animation episodes, rich with the effects of traditional ink paintings. These were contributed by Hao Zhiqiang, another independent filmmaker who took the Cultural Revolution or general mass social movements as his metaphors. They are more a maiden attempt to personalize historical narration than a reflection on the Cultural Revolution or a dialogue between the nineties reality and past memories. Rather than a desperate revival of an individual's historical memories, the film is a description of how history and memory are thoroughly buried. *1966* not only wallowed in the rock rhythm of "1966, the red train loaded with happy sheep," it was also submerged in memories constantly tinted and hidden by sentimentality and lies. As the interviews came to a close, the camera captured an interesting detail. The interviewees carefully picked up one by one their treasured traces of history: the yellowing pages of songbooks, the armbands and notebooks. Disappearing like magic into the elaborate, imitation, ancient, composite cabinet, these traces were wiped out with a disharmony of memory and reality, as if they were merely a dream dissipating at dawn. Thus, "History is the history of the present. Future is the future of the present."

A View in the City of Mirrors

In the early nineties, when the empty stage excited Wu Wenguang, the young people who began their independent work were unaware of their impending encounter with a bigger, more special historical opportunity. When *Roaming Beijing* was exhibited at the Hong Kong Film Festival, the new documentarist aroused world attention. Zhang Yuan's *Mother*, released at the same time, was touted as representing a new Chinese film mode, as "astounding", and as a "courageous achievement," provoking the Western world's expectation of Chinese film. Both *Mother* and *Roaming Beijing* made the enviable journey through a dozen Euro-American film festivals. If this achievement originated from the fact that Zhang Yimou and his Fifth Generation created the world's hunger for Chinese film, especially alternative films (not only for one director, Zhang Yimou, in one of his many modes, and not only for one actress, Gong Li), and if it also originated from the unique perspectives, landscapes, and charm that the independent, or Sixth Generation, filmmakers registered, this unfolding, complex cultural phenomenon was also surrounded by a far more complicated cultural condition in the nineties.

The significant point is that all of the independent features and most of the new documentaries, not just the outstanding ones, won glorious victories at film festivals. At the apex stood Wang Xiaoshuai's *The Day in Winter-Spring*, which not only won Best Film and Best Director prizes at Italian and Greek film festivals, but was also collected by the New York Museum of Modern Art and selected by the BBC as one of the one hundred films chronicling world film history. Independent works, including the coarser and weaker ones, were highly praised not only at Euro-American film festivals, but also by renowned and usually harsh Western film critics, who made an exception of the Chinese films. Their criterion in selecting Chinese films for international acknowledgment was no longer based on given Western art standards (even orientalist ones), but exclusively on the films' production style and the official Chinese filmmaking system.

After Zhang Yimou's *Iron Prison* (the story of desire suppressed in an old house) and the modern and historical tragedies – Tian Zhuangzhuang's *Lan fengzheng* (*Blue Kite*), Chen Kaige's *Farewell My Concubine*, and Zhang Yimou's *Huozhe* (*To Live*), for instance – independent filmmaking emerged as the West's third channel for naming and accessing Chinese films. In 1993, when the Chinese contact person notified the Notre Dame Film Festival that the Chinese government had decided to revoke Huang Jianxin's permit to attend, the organizer remarked without the least complaint, "We've got the films we needed." These films included Zhang Yuan's *Beijing Bastards*, which was flawed but original, and *Ting ji* (*Shooting Finished*), which was shot with a domestic camera, without postproduction, and was far below professional standards. Furthermore, *Shooting Finished* was not exhibited as a domestic video work, but as one of "the important Chinese films."

There is food for thought here. The Sixth Generation's creative style and path were typical of dedicated young filmmakers outside Hollywood, especially in the Third World. The tolerance and goodwill extended to the Sixth Generation had never been expected from the refined and arrogant European festival circuit or in conceited

American film circles. Perhaps the answer to this phenomenon lies in the name "underground film," which referred to the Sixth Generation but bypassed its artistic reality. Reviews of the Sixth Generation appearing in key Euro-American newspapers and journals seldom mentioned the films' artistic and cultural achievements, but simply stressed (if not fictionalized) their political significance. The consensus was that the artistic achievement of these films consisted in their similarity to Eastern European film before the radical change in 1989. Sixth Generation films did suggest a certain "political" gesture in terms of their rejection of mainstream ideology and the usual ideological operation of images. But even if independent filmmaking did constitute revolutionary subversion of the official Chinese filmmaking system, and the filmmakers' creations and potential did point to a new future for Chinese film, this did not concern most Euro-American film festivals or film critics.

Just as the films of Zhang Yimou and his imitators satisfied the West's old orientalist mirror image, the West again privileged the Sixth Generation as the Other, reflecting Western liberal intellectuals' anticipations or expectations of the nineties Chinese cultural condition. Created as a mirror image, it again validated Western intellectuals' mapping of China's democracy, progress, resistance, civil society, and the marginal figure. They disregarded not only the cultural reality displayed directly in the films, but also the filmmakers' cultural intention. Most independent filmmakers rejected the label "underground film." Zhang Yuan once observed that if there had to be a "way of speaking," he preferred "independent filmmaker."[17] Wu Wenguang also pointed out that they were facing a two-fold cultural resistance from both mainstream ideology and new-imperialist cultural interpretation.[18] What the Western promoters stressed was neither the reality expressed in the film nor the reality of the film, but the "reality" *outside* the film. In my view, this is a cultural fact in the post–Cold War period. Promoters both blessed the Sixth Generation filmmakers with exceptional favor and generosity and ruthlessly rewrote the filmmakers' cultural expression according to their own preexisting interpretive horizon. In a sense, their "penetrating" view moved away from the reality of Chinese films toward an imaginary China, and landed in a tragicomic situation. At least in the early nineties, the Sixth Generation became a scene in the fog, highly exposed in the "outside world," but little known inside China. Except for *Mother*, news about "China's underground films" – the Sixth Generation works – was communicated to me only through overseas publications and friends. They were seen only at Western film festivals and foreign embassies in Beijing, and in the cramped, small rooms of friends.

Nevertheless, they constituted a particular cultural position and a particular cultural gesture. The independent filmmakers began by breaking out of the Chinese cultural predicament. It was a pauper's moving and dramatic infatuation with the art of film. Some of their successors copied and benefitted from their cultural posturing. In a sense, on the nineties cultural stage, in the repertoire co-directed by conflicting power centers, the role of "independent filmmaker" acquired specified meanings and clear pros and cons; it became a role worthy of imitating and performing. If the "Zhang Yimou style" used to be a narrow door through which Chinese directors could move on their "march toward the world," independent filmmaking now became a shortcut to the power base in Western cinema.

Dialogue, Misreading, and Barrier

In the 1990s, there is an absurd cultural experience and reality in the Chinese city of mirrors: the efforts at cultural dialogue (especially between the East and the West), even the successful ones, constantly proved the "incommunicability of cultures." The reasons were not only the inevitable misreadings or the fact that "dialogue on an equal basis" and "reciprocal communication" can be no more than wishful thinking given the specific power structure, but also the fact that the inferior party is predetermined to internalize the superior party's cultural expectation and intentional misreading. The success of Zhang Yimou and Chen Kaige's nineties works in the West and the popularity of Zhang Rong's *Wild Swan* and Zheng Nian's earlier *Life and Death in Shanghai* indicated not that the West was beginning to understand China, but that these works had validated once again the Western orientalist imagination about China.

But the predicament of the Sixth Generation was particularly absurd: for not only was the West's lionization of Sixth Generation film produced by consistent misreading, but this misreading then constructed the reading of these films within China.

While the works of "independent filmmakers" were structuring the preconceptions about new Chinese films that invaded the Euro-American film festival circuits, Chinese delegates would have to refuse or were forbidden to attend any film festivals where independent films were also exhibited. This led to complex and subtle phenomena at various film festivals. A typical case – in fact, a climactic moment – was generated by the exhibition of the unsanctioned *Blue Kite* and *Beijing Bastards* at the 1993 Tokyo Film Festival: the Chinese representatives arriving in Tokyo were forbidden to attend any festival-related activities. That same year, Zhang Yuan was forced to stop shooting *Yidi jimao (Feathers All Around)*. The Chinese Ministry of Broadcasting, Film, and Television also issued a ban on the seven directors of *Blue Kite, Beijing Bastards, Roaming Beijing, I've Graduated, Shooting Finished, The Day in Winter-Spring,* and *Suspended Love.* This tense situation was undoubtedly a result of traditional struggles between rival global ideologies. Yet, just like their fame in the West, their maltreatment in China was more a response to the Western misreading than it was a decision based on the merit of the films. It was undoubtedly targeted on the films' subversion of the Chinese filmmaking system, but I believe it was more a grudge against overseas naming and definition of the "underground," "anti-government" films. And it was a powerful proof of the "truthfulness" of Western film circles' misreading. This was a vicious circle, a mapping of rival ideological camps' strange correspondence and mutual reference to each other.

In the cultural landscape of 1990s China, another discourse on the Sixth Generation also bypassed the reality of the films to constitute a picture of postmodern, postcolonial cultural resistance. The Sixth Generation's narrative techniques, including their flaws and failures, were gilded with postmodern art description. Some of their obvious or naïve modernist attempts were described as Third World cultural resistance in accordance with postcolonial theories of "mimicry" and "appropriation."[19] The image of smooth sailing was again buoyed up by the cultural phenomenon of the Sixth Generation.

"New Humans" and the Story of the Ruthless Youth

As opposed to some optimistic and arbitrary postmodernist imaginings, I think that Sixth Generation works exhibit more or less modernist, occasionally "new enlightenment" cultural traits. Speaking about his motives for making *Roaming Beijing*, Wu Wenguang, the new documentary director, said that for him roamers displayed a "human self-consciousness. They began to walk with their own bodies and feet, to think with their own heads. This is the primary stage of the beginning of humanity in Western humanism. What is taken for granted in the West, like roaming, takes some courage in China."[20] Zhang Yuan noted that *Beijing Bastards* described the "new humans" because "the real renaissance means the resurrection of the individual and the individual's recognition of his or her own revival."[21] "The consistent action" in *Beijing Bastards* was "seeking" since "the director is also seeking in life – seeking for his own style of life." Zhang thought that "our generation should not be the Beat Generation. This generation should stand up through seeking, achieving real self-perfection."[22] Hidden behind the rhetoric of humanity, individuality, humanism, and renaissance was the new generation's manifesto for its ascent onto the Chinese historical stage. This was true not only for this one generation, this Sixth Generation. Rather than looking upon the Sixth Generation works as yet another new wave film or new Chinese film movement, I suggest we designate it as the fading in of the social culture just emerging in the transformative nineties.

In a sense, the common theme was the city, the city in transformation. In the small number of Sixth Generation masterpieces, such as *Beijing Bastards* and *Weekend Sweetheart*, Chinese cities, such as Beijing and Shanghai, were finally emerging from various power discourses after a long, long delay. These works dealt with young people of the nineties as urban roamers, various kinds of marginal urban figures, with fading childhood memories of the city in transformation (sometimes the childhood during the Cultural Revolution specific to nineties culture). The core of Sixth Generation films was rock and roll, the lives of rock stars. Their age at initiation into cinema and their experiences as a cohort decided their common interest in the archetype of the *Bildungsroman*. Or, more precisely, their common scripting of "the story of ruthless youth" was written in different, yet similar styles. Taking as their metaphor a retarded child who cannot or refuses to have linguistic ability (*Mother*) or a psychotic patient abandoned to illusion (*Suspended Love*), Sixth Generation films and filmmakers displayed more or less countercultural traits. Facing rejection and loss, seeking out trauma, the glorious moment created by rock and roll achieved a momentary perfection. As they roamed the dilapidated back alleys of the metropolis, they existed between legal and illegal boundaries, seeking and roaming, vulnerable and ruthless. Their stories of youth were not about love. Rather they revealed the reality of a thawing swamp once the artifices of "youthfulness" had been torn away. The reality within the film (its content) and the reality about the film (its processes and means of production), which were distinctly separate in mainstream films, almost merged together in most Sixth Generation films.

The "ruthless youth" told their own stories, and displayed their own lives; they no longer adopted the forms of autobiographical masquerade or mock confession of the soul. "Parable is the Fifth Generation's core," Zhang Yuan admitted.

> They have done a terrific job writing history as a parable. But I can only be objective. Indeed, to me objectivity is crucial. Each day I pay attention to what happens immediately around me. I can't see beyond a certain distance.[23]

In Wang Xiaoshuai's words, "producing this film (*The Day in Winter-Spring*) is like writing our own diary."[24] Indeed, lack of financial backing and the fundamental characteristics of the film meant that amateurs started out using amateur actors; sometimes they just played themselves. For instance, Wu Wenguan was an important absent character in *Roaming Beijing*; the scriptwriter Qin Yan played the mother in *Mother*; and rocker Cui Jian played his namesake in *Beijing Bastards*. Wang Xiaoshuai's friends and the young avant-garde painters Liu Xiaodong and Yu Hong starred in *The Day in Winter-Spring*. Wang Xiaoshuai and Lou Ye played roles in each other's films. These filmmakers also cast professional actors, even stars like Wang Zhiwen, Ma Xiaoqing, and Jia Hongsheng, who collaborated in *Weekend Sweetheart*; Shi Ke, in *Suspended Love*; and Feng Yuanzheng, in *Postman*. Nevertheless, the basis of Sixth Generation collaboration was "contemporaneousness."

In a sense, Zhang Yuan's so-called objectivity and passion constituted the two opposite poles of Sixth Generation narrativity. The Sixth
Generation rejected parable and sought instead to turn their attention
to people and happenings around them. Their most conspicuous trait
was the on-site presentation of culture. In this style the narrator was
(or sought to be) a witness of the nineties cultural scene. "Objectivity"
presupposes a cold and nearly cruel style, in which the camera, replacing the witness, approaches the location in a sadistic, masochistic
manner. This chilling, savagely poetic camera-eye style became the
common trait of the Sixth Generation. Yet they also had somehow to
inject passion into the scenes and stories that the camera was objec-
tively recording, passions such as the confessions and appeals of their
generation. It is unlikely that they were really the witnesses of their
works; they were more like the poly-subjects of dream logic who exist
simultaneously in different places.

Certainly not all films achieved the Sixth Generation's expectations. Their Achilles heel was their inability to erase their rather
artificial youthful miseries or to suppress their profound, youthful self-
pity. I think this narcissism harmed the presentation of their own
cultural condition in *The Day in Winter-Spring*. Lou Ye's *Weekend
Sweetheart*, on the other hand, was outstanding among the films about
youth. The way it adapted the conventions of subtitling from silent
films, the studied, casual adoption of old techniques, its cold, poetic
documentary style, and the use of coincidence in narrative and epi-
logue were all means of enabling the film to transcend the self-pity
inherent in the Sixth Generation's naked narcissism. Style endowed
Sixth Generation youth narratives with a certain postmodern import.

Maybe the Sixth Generation's cultural experiences and the contin-
gencies of the moment they took the stage predetermined their
constant abandonment to the absurdity of Being and their profound
experience of how human existence is fragmented through continual
wounds and shocks. Either way, they were not able or actually refused
to integrate the fragments of their momentary experiences. Also due to
their long-term involvement in advertisement and MTV production,
they not only introduced ad "language" into film narrative, but also
formed a new narrative style through collage. This style combined the
spasms of desire characteristic of MTV and its momentary images and

sentiments with narrative scenes that drew on the fragments of the
dream, the stories of ruthless youth, and the long shot of the cold,
wandering gazes of indifferent witnesses. Of course, used indiscrimin-
ately, this pursuit of style could lead to a purposeless medley and naïve
technical bravado. Such flaws were not rare in Sixth Generation efforts.
Beijing Bastards was a success. Fragmented narratives, momentary
moods, broken scenes, the "spectacle" of Cui Jian's performances all
collapsed into the nameless urban roamers' perceptions of the monot-
onous city and its shabby alleys. Narrative, or the delays following a
dramatic passage, conveyed a particular sense of urbanity and time.

Epilogue or Prologue

As a cultural phenomenon, surrounded by cultural discourses and
power centers, and as an object for the projection of desire, the Sixth
Generation has become a scene in the foggy nineties cultural landscape. To the Sixth Generation, it is perhaps only a prelude, a mere
interlude. The Sixth Generation is a new phenomenon, just beginning
to shift from the margin to the center of a social, public space, itself in
formation. The initiators of the new documentary style have become
increasingly involved in producing mainstream TV programs.
Sometimes they are contractors or quasi-producers of programs. Their
imagistic style and the new documentaries' specific cultural appeal
are forcefully rewriting the mainstream TV scene. A case in point is
CCTV's "Dongfang shikong" ("Eastern Time and Place"). Mainstays of
this new generation, at the behest of Fifth Generation director Tian
Zhuangzhuang, have gathered at the nation's premier film studio, the
Beijing Film Studio. There, gathered around Tian, they begin or con-
tinue to create within the system.[25] Commenting on this experience,
Wang Xiaoshuai asserted, "For the first time I feel completely a direc-
tor." Although they persist with their stories of youth – Lu Xuechang's
Gangtie shi zheyang liancheng de (*How the Steel Is Made*) and Wang
Xiaoshuai's *Yuenan guniang* (*Vietnam Girl*) are good examples – they
are also combining creativity and commercial appeal. Lou Ye's earlier
The Bewitching Girl, for instance, is redolent of David Lynch's commercial style. Li Jun's *Shanghai wangshi* (*The Old Days of Shanghai*)

packages a commercial story with great nostalgia. Li admits to "leaning toward mainstream film," while Lou Ye puzzles over the fact that "now it's more and more difficult to know what is closer to the essence of film, Antonioni or Jackie Chan's *Hongfan qu* (*Rumble in the Bronx*)."[26] Is this a final salvation or is it a submission? Is the margin undertaking a successful march to occupy the center? Or has the omnipresent cultural industry and its market engineered a takeover? Is a new generation of filmmakers injecting vigor into the shaky Chinese cinema or is the system overwhelming the feeble individual artist? Actually, I hope neither is the case and that this moment marks the beginning of a new landscape.

Notes

1 See Liu Xiaofeng, "Guanyu 'siwu' yidai de shehuixue sikao zhaji" (A collection of sociological thoughts on the May Fourth generation), *Dushu* (Reading), no. 5, 1989, pp. 35–43.

2 For the Third Generation's positioning of "the old recruits" and reeducated youth at the rise of reeducated youth literature, see Zhao Yuan's *Di zhi zi: xiangcun xiaoshuo yu nongmin wenhua* (The son of the earth: rural fiction and peasant culture) (Beijing: Shiyue wenyi chubanshe, 1993), chapter 4, pp. 229–47.

3 Zhang Yongjie and Chen Yuanzhong, *Disidai ren* (The Fourth Generation) (Beijing: Dongfang chubanshe, 1988).

4 See Liu Xiaofeng, "Guanyu 'siwu' yidai de shehuixue sikao zhaji," pp. 35–43.

5 See Wang Gan, "Shixing de fuhuo: lun xinzhuangtai" (Resurrection of the poetic: on the "new human condition"), *Zhongshan*, nos 4–5, 1994; and Zhang Yiwu, "Xin zhuangtai de jueqi" (The rise of the "new human condition"), *Zhongshan*, no. 5, 1994.

6 In my opinion, the First Generation should include the important directors of silent films, such as Zheng Zhengquin, Zhang Shichuan, and Sun Yu; the Second Generation includes directors of the 1930s and 1940s, such as Cai Chusheng and Fei Mu, who started making films with soundtracks.

7 See my discussion of this phenomenon in chapter 1, "Severed Bridge: The Art of the Sons' Generation," and Huang Jianzhong, "*Disidai* yijing jieshu" ('"The Fourth Generation" Has Come to an End'), *Film Art*, no. 3, 1990.

8 See Ni Zhen, "Hou wudai de bufa" (The marching of the post-Fifth Generation), *Dazhong dianying* (Popular film), no. 4, 1989, p. 11.

9 Liu Xiaofeng, "Guanyu 'siwu' yidai de shehuixue sikao zhaji," pp. 35–43.

10 See Dai Jinhua, Zhang Yiwu, Chen Xiaoming, and Zhu Wei, "Xin shi pipan shu" (The ten new critiques), *Zhongshan*, no. 2, 1994, pp. 185–203.

11 The first "youth production team" was established at the Guangxi Film Studio, mainly made up of members of the 1978 class of graduates of the Beijing Film Academy. The result was the first work of the Fifth Generation, *Yige he bage* (*One and Eight*). From then on, many other studios followed suit, establishing youth teams and giving rise to a group of representative works of the Fifth Generation.

12 Zheng Xianghong, "Zhang Yuan fangtan lu" (Interview with Zhang Yuan), *Dianying gushi* (Film story), no. 5, 1994, p. 9.

13 Some young graduates volunteered to work at the marginal film studios such as Guangxi and Fujian, emulating their predecessors the Fifth Generation's early career moves and hoping that they would take off like them. But the production formula which enabled the Fifth Generation to succeed in the margins in those early years, no longer existed for the younger generation.

14 Tony Rayns, "Future: Astounding!" originally appeared in *Sight and Sound*, supplement to the 1992 London Film Festival. Translated by Li Yuanyi, "Qianjing: lingren zhenjing!" in *Dianying gushi*, no. 4, 1993, p. 11.

15 From a personal interview with Wu Wenguang, August 1993.

16 See 1992 Hong Kong Film Festival propaganda material, p. 35.

17 Zheng Xianghong's "Duli yingren zai xingdong: suowei Beijing 'dixia dianying' zhenxiang" (Independent filmmakers in action: the true face of the Beijing "underground films") *Dianying gushi*, (Film story), no. 5, 1993, p. 4.

18 Wu Wenguang, quoted from the workshop on new urban cinema in *Dangdai dianying* (Contemporary film), no. 11, 1994.

19 Quoted in Zhang Yiwu, "Hou xinshiqi Zhongguo dianying: fenlie de tiaozhan" (Post–New Era Chinese film: the challenge of fragmentation), Dangdai dianying (Contemporary film), no. 5, 1994, pp. 4–11.

20 My interview with Wu Wenguang, August 1993.

21 Zheng Xianghong.

22 Ning Dai's captions in his "*Beijing Bastards*' Plot Briefing," *Dianying gushi* (Film story), no. 5, 1993, p. 9.

23 Ibid.

24 *Dianying gushi* (Film story), no. 5, 1993. See captions to the color plate of *The Day in Winter-Spring*.

25 Zheng Xianghong, "Gangtie shi zheyang liancheng de: Tian Zhuangzhuang tuichu diliudai daoyan" (*How the Steel is Made*: Tian Zhuangzhuang promoting the Sixth Generation directors), *Dianying gushi* (Film story), no. 5, 1995, pp. 16–17.

26 Ibid., p. 18.

Translated by Yiman Wang

4

Gender and Narration: Women in Contemporary Chinese Film

Amidst Earth-shattering Change

After the founding of New China in 1949, the new political regime instituted its first comprehensive law, the Marriage Law of the People's Republic of China.[1] China's Communist Party also implemented a series of social reform measures explicitly designed to forward the goal of liberating women.[2] Contemporary Chinese women came to enjoy the same rights of citizenship as men: equal pay for equal work, the right to enter into and dissolve marriage contracts, the rights to give birth, raise children, and have an abortion. They were also granted certain privileges – such as the vote – that had been gender-based. The All-China Women's Federation (hereafter Women's Federation), a megalithic, quasi-official institution with branches located throughout China, became the mouthpiece of women's issues and the guardian angel of women's rights. This unprecedented bestowal of benefits definitely marked a cataclysmic change for women. There is no doubt that contemporary Chinese women did indeed become "liberated" women as Mao's sayings claim: "The times are different, men and women are now all the same," "Anything a male comrade can do, a female comrade can do as well,"[3] and "Women prop up half the sky." To this day, China is still one of those countries where women's liberation has reached an apex and where women enjoy a greater degree of power and freedom than they have ever done before.

Yet, in one respect, contemporary Chinese women experience an existential and cultural dilemma resembling a kind of logical fallacy, like an absurd paradox or vicious circle. After the May Fourth Movement, women emerged as a gender from obscurity and through great adversity "onto the horizon of history," where finally they shared with men the same expansive possibilities. Yet they lost the power or possibility of affirming, expressing, and exploring their female sexuality. When women entered the course of history as "liberated women," as a gender-based community, they were nonetheless lost to history's visual field. Paradoxically, the arrival of women's de jure "liberation" once again vitiated any chance Woman had to become a historical, discursive subject.

Women within the Discourse of History

Amidst twentieth-century China's colossal and constantly changing historical set, a fully developed and independent movement for female emancipation never made its entry onstage. Rather, specters of such a movement emerged, sometimes as an interlude within revolutionary history:[4] for example, a female writer's spontaneous, heartfelt expression;[5] or the various female images and female discourses in the history of film.

The cataclysmic change in women's status after 1949 was largely the project and accomplishment of an external force.[6] Yet precisely because an external force propelled the liberation of women for the most part, female consciousness at the individual and collective levels remained underdeveloped and separate from implemented social reforms. The female cultural revolution that should originally have accompanied women's de jure emancipation never made its arrival. As soon as the law asserted and protected the emancipation of female labor and improved the political and economic status of women, the "liberation of women" became a *fait accompli* in contemporary China's mainstream discourse. The authoritative historical discourse employed a political method of historical periodization that situated the narrative of women in two distinct historical eras: then and now. As Mao said, "Old and new society are like day and night" or "The old society turned people into ghosts, the new society turns ghosts into people." Between 1949 and 1979 all narratives about women asserted that women were tragically enslaved, mistreated, and victimized in the dark abyss of (pre-1949) Old China.[7]

In the early discourse of "women's liberation," the founding of New China not only signifies the termination of the historical fate of women suffering as subalterns and the toppling of women's eternal status as the "second sex" in patriarchal, male-dominated society; it also signifies the collapse of the inertial institution of Man's historical and cultural superiority. This way of dividing history, relying on distinctive boundary markers to delimit two completely different eras,[8] not only blocked the view of the new social, cultural, psychological problems the women of New China confronted, it also insulated the contemporary Chinese female cultural field of vision from premodern or May Fourth practices of women's culture. Thus, class discourse highlighted women's historical experience and fate. It also concealed the new life and cultural circumstances liberated women faced.

Male Domination, Patriarchy, and the Language of Desire

As a particular type of cultural practice, film in New China accurately manifests and articulates the paradox of women's de jure social condition in relation to women's culture. It is both accurate and appropriate to take 1949 as the year dividing modern and contemporary periods in the history of film.[9] As a result of the great social changes the new government instituted in 1949, mainland China experienced a political change and supersession of political authority. A distinctive rupture was also registered in the history of Chinese film that year.[10] Film in New China simultaneously dissolved its reliance on the ideology of Hollywood film on the one hand and the culture and tradition of Soviet socialist film on the other. The only remaining blueprint for film was the political schema that the new authority prescribed and the dynamic new state's orthodox ideological discourse. Consequently the bulk of Chinese films between 1949 and 1955 rested on simple, undeveloped artistic language to project ideological affirmation. Around 1959, however, following a process of gradual development, New China's films evolved into the mature form of the classical revolutionary film, a fusion of the tradition of China's left-wing cinema and the ideology of films produced in the first post-1949 era.

The sexual order and gender narrative intrinsic to the cinematic mechanism of the new classical revolutionary genre, in tandem with China's social changes, experienced a profound transformation. Not only did the image of Woman, as contained inherently in the spectral structure of male desire, gradually disappear, but both the gaze of desire – built in a structural sense into the camera eye – and the narrative of desire were gradually wiped away by the political rhetoric of the rigid cinematic narrative produced in line with New China's ideological discourse. The new classical revolutionary film genre successfully dispelled the particular discourse inherent in Hollywood's classical cinematic narrative mechanism (that is, the shot sequence of male desire/female image and male gaze/woman as object of gaze) when it eliminated the narrative of desire along with the language of desire.

In some ways, phallocentric cinema form was truly shaken up. But it is also apparent that through a process of revision the stalwart patriarchal ideology was reaccommodated in cinematic narrative. Almost without exception in this new classical revolutionary mode of cinema, women were narrated in the gaze of the authorities (this gaze is of course male, though it is not the gaze of male desire) and emptied of their own narrativizing subjectivity. Also, because the image of Woman no longer served as an object of the gaze of male desire, women also ceased to exist as a gender group distinct from men. Women could not possess the central subject position and perspective in the new classical revolutionary cinematic narrative. And just as the social organization of contemporary Chinese society failed to produce a female cultural revolution, so the elimination of cinematic narratives' language of desire and the character's gaze of desire meant that characters on screen lost their gender identity. As the gender difference between men and women weakened, political and class difference replaced it.

Qin Xianglian and Hua Mulan

In the intellectual and cultural history of modern and contemporary China, two mirror images of Woman dominate discourse on the female gender and liberation of women. Qin Xianglian represents the traditional girl who is exploited and abused; Hua Mulan is the normative heroine who transgresses patriarchal society and joins the ranks of men in history by fighting in the service of her country. The only additional image is that of Nora, the woman who rebels by walking out of the family.

In retrospect, it gradually becomes clear that the Maoist discourse, "The times are different, men and women are now the same" and its social practice, while establishing a social system and cultural tradition that countered sexual discrimination, also instituted the denial of Woman as a distinct, collective gender. Although the discourse of "men and women are the same" vigorously expedited and safeguarded sexual equality, gender-based cultural differences – deeply inscribed in a thousand-year-old male history – were also erased in the process. Consequently, another absurd paradox came into play. Once women were released from the female norms set by a male-dominated culture that required their subservience and silence, the masculine norms (not the norm created by men for women but the norms created by and for men) became the only absolute set of norms available to women. This is encapsulated in the Maoist saying, "Anything a male comrade can do, a female comrade can do as well." Paradoxically, women were losing their spiritual gender, while at the same time finally casting off the yoke of history. Because of the elimination of sexual difference in official ideological discourse, women, women's discourse, and women's self-expression and self-exploration became unnecessary and impossible.

Since the official ideology only provided new, liberated women with two female models – the tragically miserable girl of Old China and the masculine woman warrior – the "new women" (*xin nüxing*) and the "liberated women" (*jiefang de funü*) fell through the cracks of history. A new form of cultural oppression accompanied the political, economic, and legal liberation of women. After 1949, then, any discussion or analysis of women's issues based on a recognition of gender distinctions was treated as reactionary, a political and cultural affront to the Maoist regime. Given the supposition that women never had a language of their own, that they were always weighted down by the yoke of male-dominated culture, contemporary Chinese women even gradually lost their ability to maintain a distinct subject position in a uniquely feminine discourse.[11] Granted, the image of Nora and her renowned rebellion created an ephemeral moment of historical possibility for women, but May Fourth women instead oscillated between the authority of their fathers and their husbands.[12] The contemporary narrative of women related by the official discourse of New China described a trajectory "from slaves to soldiers" and did provide women with an ostensibly liberating historical moment: women only became "liberated" the moment they left the "dark, bitter ten-thousand-foot-deep well" and marched into the bright sky of New China's warm haven (represented by the liberated areas, the CCP, or PLA).[13]

Within this official narrative, a particular rhetorical strategy makes the signification of gender a function of the discourse on class and class struggle. For example, only class enemies – exploitative classes – view women with a gendered gaze of sexual desire, which thus signifies an evil and base gaze characterized by discrimination and derision that inflicts violence on women.[14] In accordance with this rhetorical strategy, once Wu Qionghua, in "Hongse niangji jun" ("The Red Detachment of Women"), becomes a female soldier in the unit, she wears women's attire only two more times: once, when she goes on a reconnaissance expedition into the enemy's territory; the second time, when she accompanies Hong Changqing, who is dressed up as a concubine, on a mission to break into Coconut Grove Manor. In other words, it is only necessary for women to "dress up" and perform their gender – sexual identity is an act of seduction when positioned within the enemy's gaze. Therefore, when contemporary Chinese women obtained the right to enjoy a certain degree of social and discursive power, their gender identity and gendered speaking position (*huayu de xingbie shenfen*) were lost as a consequence. When women finally became active agents in history, their subject position lay concealed behind a desexualized (or more accurately masculinized) façade. Although the new legal and social system certainly helped contemporary Chinese women avoid the tragedy of Qin Xianglian, the Hua Mulan predicament was nonetheless exacerbated.

With the Family-Nation

If we examine the Hua Mulan legend, it is not difficult to discover why the story, despite its transgression of the gender order, has gained acceptance within China's cultural tradition. Its legitimacy stems precisely from the fact that the story's dominant device is a woman's commitment and utmost loyalty to her family and country. A more accurate title for the story "Hua Mulan Joins the Army," would really be "Hua Mulan Takes Her Father's Place in the Army."[15] In the legend, when Mulan first appears, her image conforms to the traditional female norms: "Alack, alas! alack, alas! / She weaves and sees the shuttle pass."[16] Mulan joins the army only because she has no other choice: "I read the battle roll last night; / The Khan has ordered men to fight. / The roll was written in twelve books; / My father's name was in twelve nooks. / My father has no grown-up son, for elder brother I have none."[17] Actually, in China's traditional folk culture, narratives with the "mounted female warrior" (*dao ma dan*) generally include this particular device: the woman warrior devotes herself entirely to the country by replacing her father or husband in the army.[18] Consequently, in the widely known story *Yang jia jiang* (*Yang Family Generals*) the relatively famous acts when performed in vernacular opera are "Bai sui gua shuai" ("Centenarian in Command") and "Mu Guiying gua shuai" ("Mu Guiying Takes Command").[19] (It was not until the sixties that these sections became popular acts in the Beijing Opera repertoire.) These are all legends about women who heroically joined because all the men in their families had died on the battlefield and the country was perilously teetering on the brink of extinction. Interestingly, although the heroine once again appears against the backdrop of a battlefield in the heart-rending act "*Lianghong Yu leigu zhen Jinshan*" ("Battle of Jinshan"), beating the battle drums for her father, she maintains a position more "properly" in accord with traditional gender norms.[20] Other acts of *Yang Family Generals* in which females play the part of men, such as "Muke zhai zhao qin" ("Finding a husband at Muke zhai") and "*Yuan men zhan zi*" ("Captive at the Barracks") are no more than comic divertissements.[21] These divertissements are much less enjoyable even than the comedy "Da jin zhi" ("Rebuking the Princess"), which lacks the motif of gender transgression and affirms the traditional female stereotypes.

The tradition of the "mounted female warrior" in China's folk culture reveals an interesting fact: to a certain extent, premodern Chinese women were situated within a powerful and effective ideological framework of loyal identification with their country's rulers. Of course, although "cultivating the self, uniting the family, governing the country, and maintaining peace under the heavens" were criteria for exemplary men, when a woman fortuitously "emerged onto the horizon of history" she had first to meet the prerequisite of being pious to her family before being allowed to adopt the standards of the virtuous man. Consequently, Hua Mulan's transgressions of gender norms were permitted and exonerated because she displayed filial piety when deferentially "taking her father's place." Likewise, though in choosing her own husband, Mu Guiying transgressed the gender norm, the Song court eventually pardoned her and commanded the "female generals" of the Yang family in recognition of Mu Guiying's loyalty: she convinced the rebels of Muke zhai to pledge allegiance to the Song court. Here, both Hua Mulan and Mu Guiying are used to prove that the fate of the country depends upon each and every woman, as well as each and every man.

Even a very superficial "cultural" comparison reveals that this "family" of premodern China – the patrilineal, patriarchal feudal clan – is very different from the "family " of modern society – the male-dominated nuclear family. The "country" of premodern China – a feudal kingdom – is likewise very different from the "country" or nation-state of modern times. Tragic masterpieces such as *Kongque dongnan fei* (*Southeast Fly the Peacocks*), *Chaitou feng* (*Hairpin Phoenix*), and *Fu sheng liu ji* (*Six Records of a Floating Life*) reveal women's position as accessory and subordinate of the entire patriarchal household rather than simply of the male himself.[22] They also expose the impotence and frailty of the men who occupy the relationally subordinate positions of minister or son when opposing the power of the Father (or Mother, acting on behalf of the Father). In relation to the authority of the patriarchal household and nation, men too have few alternatives other than "hanging themselves" – showing rebellious spirit, having a concubine "bestowed" upon them and "entering the erotic dreamworld again" – or dragging out an ignoble existence, "guided by deceit and forgetfulness."

It is not surprising that the narrative of the wife "walking out" of the modern nuclear family was rewritten during the May Fourth period as the daughter or son's rebellion against the feudal family. Only belatedly did Nora, who walks out and is ostensibly liberated but only really goes from her father's family directly into her husband's family, appear on the Chinese screen. Even with the arrival of "supplements to the May Fourth new cultural revolution," such as "the movement for the revitalization of domestic film" and the "leftist film movement" of the 1930s, women on the screen, positioned in urban settings, were defined as those with no home to return to. Not only was the connection between a woman and her "family" – that is, her father's family – always already severed or shelved; her class status was also signified and differentiated before the signification and differentiation of her gender status: see, for example, *Shennü* (*Goddess*, 1934), *Ye meigui* (*Wild Rose*, 1932), *Shizi jietou* (*Crossroads*, 1937), and *Malu tianshi* (*Street Angel*, 1937).[23]

Without a doubt then, the flashing act of Nora walking out of her father's house foreshadowed a tragic denouement: see *Xin nüxing* (*New Women*, 1934).[24] Here the fate of Woman is used not simply to evidence patriarchal and male-dominated society but also to illustrate the tragic fate of individualism in modern China. Indeed, images of Nora and accompanying narratives most closely resembling Ibsen's vision only appeared belatedly on Chinese screens after the war, in the forties: see, for example, *Guan buzhu de chunguang* (*Impossible to Imprison the Light of Spring*, 1948); *Ruozhe, ni de mingzi shi nüren* (*Frailty, Thy Name Is Woman!*, 1947); *Yaoyuan de ai* (*Far Away Love*, 1947).[25] In these films, fully developed and determined women do indeed walk out of the modern, nuclear family's "doll house" in rebellion against the monogamous patriarchal order of modern society. Here again, however, Nora's walk-out is a simultaneous return. Women walked out of the doll's house and right back into the collective body under the name of the "people" and the "revolution." Once again, the emergent problematic of women's liberation became a metaphor.

Although, apparently, the issue of "enlightenment" often highlights the historical mission of women's liberation, condemning and opposing patriarchal power because it emphasizes the issue of feudalism and at the same time obscures, regardless of intention, modern-day patriarchal culture and the feudal order of male authority's inherent continuity. In this sort of literary and film narrative, women victims or women rebels are inadvertently circumscribed as metaphors or empty signifiers to designate the darkness and backwardness of feudal society and the anguish of society's exploited underclass. At the same time, the discursive presentation of traditional women as dead, as a sacrifice to history, precludes any probing of female experience and forecloses the possibility for a continuous, unbroken female experience, practice, cultural tradition. The imperative of national salvation as the nation faced the peril of extinction, however, superseded the issue of women's liberation. Women once again became amalgamated into the narrative and identity of the all-powerful nation-state.[26] So, women who experienced the democratic revolution nonetheless still found themselves circumscribed in the family-nation. A nuclear family constructed through the discourses of love, the division of labor, responsibility, and duty replaced the patriarchal feudal household. But the nation-state's vigorous "interpellation" administered a more constant and powerful effect on the subjective consciousness of women.

The Shared Horizons of Women and Individuals

It can be argued that one of the predicaments of modern Chinese women's culture is its association with the ambiguous, inchoate position of the individual and the discourses of individuality in Chinese culture. It was science and democracy (*kexue yu minzhu*) rather than freedom, equality, and universal love (*ziyou, pingdeng, bo'ai*) that came to form the core of China's enlightenment culture and the literati's spirit.[27] Therefore, within the history of China's modern culture, the possibility of the solitary individual becoming a cultural hero was foreclosed. Individuals (*ge ren*) could only be indecisive cowards vacillating at the historical crossroads or stooges ridiculed amidst the shifting winds of the great era. Since the emergence of women as a collective gender always faced the joint assault of the male-dominated and patriarchal discourses, women often adopted the strategy of aligning their own narrative with the discourse of the individual. Due to the ambiguity and fragility of the culture of individuality in Chinese culture, this type of discursive strategy became a potent, yet limited possibility.

Consequently, although autobiographical writing has always been one of the most important literary genres for women, it never really gained recognition. Even when it was actually identified as representing a marginal voice, more often than not it was dismissed as a symptom of the times or a social symbol. In China's intellectual and cultural history, *female* and *individual* were high-sounding terms, but they possessed, at the same time, a precarious existence. If, among women's works, Zhang Ailing's *Qingcheng zhi lian* (*Love in a Fallen City*) presented an alternative myth about history and women, Xiao Hong's story – her life of solitary struggle, pregnant amidst the chaos of war on the docks of Wuhan, and her lonely death in Hong Kong under siege – became a prototype of revelation for women. But these discourses about women, individuals, and their cultural predicament have always belonged to the discourse of leftist, elite intellectuals.

Such discourses, however, did not successfully surface in Chinese film, generically a part of urban/commercial/popular culture. Or, more precisely, they never crystallized in a successful or effective cinematic expression. Take as an interesting, complex example the career of Ai Xia, one of the handful of female screenwriters during the development period of Chinese films (1905–49): Ai wrote a script rather like a female *Bildungsroman* before collapsing under life's pressures and committing suicide. In *New Women*, the famous movie based on her life story, directed by Cai Chusheng, the illustrious actress Ruan Lingyu acted out her own tragic fate on screen. In the film narrative, the heroine escapes from the darkness of the oppressive patriarchal household and gains her independence, only to decide once again that she must walk out of the modern "doll's house." She commits suicide once she has written an autobiographical short story, "The Tomb of Love," because she cannot escape being a toy of male desire, manipulated by the voyeurism of the publishing industry.[28]

The oppositional, new woman's reverberating record of destruction and self-destruction – as a female-authored, multi-layered story – exhibits with much clarity both the complicity and the bankruptcy of the constructions of woman and the individual. Beyond being seen as a female tragedy produced by the system of commercial stardom or as the tragic result of a collision between the new woman and a patriarchal/male-dominated culture, the death of Ruan Lingyu should also be viewed in terms of the 1930s conflict between leftist film and rightist journalism industry.[29] So in relation to the new woman, the individual (man), who is cast into an era where the old and the new are in conflict (that is, old literati versus new youth), is even more frail and perplexed. And this is perhaps the other meaning to be found in the legendary romance between Zhang Ailing and Hu Lancheng.[30] Zhang Ailing, who wrote screenplays for *Taitai wansui* (*Long Live the Missus*, 1947) and *Bu liao qing* (*Love without End*) during her mainland film career, used her unique humor and tactful slickness to write about women's lives of compromise. In the particular context of postwar China, under the directives of Nationalist and Communist Parties, mainstream writing used stories about the fragmentation of traditional families and the nuclear family to serve as a means of opening space for sociopolitical mobilization and assimilation. In contrast, Wenhua Film Company, which produced the two aforementioned films scripted by Zhang Ailing, took the middle path and preserved the nuclear family in order to protect a space for the individual. Without a doubt, this protection of the individual was necessarily won at the cost of woman's self-sacrifice. However, Zhang Ailing, intriguingly, used the royalties she acquired from the two screenplays to provide her estranged husband Hu Lancheng with alimony and support after their separation. The relationship between Zhang Ailing and Hu Lancheng is commonly read as the classic tale of the infatuated girl deserted by a heartless man. In fact, in their story gender roles undoubtedly experienced an intriguing inversion.

Stories of new women, the narrative strategy of a culture of individual/males and non-females, were not just simply masks for men's writing once again, but often they also structured the new categorical requirements for the individual: the sacrifices that class, nation, or the ethics of bourgeois individuality required. It was precisely in male writing about women that the new woman as signifier of the vulnerable individual, while actualizing an oppositional stance, was in fact banished from society and culture as a selfless exile. As for works by women, most are read as expressions of social and cultural symptom, representing subordinates, loners, those who have lost their way. They also, simultaneously, signify the fate of the nation and the class. Stories dressed up as women's stories are basically mythic and greatly limit women's horizons.

Within the Family-Nation

With the establishment of New China, women collectively entered onto the social and historical stage from which they had been long excluded. This was certainly the first time since the early twentieth century that the ideal of the nation-state had been realized in a vigorous, powerful cultural and political assimilation. It is also the first time in the cultural history of contemporary women that the interpellating call to assimilate into the nation superseded women's devotion to the family. But this time, liberation's arrival did not mean, or did not only mean, that women would enjoy freedom and happiness as new women. Rather it meant that they should devote their newly freed hearts and bodies without restraint to their saviors, their liberators – the CCP, socialism, and the grand Communist project. The road from slave to warrior was the only one available to women; they would share equality and equal status with men not as women but as warriors.

There is another important aspect of Hua Mulan's metaphoric representation of women's circumstances. The most garrulous, detailed account in "Song of Mulan" is not given until Hua Mulan returns home:

> She opens the doors east and west
> And sits on her bed for a rest.
> She doffs her garb worn under fire
> And wears again female attire
> Before the window she arranges her hair
> And in the mirror sees her image fair.
> Then she comes out to see her former mate,
> Who stares at her in amazement great:
> "We have marched together for twelve years,
> We did not know there was a lass 'mid our compeers!'"[31]

It is clear that in the Hua Mulan story the attire of men in the army and the clothing women wear in their boudoirs clearly distinguishes two separate realms and spaces. The door, here, unquestionably delineates man's social space from woman's internal place within the home. China's new women, however, did not possess Hua Mulan's good fortune.

The vigorous call to assimilate into society alienated the gender identity of women by requiring them in the same capacity as men to undertake public responsibilities and duties, and to accept all male behavioral standards. Furthermore, in making the moral order more ideological (that is, intensifying the dichotomy between positive pro- letarian sentiments and negative bourgeois lifestyles), the household was promoted as the fundamental unit in the organization of society, and marriage became emphatically the foundation of values regarding the family. Under inflexible class and political standards, marriage and the family became endowed, though not sanctified, with an extremely tenacious practical value. Women's roles in the family remained traditional: they were responsible for elder care, childcare, childbearing, supporting their husbands, instructing the children, and altruistic devotion. The familiar saying "carrying loads on both shoul- ders" accurately depicts the image and burden of a generation of new Chinese women.[32]

In the family-nation, women were the same as men in their devo- tion and loyalty to the nation – CCP, proletariat, and the Communist mission – and in their recognition of its primacy. Tacitly, however, women in the family still maintained the same responsibility, the same obligatory duties as before. Women's daily life already adhered to the saying "devote utmost loyalty to the nation." In addition, the manifest and subconscious gendered double-standard, as a discursive structure and standard of behavior, created a female internal experience of rup- ture and conflict and a psychological burden of guilt. These women are the "heroines who have never left the home and family."[33] From one perspective, in the revolutionary barracks, the social landscape and discursive structure of the harmonious equality of "class brothers and sisters" not only concealed the existence of a double-standard, but at the same time buried the language of desire and desire's impulse in culture's interiority, vigorously transforming them to strengthen soci- ety's consolidation and centralization. In other words, a scattered and de-centered male power was replaced by a patriarchal form appearing in the name of the Nation, which once again became Woman's almighty overlord.

Writing Gender

In her deep and detailed study of the literature of the Seventeen-Year Era (1949–66), Chen Shunxin points out:

> In the investigation of [this period's] narrative discourse, it is not difficult to discover that the dominant discursive narrativity changes "femininity" to "masculinity" producing what appears like a "genderless" society. What is oppressed in the cultural arena is actually "the feminine" and not gender itself. Moreover, the extrusive or excess "masculine" was bolstered again in the ensemble of the names of the "party" and the "father" to support its higher authority, thus becoming the only acknowledged gender label. When the male became politically marked, then that which the powerful male discourse conducted possessed an ideological as well as a gendered function. The main point is that the traditional relation domination/subordination between man/woman was never in fact eradicated. Rather, the deepening of the relation of absolute power and submission between the party and the people directed more effective results within the levels of politics, society, culture, and psychology.[34]

Consequently, the male heroic image is still the pioneer and the leader in narrative works (that is, novels, films, narrative poetry). For example, in *Bai mao nü* (*White-Haired Girl*), Da Chun, Xi'er's former lover, who had already joined the ranks of the CCP's Eighth Route Army, leads Xi'er out of the damp, dark mountain cave, ushering in a glorious and happy new life. In *The Red Detachment of Women*, also, the CCP's Hong Changqing provides the ransom to rescue the bondmaid Wu Qionghua from the dungeon; he subsequently instructs her to head for the Revolution, steering her each step of the way as she becomes a revolutionary heroine.

The fate of the feminine gender during this era is even more complex. In the narrative works that manifest and submit to the artistic orientation of the workers, peasants, and soldiers (*gongnongbing*), the feminine as a quality and unique characteristic was destined to be abandoned and reinscribed. Against the backdrop of the revolution, the only female figure whose gender identity remained secure and "legitimate" was the endlessly devoted and persevering mother – the mythical Earth Mother, mother of the male soldiers, mother to the people, nation, and land. The female image filled with the most vitality is that of the girl/maiden, more specifically, the peasant maiden. Examples of the maiden awaiting suitors in her symbolic boudoir include Xi'er in the opera and film *White-Haired Girl*, Er mei zi in *Liubao de gushi* (*Story of Liubao Village*, 1956), Chunlan in the novella and film *Hong qipu* (*Red Flag Chronicle*, 1960), Wu Qionghua in the film *The Red Detachment of Women*, and Gaoshan in the film *Zhan huo zhong de qingchun* (*Youth in the Flames of War*).[35] The unknown and suspended position of these images was appropriated to assume a type of social and historical narrative. What is particularly striking is that, in these narratives, the typical image of the maiden is still placed in the classical object position as the recipient of the Other's actions and intentions. These maidens have no other choice than to pursue love and a happy marriage.

In the suppression of Woman in contemporary Chinese culture, Woman became an empty sign and a potent social symbol. The rhetorical pattern reflected in the ideology of Party/nation = mother succeeded in sanctifying the Name of the Father. Another important method of constructing the image of the revolutionary household was the "strict father, loving mother" characterization in the narratives of Revolutionary War. Consequently, this essentialist representation of Woman gained a kind of indispensable cultural function, a position that could be occupied by a man, woman, or symbolic character. At one end is the female slave girl–becomes–soldier narrative, within which the female is a symbolic label that gradually must be concealed. At the other end is the omnipresent female, the mother who generously illuminates the texture of the classical revolutionary narrative. She can represent the Party, country, people, and homeland. Furthermore, she carries an abundant and enchanting function not only within the two-tiered authoritative discourse – "There could be no New China without the CCP" and "Only the people are the motive force of world history"[36] – but also in the real-life dynamics of the savior/rescued (the Party-Army/the people).

Within the representation of the revolutionary family, she can surface in any one of the patient, gentle, and protecting political leaders. Those numerous negative and positive representations of the "female essence" are continually drawn, on multiple levels, by the political and cultural needs of the new China.

Empty Signifiers

In the production of classic revolutionary cinema, the film *Qingchun zhi ge* (*Song of Youth*, 1959), adapted from the novella of the same title by female author Yang Mo, is a most important and interesting work. *Song of Youth* is a model of socialist realist cinema. Taken out of context, one may instantly classify this film as a feminine *Bildungsroman*.[37] Woman, however, in terms of discourse, remained an invisible and suppressed identity, while at the same time it became an important and poignant empty signifier. In the narrative, woman acquired its identification and representation as the concealed metaphor for the social status of the intellectual.[38]

Actually, there has always existed a subtle parity and correspondence between the discourse on intellectuals within the mainstream ideology of the Mao Zedong era and the discourse on women within traditional ideology. Just as the position and value of Woman relies upon and is confirmed by her subordination to men – fathers, husbands, and sons – the intellectuals' position and worth stem from and are defined by the specific classes to which they are "attached."[39] Woman's existence is both internal and external to male-dominated culture, as a type of indispensable but distrusted threatening power; this is precisely the role of intellectuals within society.[40] In the classic ideology, the negative representation of Woman depicts her as callow, ignorant, manic, and frivolous, precisely the stereotypical negative features of intellectuals.[41] Thus, it is an apt choice to make a woman's story and fate represent the condition of the intellectuals.

Within *Song of Youth*, the fate of Woman and the condition of the intellectuals continually displace each other on a symbolic level as one of the film's most important textual strategies. The object of the fiction is historically recognized to be the intellectual transformation and rectification of the bourgeoisie or of petit-bourgeois intellectuals. Because of this, *Song of Youth* falls within the array of literary works dictated by the "worker, peasant, soldier" artistic orientation and policy, an allegorical text of great importance. It illustrates the process through which an intellectual who values individuality, democracy, and freedom develops and transforms into a Communist. It conveys a particular hegemonic discourse: a petit-bourgeois intellectual (woman) can only obtain a true existence and true liberation by following a course of pursuit, austerity, reform, trials, and devotion to the Party and the people as guided by the leaders of the Party.

Actually, within the various "history textbooks" devoted to the mainstream artistic orientation and policy of the Seventeen-Year Period, *Song of Youth* became a special reader: it became a manual for the thought reform of intellectuals. Yang Mo's *Song of Youth* is one of the models of mainstream writing in the Seventeen-Year Period of literature, depicting a norm for the cultural and social practices of intellectuals; this particular style of political rhetoric inadvertently reveals the similarity between women's and intellectuals' positions of cultural marginality. In other words, *Song of Youth* displays for us a marginal narrative organized successfully in the center: or, it provides a discourse about the center from the position of the margin.

The Dynamics of Negative Desire

In classical socialist ideology, class difference became the substitute for and yardstick of all social difference. Therefore, in the "worker, peasant, soldier" orientation and artistic policy, class narratives constantly negated gender; within these negative dynamics, an important ideological discourse, or self-evident truth, was that desire, the gaze of desire, the language of bodies, and the signification of gender were all designated as trademarks of the class enemy, as contrasted with the proletariat, the revolutionary, and the Communist. There could only exist the class camaraderie in the military barracks of the Revolution and the solidarity of the people.

Song of Youth's unacknowledged female narrative is symptomatic of the subtle experience of women's culture in New China. In tandem with the implementation of the new social equality, as represented by the Maoist saying "The times are different, men and women are now all the same," the feminine gender was successfully concealed and women only existed on the level of biological difference. While narratives by and about women, as important components of powerful ideological discourses, continued to rely on discourses of women's social gender (female as the socially underprivileged and female as intellectual), gender itself – and the narrative of the body and desire – was banished. However, banishment always implies an effective christening. In accordance with the "worker, peasant, soldier" artistic orientation and policy, any narrative of the body or desire was either deemed reactionary, corrupt, or a degenerative hallmark of the bourgeois culture, or it was a forbidden infraction of naturalism. However, in those "pure" narratives in which gender is never absent, desire still latently serves to move the narrative. The conventional relationship between a man and a woman, in fact, still supplied the a priori representational and ideological economy of the narrative.

For example, the displacement and transplanting of women in the space of men, which truthfully represented the era and history of the time, is still one of the main themes of the "worker, peasant, soldier" artistic orientation and policy, and manifests as an awkward yet, just as before, charming love story. Within *Song of Youth*, the heroine, Lin Daojing, abandons love, or rather feelings of friendship and selfish desire, which is the first step in the process of devoting oneself to the cause of the Revolution. However, the real love story is not that of Lin Daojing's "romance" with Yu Yongze but that of her romance with Party member Lu Jiachuan. Since this romance remains unacknowledged and lacks sexual intimacy, it is characterized as a very pure emotion, closer to an allegorical myth than to an enchanting love story. In the narrative, the woman is not enticed by a man to fall in love; rather, a disoriented intellectual encounters a Party member who enlightens her about the Revolution and guides her toward it.

But like the classic revolutionary film *The Red Detachment of Women*, however, this narrative contains a latent gender order (man/woman, respected/vilified, high/low, enlightener/enlightened, leader/follower) which establishes the legitimacy of both its narrative and its reception. The repeated concealment of desire is one of the heroine's main motives for action.[42] Therefore, as soon as this love story without love is established and after the ideological discourse based on it is reaffirmed, the story must resort to the destructive violence of history to complete the exile of love and the object of desire. For example, when Lin Daojing's love for Lu Jiachuan is finally given expression, in the poems she has written in prison, her only love letter from him, a posthumous one, is finally read: "I have already been buried at the cemetery." Also, in *The Red Detachment of Women*, Wu Qionghua's highest trial is to witness her lover's immolation in the enemy's pyre.

Thus, the body is exiled rather than love itself, not only to support self-control and the disavowal of desire, but also the banishment of love, as the discourse of love could possess a certain subversive potential or espouse individualism. The sacrifice, or disappearance, of the object of desire and love creates the suspension of desire, which progressively is transformed into zeal for the revolutionary project. Therefore, this type of love story becomes an important mode of cultural assimilation: devoting the body of the pure girl to the great Communist project. From one perspective, this type of narrative effectively pulverized the limited yet poignant, complicitous association between Woman and the individual, and between Woman and the body, since the May Fourth Movement. It should be kept in mind, however, that this situation is much more complicated when looking at it from the perspective of reception.

However, even in the narratives in which the love story was not central to the plot, the body still had to be banished, or the narrative had to be limited to the period just prior to and including marriage. Actually, this is one of the most important ways in which the "worker, peasant, soldier" artistic orientation and policy revised the original old-culture narratives. For example, the marital bond between Xi'er and Dachun in *White-Haired Girl* had already been made prior to the narrative's beginning in the film. In the joyous denouement, in which Xi'er and Da Chun labor side by side in the fields, displaying the "good life" of the liberated areas, Xi'er's white hair is already fashioned into the wife's conventional hairstyle. The need for assimilation, as demanded by class and politics, once again strengthens the system of family and marriage. Consequently, one of the lines from *Li Shuangshuang*, one of the most celebrated films of the sixties, "Marry first, love after," is endlessly repeated as a maxim. Even in the most extreme form of the "worker, peasant, soldier" artistic orientation and policy, the Cultural Revolution's model opera (*yangbanxi*), the lone or widowed adult woman, depicted as one of the solitary main heroes, nonetheless must show her marital status by displaying the "honorable family" plaque on her door frame.

Rewriting Woman

The main paradox of contemporary female historical experience is the submersion of women in the depths of history at precisely the moment when they had achieved liberation. Since 1976 and particularly after 1978, the liberated woman as defined by revolutionary (male) norms was replaced by the return and reinscription of an explicitly male-dominated traditional cultural norm. It seems as if China's contemporary history, once again, is relying on the "restoration" (*fuwei*) of the female image to complete the reestablishment of order and the process of "dispelling chaos and restoring order" (*boluan fanzheng*).

Exemplifying this historical regression of the female image are the revolutionary melodramas that Xie Jin pioneered and refined as one of the important forms of the "worker, peasant, soldier" artistic orientation and policies. Xie Jin's 1978 work, *Ah yaolan!* (*Oh Cradle!*) is an important and interesting instance of the "reinscription" (*chongxie*) of Woman. In the beginning of *Oh Cradle!* the film's heroine is a commander of a male battalion. Amid the inferno of combat, the company fights bravely and with resolve on the brutal front lines. When the heroine is then transferred to a new posting in the army kindergarten, Xie Jin shows, in his characteristically sentimental and dramatic style, how femininity and maternal instincts awaken and blossom in a woman who has experienced alienation in battle and through suffering. At the film's denouement, the heroine, embracing her child, is filled with ardent yet tender feelings while earnestly gazing after her husband, who is galloping off to the battle front. With little doubt, she/Woman remains behind, as mother and wife, protecting the children. We could almost read this as a parable: if Mao Zedong had made women step into the historical limelight in the name of class liberation and revolution, then in the era of Deng Xiaoping History demanded that women retreat to the back of the stage in the name of liberating Humanity.

This retreat was replete with symbolic significance, as both the expansive foreground and the historical space of social life were once again restored to Man. The nuclear family in the denouement of *Oh Cradle!* resembles "families" of the classic revolutionary films: it is a family unrelated by blood. However, in a transposition of the revolutionary classic's narrative style, the new narrative no longer has Woman abandon the traditional course to devote herself to historical progress (that is, the grand Communist project), impelled by violent historical force. Rather, it depicts the restructuring of the new era's mainstream film; the reentrenchment of the image of woman put into practice the new ideological requirements of the Deng Xiaoping era.

Following *Oh Cradle!*, Xie Jin provoked an enormous social sensation in 1979 with his film *The Legend of Tianyun Mountain*. This film brings to completion both the model gender narrative and the model political narrative in the new era's (*xin shiqi*) mainstream film. It is a story about one man and three women. The film's main male character, Luo Qun, the son of a CCP martyr (representing his true "redness"), is a quasi-intellectual CCP member who is victimized in the 1957 anti-rightist movement. By enduring the anguish of his purging, he becomes a saint and assumes the historic role in the new culture's (that is, Deng Xiaoping's) ideological structure. As one of three female characters in the film, Feng Qinglan, Luo Qun's wife, is very loyal, self-sacrificing, and supportive. By playing the role of the woman who possesses "traditional Chinese morality," Feng becomes the true and visible victim of the historical violence. She consequently becomes her man's shield, protecting him from harm. In the film's grand denouement, which occurs at the start of the new era, or the "moment of dawn," Feng peacefully passes away, leaving us with a new grave. As a "good woman," whose life was taken away and destroyed by historical violence, she is an icon who represents the total negation of the Cultural Revolution and even the authoritative conclusion and political subtext of the Mao Zedong era after 1955.[43] As a corpse, she clearly draws the absolute boundary between the Cultural Revolution and the New Era. This delineates the Mao Zedong and Deng Xiaoping eras as two essentially different periods, and consequently preempts our ability to interrogate history. It is worth noting, however, that the hero's perseverance through calamity and his subsequent revival passes on the logical continuation of socialist history and its Communist political authority.

A second woman, Song Wei, Luo Qun's former lover, is the main female protagonist; she plays the dual role of innocent traitor (deceived by History) and accomplice to historical violence. The widely prevalent impression at the beginning of the Deng new era that historical reflexivity and historical repentance were absolute necessities was projected onto this character. Yet because her only real culpability was her lack of faithfulness in love – she abandoned Luo Qun only after he was purged – her case did not make a completely identifiable fit with the process of reexamining the tragic historical era itself. Nonetheless, Song Wei was the fictional character who evoked the strongest personal identification from audiences. Moreover, in this character we can see how Xie Jin's film is revising the logics and the rules of narratives about desire and politics in Chinese socialist mainstream cultural narratives in the new era. Given that desire, sex, and gender were latent, invisible discourses in the classical revolu- tionary cinema/revolutionary melodrama, one could say that in the new era's mainstream cinema, such stories of desire, sex, and gender were reshaped and became the vehicle for or vessel of post- revolutionary narratives explaining the history and politics of the bygone era. This led to the staging of a unique new moral value in which those who remained upright and righteous during the Cultural Revolution reaped their reward; on them is bestowed the united and perfect family, and all their desires are fulfilled, whereas the unfaithful, and thus unrighteous, families are shattered and spread to the winds, suffering the painful fate of drifters.

It can be asserted that the objective of this type of revision of nar- rative style is to elide the ideological and structural rupture between the Mao Zedong and Deng Xiaoping eras, as well as the profound con- tradictions bound up with the perpetuation of political authority and Party rule. At the same time, this revision also begins the process of a powerful rewriting and renewing of the gender order's norms. Zhou Yuzhen, the only female character from the younger generation, first appears in *The Legend of Tianyun Mountain* as the classical narrative's messenger. She is not only a literal go-between for those involved in this quadrangular romance, but on a more symbolic level she also plays the "one who heralds the spring of the new era." However, intriguingly, as soon as the main part of the narrative about love and politics is completed, Zhou totally discards her spry, independent, and "new" female personality. Both in terms of characterization and in the space of the narrative structure, she replaces the martyred wife as a capable and sensible new wife. Although the women are the text's internal narrators, their significance and value are determined in accordance with their relationship to Man and the social and political function they serve. They endure calamities, interrogations, martyrdom, hardships, and punishments, just so that men can be rescued from history and their complicity atoned for.

Women entered history's field of vision only fleetingly, to be banished again from history. It is by means of the women's exile that men can succeed in banishing the specter of history and burying the skeleton of the catastrophic era in their imaginations. Relying on these three women, the male characters are the heroes/main subjects of history, yet they are able to transcend the historical turbulence without injury, continuing to direct the progress of unfolding history.

The Vicious Cycle of History

From one perspective, Xie Jin's works are mainstream films that succeed in passing through and linking ruptured ideologies. They aptly display the reinscription of Chinese women's culture in the new era and are symptomatic of the new era's cultural reorientation, as can be seen in the narrative absurdities to be found in the dynamics of "progress" and "retreat," "liberation" and "oppression." But if it is said that this new feminine predicament is nothing but an example of the so-called rifts in the "enlightenment discourse" that the promotion of modernization and development have once again made prominent, then, in particular reference to contemporary China, the problem is really not that transparent. Actually, the absurdity of contemporary Chinese women's culture has always been a vicious cycle between reality – in relation to class and gender (and to rural and urban) – and its discursive manifestations.

If we accept that the Mao Zedong era's unprecedented and massive women's liberation movement really inflicted historical violence on women, then it is precisely the same violent element that thoroughly shattered the old system of patriarchy (and with it, the Name of the Father and the husband) and that occasioned the community of women's ascent upon the social stage. Those women who most poignantly experienced this violence were the middle bourgeoisie or petit-bourgeois intellectuals, apparitions existing in the male imagination both during Mao's era and now.[44] In China from 1949 to 1979, women were obviously burdened, and not just with the obligations of their new social role, for, without a doubt, the industrialization process in any nation must inevitably involve the infliction of some degree of violence and inhumanity on everyone, not just on women. But women had to make a double payment, as required by the superpositioning of their roles as citizens and housewives. The reallocation of housework is one of the important components of socialist production but, as a matter of course, housework has been assigned solely to women. This fact is not only concealed by the culture embodied in the maxim "men and women are all the same," but it represents a type of national violence being inflicted exclusively on women.

The emergence of a "women's culture" (*nüxing wenhua*) in the new era could verify the arrival of a new liberation. But it is without doubt the projection of a spiritual legacy of the former women's liberation. The new women's culture, therefore, immediately became a type of oppositional form and voice: "Woman is not the moonlight and she does not rely on the projection of man's brilliance to illuminate herself."[45] At the same time, though, because the prerequisite for the legitimacy of the new women's culture is sexual difference, numerous discriminatory and oppressive discourses were as a result ushered into the social arena. During the Deng Xiaoping era, the emergence of gender (or women's) culture was still instantly appropriated as a screen to conceal the new class structure and class differentiation.

The Reconcealment of Gender Discourse

Intriguingly, within the elite discourse of intellectuals, the China of the seventies and eighties was narrated as a counterpart of the May Fourth era. This time, however, at the every least it is evident to the intellectual community that men and women cannot form an alliance or coalition working toward a collective goal as the "sons of young China" (*shaonian Zhongguo shi zi*) and the May Fourth women attempted to do.

Rather, as "intellectuals" they identify with and are assimilated into the male intellectual's social agenda.

During the advent of the new era, the most celebrated group of women writers within the literary circles consisted of many of the most vigorous and effective intellectual-elite constructors of intellectual discourse in the eighties. The main theme in their array of discursive representations is a contemporary Chinese version of the enlightenment discourse, an expression of humanism, in which tropes like "human rights" (*renquan*) and the mission of "human liberation" (*ren jiefang*) underlie the narrative's expression of "love" (*ai*). Yet the history of the narrative of "humanity" (*ren*) was always already endowed with a male's image. Within the representation of man (and even woman), the subject and hero of the "catastrophic history" (*zainan lishi*) was clearly written as male. Moreover, these narratives were a type of effective strategy whose main objective and true meaning resided within "parting with the revolution" (*gaobie geming*) or, more candidly, "ending the Mao Zedong era" (*jieshu Mao Zedong shidai*). Therefore, the Mao Zedong era became a period to be concluded; thus, great social acts such as the "liberation of women" and the institutionalization of equality of the sexes were deprived of their historical and cultural legitimacy in a historical purge.

To mend and transcend this ideological rupture and to terminate the purge of Mao's era, the new political authority in its quest for continued ideological legitimation resorted to a popular and effective social truism, arrived at consensually; namely, the "cost argument" (*daijia lun*) or "tuition argument" (*xuefei lun*). As a kind of mainstream ideology, it labels contemporary China's historical miscarriage and casualties as the "price" (*daijia*), or "fees" (*xuefei*) that must be paid before entering the Elysian fields. Therefore, "price" became a euphemism for "mistake" (*cuowu*), resulting in a gentle historical verdict that did not require vigorous investigation. Within this theoretical strategy, the male-dominated culture discreetly latched itself onto "thought emancipation" and the "rectification of chaos." Initially tacit, "cost" became publicly disclosed as the main issue in the discussion of the liberation of women in contemporary China.[46]

Implicitly, women's liberation, sexual equality, and the widespread employment of urban women became "historical mistakes" (*lishi cuowu*), in the style of the Great Leap Forward or even an absurd comedy, that had to be "rectified." At this time, an anonymous, biased debate emerged concerning "the ethics of intellectuals" (*zhishi fenzi lunli*). The "intellectual's integrity" (*zhishifenzi pinge*), "image of self-reliance" (*teli duxing de xingxiang*), and "independent human dignity" (*duli renge*) constructed a monolithic but ambiguous reference system employed to evaluate the ethical positioning of intellectuals. In this reference system, the intellectuals were judged in terms of their oppositional positioning vis-à-vis the "authority" (*guanfang*). Therefore, a reproach that accused an intellectual of "complicity with the authority" (*yu guanfang hemou*) became the ultimate humiliation, or an even unpardonable crime, for the intellectuals. In this system of ethics, the "authority" included the political authority, Party leadership, and central political and systematic power, but it did not include ideas about ideological state apparatuses and social structure. This "authority," most often, was an imaginary, monolithic apparatus of power. However, throughout the eighties, intellectual communities in different fields were almost entirely reliant upon the state's system, since they were placed within the state's political, academic, or educational institutions. This remained the case even though after 1979 the so-called authority – state power and mainstream ideology – itself underwent constant vicissitudes and self-rupture.

Without a doubt, the intellectuals' discursive structures and myths of origin drove the expression of the subjectivity of female intellectuals into an awkward position. Since women's liberation in China was promoted and actualized by the "authority," and the protection of women's power, to a fairly large degree, relied on that authority's system (for example, the institution of the National Women's Federation), the issue of women's liberation or sexual equality could as a result be tainted by the suspicion of its "complicity with the authority." Therefore, due to the intellectuals' resolve to "part from the Revolution," a resolve that women shared with male intellectuals, women faced a great difficulty in creating an alternative appraisal of China's Revolution and the historical process of Chinese women's liberation. A typical example of the "ambivalence of the enlightenment discourse" consists in its adherence to the narration of "progress" in a linear history and to the notion of historical periodization. More specifically, this ambivalence also consists in its insistence upon narrating history from the abundance of "humanity" and from the vantage point of humanism, both of which intensified the representational and expressive predicament of women's subjectivity.

For instance, popular opinions about Chinese women's liberation expressed concerns that the movement had progressed too far ahead of the epochal logic of development. This is to say, How can we even talk about women's rights before the problem of human rights in China is solved? Another common attitude was the characterization of Western feminism as a luxury inappropriate for a country that has been underdeveloped throughout its modern and contemporary history. It was even asserted that the field of women's issues was too parochial and narrow. Why can't we, with the broad-mindedness of humanity, think about the struggles of humanity, China, and the Chinese people?

Thus, the domain of the intellectuals became defined by the extirpation of women, and even gender and gender identity. The feminine, since it could not be interpreted as bearing "universal relevance," had to face the neglect and profound animosity of China's intellectual communities. Since the eighties, enveloped under the weight of the hegemonic discourse of modernism and enlightenment, feminists lost their opportunity to examine the pluralistic possibilities of such discourses or the alternative of deconstructing them.

"Genderless" Narratives and Gender Landscape

While Xie Jin's revision of mainstream film continued to define the cultural arena of Chinese cinema during the seventies and eighties, an embryonic form of artistic cinema was developing unnoticed. This style of cinema later became identified with the films of the "Fourth Generation" and "Fifth Generation." It gradually formed an alternative mainstream within China's screenwriting and cinematic culture. The Fourth Generation films selected a writing style characterized by a manner of subservient supplication and a tender, sentimental tone, similar to the writing style of women writers in literary circles. Fourth Generation directors also embedded the individual experience, the "minor story of the great era" (*da shidai de xiao gushi*),[47] into the "grand history" by borrowing the "female" position and manner of representation.

Interestingly, although the Fourth Generation adopted a "feminized" narrative tone and style, the individual, who was depicted as the "hostage of history" within the "grand history" or "minor story," was nonetheless an image of a male subject. In the Fourth Generation director's heartbreaking stories of unrequited love, women are depicted more as a portal to humanity suddenly demolished by violence rather than the object of man's desire. Women in these films are positioned between the beautiful goddess and the beautiful sacrificial offering. They are the illusory image that evil has plundered. Once dispelled from the landscape of history, namely the Cultural Revolution, they are never to return. It can be asserted that these stories are still "sexless" (*wuxing*) or at least degendered. Within the landscape of the sorrowful, emotional utopia or Platonic love, any expression of desire and any expression of the body is washed away by women, who assume a rarefied meaning.

In Yang Yanjin's film *Xiao jie* (*Little Street*, 1980), the heroine's gender status is never even identified. Despite this, the story certainly differs from the gender narrative of the classic revolutionary film. Not only is this a male/individual growing-up story, inevitably containing the latent narrative of sex/body/desire, but also these stories which narrate man as the subject also make him the absolute and only historical subject within the story. He is the one who bears the calamity of political violence and denounces and rebels against violence. We can say that the cultural rhetoric adopted by the vigorously fashioned works of the Fourth Generation takes up the same political/cultural strategy as the elite intellectual's discourse that emerged during the advent of the new era. Namely, although man does not appear brazenly as the only subject in the narrative, he is nonetheless constructed as the sole subject in the historical landscape. Woman is fashioned as the absolute object of man's desire as well as, importantly, the victim of historically anonymous violence. Therefore, in this narrative in which desire, body, and even gender seem hidden, male desire and women's bodies form an allegory about history, politics, and society. Consequently, a common thread running through

China's culture in the new era is the unique equivalence of political expression and gender expression. If this does not include the rhetorical transformation of "sex" into "politics" and the equivalence of sexual expression and political expression, then, at the very least, it is obvious that the majority of writings about gender can be successfully identified with and read from a political (that is, oppositional) position.

The sudden cessation of both the literature of the wounded and the works of political reflection exhibited China's most profound ideological contradiction and fissure during the Deng era. The Fifth Generation filmmakers rapidly made their entrance onto the Chinese film scene, provoking a " revolution" in cinematic language and forging a break with earlier Chinese film. However, the later work of the Fourth Generation – created after the Fifth Generation had become normative – rather intriguingly narrated tales featuring women not only as the main protagonists, but as desiring subjects. This rhetorical style would eventually become a legacy, via Zhang Yimou's *Raise the Red Lantern*, to the Fifth Generation directors, even though it would be a vehicle carrying a different theme and a different context. In the eighties, the "discovery" of female desire in Chinese cinema actually originated from an age-old male rhetorical style or, at the very least, from the Chinese literati's tradition of "comparing oneself to fragrant beauties" (*xiangcao meiren zibi*). In essence, within this rhetorical style, man's cultural predicament and confinement were transferred and displaced onto the female role; a story about a woman's desires and cravings was only a masquerade for man's real predicament. Within this "new" array of female images, appearing in connection with the "movement of historical and cultural reflection," the majority are, without a doubt, "empty signifiers" (*kongdong de nengzhi*): they are estranged from the actual lives of women and are rather allied with man's imagination. The multiple significations of Woman are employed to transplant and relieve the profound contradictions and self-entrapment of contemporary China's political and gender culture.

In the early and mid eighties, a favorite theme of the elite culture was the conflict between civilization and backwardness (*wenming yu yumei*). Within this context, the image of Woman was constructed as a sacrificial lamb of backwardness, an offering to civilization, an iconic victim of political and historical violence, the imprint of historical evolution, and the location of an ethereal redemption. There are two main motifs in roots literature (*xungen wenxue*), in both of which women's images elicit different, mystifying effects while providing the male narrating subject with a narrative purpose through the representation of an essentialized and functionalized female character: he must repay (male) historical debts and release (man) from his real predicament. The first fundamental motif is that of a thirsty and companionless man amidst the arid and parched landscape; there are two main male characterizations and narratives in this narrative schema. In one, the search for the source of water and the struggle to procure women become the Chinese people's (male) national allegory.[48] In another, elderly, authoritarian men, "fathers" who have lost their reproductive ability, nevertheless possess women, a theme that forms the backbone of the narrative of "oriental infanticide" (*shazi wenhua*).

The second main motif is an allegorical representation of the conflicts between nature and culture, images and words, life and power. Appearing outside writing, language, and history is the eternal and immense space of nature. Within this transcendent nature, full-bosomed and fecund women become the signifiers of nature and symbols of the primordial life force. In these representations, premodern and prehistoric mothers became the retainers of life and salvation. They were intrinsic to humanity and Chinese society and extrinsic to Chinese culture, history, and tradition. "New woman," an appellation that all but disappeared after half a century, could then only be even less than a replica or facsimile of modern man. This reinscription of Woman can be seen as a cultural symptom, inadvertently exhibiting the great cultural tension produced by the revitalized discourse of modernity.

Social Transformation and Gender Writing

Within these "genderless" narratives and gender landscapes, the Fourth and Fifth Generation filmmakers opted for different representational strategies. In most of the former's repertory, the object of desire is stripped away. As a result, the hero is stuck in a limbo of youth that forever defers fulfillment. However, the Fifth Generation filmmakers selected a posture of rejection. They rejected Woman and plot. Never mind that the woman written off here was precisely the forbidden object of desire proscribed by the moral order. Ironically, the Fifth Generation filmmakers refused to submit to and accommodate the authoritative and mainstream order and culture. They achieved this by rejecting the encroachment of the mainstream cultural/symbolic order. It is precisely this posture of rejection which gives prominence to the paradoxical situation of the Fifth Generation and the entire "movement of historical and cultural reflection." However, through its manifestation within narratives, cyclical and immutable Chinese history was constructed as an eternal and naturalized, but infertile and arid, space. If this reveals the failure of politics/socialism to solve the cultural dilemma, how could the strides of modernization touch this cultural desert? If Woman's meaning stems from her internalization of a cultural order, as a method of circulation (*liutong shouduan*) in patriarchal society, and if she signifies the posture of passive obedience, then rejection of this representation of Woman does not just mean the rejection of the old cultural order but also the indefinite deferment of a culture's coming of age and the negation of a free-flowing representation and value as truth. If Woman both is coded as non-order and non-culture and signifies life and nature, her rejection also means the rejection of the availability of any redemptive means beyond culture and history.

Supposing that woman as primitive femininity outside of civilization actually provides an alternative way out that transcends history, then her existence is still vetoed by the enlightenment discourse's linear historiography, "development" and "progress." From this perspective, Chen Kaige's *The King of Children* pushes this expression of cultural contradiction to an extreme, while also laying bare the desperate situation of his cinematic expression. Subsequently, in *Red Sorghum* – a film produced concurrently with *The King of Children* – Woman emerges with great fanfare once again onto the landscape of male desire. Satisfying male desire and constructing male subjectivity, she functions to reconcile men with the (new) order.

Nineteen eighty-seven is an important year in contemporary

Chinese history and the cultural history of Chinese film. In this year, the reform of the Chinese social system entered a key period and experienced the first "breakthrough" (*chuangguan*). "Socialism with Chinese characteristics" (*Zhongguo tese de shehui zhuyi*) was quite stable; transnational capital was beginning to permeate, at first slowly and then more rapidly, into the newly established market economy. Like a tidal wave, commercialism and consumerism burst onto the social landscape and began impinging on and rewriting people's daily lives. Mass culture began its furtive infiltration into society. Film production bore the brunt of this new trend of marketization of culture. The former classification of films into mainstream films, which adhered to the "worker, peasant, soldier" literary orientation and policy, and the artistic films of the Fourth and Fifth Generations was reformulated into a three-part division. This new division consisted of the "main melody" (*zhu xuanlü*) films (that is, propaganda), experimental films (art-house cinema), and entertainment (commercial films). Almost at the same time, Fourth and Fifth Generation filmmakers inadvertently transformed their strategies of writing gender. During this peaceful period of social transformation, once again, gender writing, or the inscription of women's images, both consciously and unconsciously served as a floating bridge on which the male discourse rested to negotiate its way out of the predicament of a trapped cultural identity, a consequence of social pressure.

Intriguingly, in precisely this period the community of mainland China's female short-story writers began to engage the subtle "rules of the game" of gender and ethnicity rendered in the global context.[49] While the contemporary discovery and writing of these rules of gender and race by female writers became a powerful means of deconstructing mainstream and male culture, a widely different system of signification came into being in Chinese film. The experiences of *The King of Children* and *Red Sorghum* in 1987 taught Chinese directors (in fact, Third World film directors in general) a few lessons. Winning awards at European art-film festivals presupposed not only the internationalization of the traditions, standards, and tastes of European art films, but also the internationalization of the Euro-American imaginary of China. This necessarily meant that Chinese directors had to turn their native history and experience into a reified object, an exotic and sensational Other, which was still accessible to the Euro-American cultural decoding machine. Thus the process of cultural subordination and the self-exile of indigenous culture unfolded.

Consequently, those Fourth Generation films that excelled at the narration of female desire were excavated once again. These kinds of stories – shall I call them stories of "women in the iron house" (*tie wuzi zhong de nüren*) – began to serve as a medium through which the exotic "orient" was exhibited to the Euro-American gaze. Examples of this genre included Zhang Yimou's *Ju Dou* (*Ju Dou*, 1989), He Ping's *Pao da shuang deng* (*Red Firecrackers, Green Firecrackers*, 1993), Chen Kaige's *Fengyue* (*Temptress Moon*, 1996), and Zhang Yimou's *Raise the Red Lantern*.[50] Facing rapid social changes during the transitional period and encountering the fetishism of money, desire, and survival and status anxieties, Chinese male writers and film-makers inadvertently adopted another narrative strategy, once again transplanting their personal and social crises and angst onto the female roles. The "new" image of Woman, which was once a sensation during the 1930s in Chinese urban literature, began to reappear in contemporary Chinese culture. Hysterical and irrational women began to be constructed as the source of evil leading to men's dilemmas and anxieties. The Fifth Generation director Zhou Xiaowen's commercial film *Fengkuang de daijia* (*The Price of Madness*, 1988) became the first example of this recuperated representation of Woman. Beginning with male voyeurism and violence, the film ends with Woman's bigotry and homicidal conspiracy. The film provides an imaginary solution to the male social crisis through the transfer of criminal behavior from men onto women.

Women Directors and Their Films

Before 1949, most of the film directors in China, as in the rest of the world, were men. After 1949, New China's cinema included only one female director, Wang Ping, a noteworthy member of the Third Generation. Shortly afterwards, women directors gained prominence within the community of Fourth Generation directors and formed a battalion within the Chinese film industry. During the era of the Fifth Generation, in which Chinese film won the acclaim of Europe and

America, women directors, although not on an equal footing with Zhang Yimou and Chen Kaige, were still visibly positioned. However, subsequently, younger women directors disappeared almost without a trace from the film industry. The regressive motions Chinese society went through after 1979, in order to resuscitate male power and reconstruct a male-centered society, were being enacted swiftly in the film industry, a field men had traditionally dominated.

In the mainstream film industry, however, contemporary China possesses the most powerful and numerous cohort of women directors in the world: more than thirty women directors have supervised the production of more than two feature-length films for large film studios. Within the socialist system of film production, approximately twenty influential women directors work at state-owned film studios. A further five or six women directors, including Huang Shuqin, Zhang Nuanxin, Li Shaohong, Hu Mei, Ning Ying and Liu Miaomiao, have won awards at various international film festivals and gained varying degrees of international acknowledgement. Yet even so, in the last fifty years of New China's film history, the true "women's film" (*nüxing dianying*) is rare, if not completely absent. In the majority of female-directed films, the female gender not only rarely manifests itself as a narrative position or a visual vantage point, but it also seldom emerges as a distinct feature characterizing the film's material structure, plot development, characterization, narrative style, and cinematic language. In contrast to the literary works of contemporary women writers, most women directors have not turned their gender position into the motivating force for their creative work.

Contemporary women's liberation and the paradoxical landscapes of women's culture can be vividly traced by reviewing women's gender writing in films in the last fifty years. For the cinematic writing of women directors materializes the precise cultural heritage within which they have lived and the multiple historical tracks upon which they have traveled. Like the cohort of women writers, contemporary Chinese women directors also "emerged on the horizon of history" during the "new era." However, women writers in the eighties and nineties adhered to one of two separate historical paths: the continuous merging and rupturing of the heritage of socialist culture or the May Fourth tradition of women's writing. So female-directed films have always been closely bound up with the history of socialist China.

Until now, it has been common knowledge, or a widespread bias that those working in the film industry shared, that the success of women directors – those fortunate enough to rise to the top in this male-dominated field – was gauged by their ability to produce films that are exactly the same as men's. In other words, women's success rested on their ability to master those subjects and materials that characterized the work of male directors. Although this may be a cultural legacy of the Mao Zedong era, it is more accurate to regard this phenomenon as one of the strategies adopted by contemporary Chinese intellectual women, both a special consensus reached by the female community and one of the profound paradoxes of contemporary Chinese women's culture and even feminist culture.

Clearly, the women betray a transparently resistant consciousness, a position that refuses to be relegated to the "second sex." However, their consensus is at the same time a fallacious option and an obsequious choice: it not only inherently accepts the centrality of male culture, internalizing men's cultural and social hierarchical logic, but also necessarily overlooks and conceals, once again, women's living reality. In other words, women directors collectively play a Hua Mulan social role: they are women who have successfully dressed up as men. The more they conceal their own gender characteristics and position, the more recognition and success they gain. Those women directors who "expose" their own gender, or select material that articulates their gender position, lose status, as if they willingly have accepted a self-positioning that relegates them to the second or third class. Therefore, the primary materials selected by women directors have been "momentous" socio-historical and political themes. Almost without exception, contemporary women directors are the makers of mainstream films. They do not experiment with radical, therefore marginal, cinema, nor did they attempt to create works that can be categorized as "anti-cinema."

As noted above, Wang Ping is the first woman director of New China's cinema. Compared to the work of her contemporaries (men), Wang Ping's array of films even more clearly manifests the cinematic characteristics of the "worker, peasant, soldier" literary orientation and policy. Unabashedly, she could be cited as a key purveyor of mainstream film during Mao's era. Her representative works, in chronological sequence, map out succinctly the canonical themes of mainstream culture enveloped within the context of contemporary Chinese culture and society: *Liubao de gushi* (*Story of Liubao Village*, 1956); *Yong bu xiaoshi de dianbo* (*Constant Beam*, 1958); *Huaishu zhuang* (*Locust Tree Village*, 1962); *Nihongdeng xia de shaobing* (*Sentinels under the Neon Lights*, 1964); the large-scale musical epic *Dongfang hong* (*East Is Red*, 1965), *Qingchun* (*Youth*, 1978); and the large-scale musical documentary *Zhongguo geming zhi ge* (*Song of China's Revolution*, 1990). As China's only female director during the Seventeen-Year Era, she expresses no particular concern with "women's material" (*nüxing ticai*) other than treating it as a political allegory of social transition. For Wang Ping, women's representation or gender positioning, without a doubt, is still an unreachable mirage.

Wang Ping is a real-life counterpart to the image of the heroine in the works by male filmmakers. As far as her cinematic production and language are concerned, her ideological identification is built on class and nation, and her representational discourse is obviously confined within the family and nation. However, intriguingly, as a successful filmmaker, she was never identified and named as a Hua Mulan. The film critics, nonetheless, in their search for a way of describing Wang Ping's fictitious "style," resorted to allusions to her gender, and conjured up a subtle order of and quest for the feminine. In such an idiom, Wang Ping is known for her natural, delicate, and lyrical artistic style. Her main theme is vivid, and her artistic expression is graceful, subtle, and refined."[51]

Wang Ping's films constructed a tradition of non-feminine women's cinema. Since the new era began, many important women directors have followed in her footsteps; and their works are symptomatic of another feature of women's culture in the new era. You will recall that in the eighties and nineties Chinese film gradually turned from the diametrical opposition of art films versus mainstream proletarian films to a tripartite configuration composed of three main genres: the "main melody," experimental, and entertainment films. Wang Ping's successors continued in the tradition of mainstream films that have been reincarnated as "main melody" films. With some success they

expelled the historical and cultural tension embedded in the newly
transformed mainstream narrative authored by Xie Jin. For example,
in *Miren de ynedui* (*Enchanting Band,* 1982) and *Shixin de cunzhuang*
(*The Village Which Lost Its Faith,* 1984), female director Wang Hao
explored two main themes: how prospering peasants constructed
socialist spiritual civilization and how the Party members in the reform
era regained their credibility among the masses. Both films won prizes
awarded by the Ministry of Culture, and the latter was even designated as a model film for political study in the CCP.

In fact, Wang Hao mastered more adroitly than her male counter-
parts the narrative style of socialist classical cinema and successfully
continued the narrative tradition of revolutionary drama. Her smooth
attempt at connecting comical episodes, her stage-like management of
camera angles and shots, and her vital and optimistic comic undertone
have made her films models of the "main melody" genre. Her films
serve to illustrate not only the profound identification between
women intellectuals who came of age with the socialist system during
Mao's era, but also the intensity with which they internalized the socialist ideology. This ideological identification undoubtedly formed an
enormous obstacle to their cultivation of a critical stance toward society and their articulation of their own gender positions.

Yet, from another perspective, what accounted for their gradual
dissociation from the mainstream elite intellectual culture of the eighties, whose agenda was spelled out by a conscious "farewell to the
Revolution" was nothing other than those female directors' self-
conscious or half-conscious recognition of the parasitic relationship
between the current system and women's liberation.

More eye-catching specimens are to be found in the experimental
films (*tansuo pian*), or art films, made by female directors who belong
to both the Fourth and Fifth Generations. Similar to the women directors of the "main melody" films, the directors of experimental films
also consciously erased their gender position. However, those women
filmmakers succeed in replacing the political prescriptions and social
principles characteristic of the "worker, peasant, soldier" arts with the
aesthetic standards emblematic of European art films and a clearly
articulated orientation of art for art's sake. For example, *Bloody
Morning*, directed by Li Shaohong, one of China's outstanding female

directors, is based on Colombian author Gabriel García Márquez's *Chronicle of a Death Foretold*, and depicts the cruelty and absurdity of Chinese society and China's rural life. *Zhao le* (*Looking for Fun*, 1993) and *Minjing gushi* (*On the Beat*, 1995), films by Ning Ying, another noteworthy female director, exhibit the microscopic political and comical landscape of the everyday lives of the urban underclass. Nevertheless, Li Shaohong's skillfully filmed and mature work, *Hongfen* (*Blush*, 1995), reveals that even films which claim to have achieved "transcendent" artistic status may still betray the paradox of gender representation. The very historical context in which a truly clichéd story about a dissolute dandy (the high-ranking son of an official) and a genuine prostitute is situated – post-1949 China, when brothels were closed down and the reformation of prostitutes was set in motion – underlined the great potential of the material. However, based on male writer Su Tong's original work, *Blush* succeeded in rendering, and even augmenting, an epochal story in which woman is oppressed, victimized by man, and compelled to eke out an ignoble existence in order to survive.

The female characters in the film are neither the narrating subjects nor are they connected meaningfully to the changing historical events, just as they would be in films directed by man. Moreover, they very rarely act as the agents of a desiring gaze; more often, they become its objects. In a world where the male sex enjoys privileges, being situated with male directors on terms of equality certainly bestows upon women directors a sense of pride and resistance. But standing shoulder to shoulder with men is also symptomatic of the negation of one's gender position, which in turn has self-destructive implications. This paradoxical cultural reality is perhaps an important and fundamental cultural and social legacy of the Mao Zedong era. But it unintentionally puts into practice the perpetuation, dissipation, and abandonment of this legacy.

Gender Writing in Film?

Around 1987, accompanying the intensification of economic reform and capitalism's rewriting of contemporary China, an obvious transformation appeared in the works by women directors. These films can

be seen as an alternative type of cinematic production. Women directors inadvertently began to select materials concerning women which
had been previously neglected or scorned. They earnestly tried to
mold a female perspective that cannot be found in male narratives.
They sought to use film as a vehicle to transmit an experience and
world unique to women. The large corpus of "women's films" thus
appeared and formed a minor cinematic fashion and a new creative
trend in cinematic production.[52] The appearance of "women's films"
does not necessarily indicate another blossoming and awakening of
female consciousness. Rather, more precisely, it only reflects indirectly
the prevalent phenomenon of the lowering of women's social and cultural status. There is no denying that, conscious of their own gender
position, female directors did arrive at an oppositional self-awareness
of the necessity of resistance. It would be nonetheless more accurate to
say that their sensitivity to subtle social "market demands" prompted
them to portray the unpleasant reality that they themselves had experienced. It is this type of film, not those which attempt to transcend or
conceal the filmmaker's gender position, that brings to prominence
with greater clarity the paradox and dilemma of contemporary
Chinese women's culture. To use one of my favorite expressions, this
is an example of "fleeing from one trap while falling into another."

The female stories in these films inadvertently stake out an articulate anti-moralistic position. However, these anti-moral or amoral
stories always convey a clear value or moral orientation; since the legitimacy of the anti-moralistic value is built on the enlightenment
discourse of the 1980s, these films both depict the imaginary of a
humanist moralism and call for its return. Therefore, these stories
about gender and sexual desire often begin by attacking "marriage
without love" and end with the consummation of love in sealed marital bond. Actually, this is one of the common themes female writers
shared at the end of the seventies and the dawn of the eighties.
Although at times the complex and often circuitous gender expression
in these women's texts violated the "dignity" of men as a gender collective, nonetheless, it is probably the only common theme both male
and female narratives during the new era could jointly endorse. This
consensus is reached not only because the motifs of "individual liberation" and the taboo subject "sexual liberation" – motifs female

subjects enact in those texts – make up the new era's enlightenment discourse proper; it is also made possible precisely because the women's narratives contain a censure of "marriage without love" that incorporates the metaphorical implication of bidding "farewell to the Revolution."

Among female-directed films with female leads, those possessing a "female consciousness" are for the most part identical in narrative style and narrative language to those of the mainstream classic cinema. Furthermore, the narrators' gender identity, perspective, and position are also ambiguous and confused. In such films, which evidently attempt to highlight the reality of women's life and culture, Woman is submerged even more deeply within a discursive quagmire. They frequently begin with an unconventional and oppositional female image and female story, yet end with a classic and conventional cultural order, morality, and marriage. Therefore, the oppositional or unconventional position of these films is subtended by a tenacious relegation and subordination of gender. Assuming that the films do construct a vacuous and vague female expression, they are still completely saturated by the normalization of male-dominated culture. At the same time as the narratives in these films depart from one kind of male discourse and patriarchal norm, they often adopt another set of male-dominated discourses, casting aside any alternative position. These hackneyed narrative schema succeed only in producing a cliché of female expression. Rather than displaying women's culture or women's real predicament, the films become texts symptomatic of the predicament of women's culture and women's social reality.

Wang Junzheng's *Shanlinzhong touyige nüren* (*The First Woman in the Forest*, 1987) and Bao Zhifang's *Jinse de zhijia* (*Golden Fingernail*, 1988) are representative of this type of women's film. In *The First Woman in the Forest*, the vacuousness of the cultural expression of women is first revealed by the confusion of the narrative perspective. The film's first-person narrator is a female college student who goes to a forest to gather material for writing a script. In the first half of the film, an old woodcutter reminisces about a lover from his youth: she was a beautiful prostitute, nicknamed Little White Shoe, who died prematurely. This is a familiar story about the cruel victimization of a woman. In the film, however, the actress who plays the college student also plays Little

White Shoe. Furthermore, the film employs classic structures of visual language which make the woodcutter the main subject/the center of the camera's perspective. The woodcutter, rather than the college student, occupies the "I" of both the outer and inner stories. Therefore, the female narrator becomes an empty form or idea existing in name only, and in reality she only exists as an object of male desire. Consequently, any identification between the college student and Little White Shoe that the visual strategy of having the same actress play both of these characters might have created fails to materialize.

The first half's narrative perspective, however, is subverted in the film's second half, which adopts an "objective" narrative perspective to tell the story of another prostitute, Big Goddess. It is apparent that this character, who could contend with men in terms of her physical strength and resolve, was close to the director's heart. However, Big Goddess's narrative nonetheless rapidly turns into a conventional and banal story of self-sacrifice, infused with maternal love and unrequited feminine generosity, culminating in the film's denouement: in a low-angle shot, she kneels down on the cliff, beside her lover. In an oath to heaven, she swears, "I will establish a home and bear children for him." She is the First Woman of the Forest, the symbolic title role of the film. Without a doubt, she represents the familiar Earth Mother. The significance and worth of her life lies in her devotion and sacrifice to a man so that his life and potential can be fulfilled. If director Wang Junzheng had intended to narrate a story about a strong-willed woman and a spineless man, what he eventually tells us is ironic: a "strong" woman can only complete her life through a childlike man – through building a home and rearing children for his sake.

Since *The Golden Fingernail*'s narrative is based on modern life and the authorities banned the film for its "immoral" erotic content, it comes across as being more complicated and interesting. The film is derived from Xiang Ya's *Nü shiren tan* (*Ten Women's Accounts of Their Lives*), which consists of ten interviews with women about their unconventional, or "immoral," marital, familial, or sexual lives. While the original work already contains an inherent commercial incentive – namely, that of satisfying the male reader's voyeuristic desires – the interviews more or less still display a degree of female reality which is difficult to fit neatly into a norm of discourse. However, the structure of the screenplay transforms the film into a classic melodrama. In keeping with its title, this ostensible "women's film" imbues the women exhibited on the screen with a voyeuristic eroticism. The film's narrative of sexual desire is still written as a morality tale, artless and humanistic, albeit unconventional. The accounts of the women's convictions and career aspirations are portrayed as displaced and pathological reflections of women's repressed sexual desires. Friendship between women exists only to induce jealousy or to play manipulative games; "open marriages" become a strategy women employ only to ensnare men. The film's denouement consists of a typical grand reunion scene, a wedding ceremony, in which the unconventional woman acquires a conventional role. The film's only unmarried woman pairs up with an anonymous man and they leave the wedding ceremony. In the film's last shot sequence, this couple is shown crossing the street holding a red umbrella. In an overhead shot, as the camera lens zooms downward, the zebra-striped pedestrian lane, signifying the norms of the establishment, fills up the screen, thus depicting the normalization of the woman under the umbrella.

In a more concrete discussion of the cultural configuration of women's narratives, it is apparent that the joint existence of a consciousness of sexual equality and an essentialistic division of gender, together with women auteurs' rejection or misreading of feminism, create a self-contradiction and structural conflict in women's narratives. Throughout the eighties and until the early nineties, the absence of a critique of modernity occasioned the female intellectuals' inability to perceive the plurality of the enlightenment discourse and the latent centrality of patriarchal discourse. Consequently, the majority of films by women directors are satisfied with just creating "positive female images." Rarely do these films become a self-conscious subversion of mainstream culture and patriarchal discourse. Their employment of the classic narrative mode and cinematic language predetermines their falling prey again to patriarchal norms while fleeing from them at the same time. The fact that the majority of women directors created films with men as the screenwriters or cinematographers – a systemic constraint in the existing film industry – guaranteed, or exacerbated, women's difficulty with forging their own style. (To this day, although there are an enormous number of women directors in China, there are very few women cinematographers, not to mention outstanding ones.) The scripts written by men determine the film's structure, narrative, and the expression or evaluation of its moral vision. The gendered identity of the cinematographer – the creator of the cinematic images, the one who truly transforms the text of the script into images on screen – determines the mode and perspective through which the film is to be viewed. Therefore, some of the scenes and shot sequences constructed by the cinematographer become a mocking revision of the plot and the director's intention. At the very least, they have the power to invert or dislocate the film's intended narrative and expression. As a result, the women directors' films could only serve an ornamental or supplemental function vis-à-vis the mainstream film.

Female Narrative and Expression

In contrast to the self-conscious "women's film" discussed above, there is another type of film produced by women that displays the vivid imprint of women's expression and alternative possibilities. In Zhang Nuanxin's *Sha'ou* (*The Seagull*, 1981) and *Qingchun ji* (*The Sacrifice of Youth*, 1986); Huang Shuqin's *Tongnian de pengyou* (*Childhood Friends*, 1985); and Hu Mei's *Nü'er lou* (*The Chamber of Maidens*, 1984) not only were women the protagonists, the center and subject of the narrative perspective, but at the same time a profoundly plaintive and refined tone became central to the film's cinematic mode. In literary circles, most women authors' pursuit of the creation of a female style was an intentional or inevitable female strategy. In film, the arrival of a female style became evidence of women's historical advance, a step along the path of the invisible woman's difficult emergence.

In terms of cultural and social motifs, films exhibiting the female style are, for the most part, similar to those made by men. They simply reappropriate female experiences, "translate" and rewrite them into a female version of the same motifs. Zhang Nuanxin's *Seagull*, which is representative of the films made by Fourth Generation directors, relies on the main motifs of her generation, such as historical deprivation, personal loss, and the feeling of abandonment. But these motifs have been translated into a life story about a woman who "loves honor even more than life itself." The female protagonist is never even given the opportunity to confront or combat the major dilemma of women within mainstream culture: the choice between career and family, or between superwoman and homemaker. History and catastrophe deprive her of everything, only unattainable "possibilities" are left. "Whatever can be burned is burned; only large rocks shall remain."[53] In Zhang's second film, *The Sacrifice of Youth*, a woman gains recognition of her own gender position through historical experience and ethnic difference. Nonetheless this realization offers nothing more than greater tribulations and chagrin.

However, the only contemporary Chinese film that can unequivocally be considered a "women's film" is Huang Shuqin's *Human, Woman, Demon*.[54] This is not a radical film filled with destructive exhilaration. Its creation perhaps derives from material which was in part determined by chance. Relying upon the story of a unique female artist, the film metaphorically reveals the existential and cultural predicament faced by contemporary Chinese women through the depiction of a female opera star who performs male roles. The life of this female artist, Qiu Yun, is depicted as an absolute struggle to escape from women's fate and the female tragedy. However, each escape only results in her encounter and confrontation with her gender destiny. Qiu Yun's attempt to escape her gender fate by "playing a male" (*yan nan de*) is not only a signifier and metaphor for the existential predicament of modern Chinese women, but it also more subtly exposes and subverts the classical male-dominated culture and male discourse. Qiu Yun always performs the stereotypical male roles and heroes of traditional Chinese culture. As a woman playing a man, however, her conscious or unconscious puzzlement over her own gender identity is intensified. Moreover, since the role and the performer playing the role cannot coexist, the dichotomies of female desire/male object and woman as saved/man as savior are informed by a rotating absence. As a result, the classical cultural condition is forever deficient and defective, becoming a dream which women can never fulfill. Qiu Yun cannot become a woman who is saved by playing a man, because the men who have the power to save her only exist within her performance. The classical historical situation between a man and a woman, in which the man is positioned as the woman's savior, becomes a lie.

Ending or beginning

The upsurge of female-directed films, just like the splendour created by the Fifth Generation, soon faded away. Not only are "women's films" gradually banished from the mainstream film industry, but China's film industry itself is sinking into a crisis and collapsing as a result of Hollywood's cultural invasion and the state's unchanging and persistent system of censorship. At the same time, women are now beginning to acquire a conspicuous influence within the mass media, especially the television industry. This is where the hope of Chinese women's film lies. And this is where we could say that the women's growing influence in the mass media partakes of the spectacle of China "in stride with the rest of the world."

Women's narrative and expression is also gradually beginning to take shape within the field of documentary filmmaking. However, while women film artists are keeping step with historical progress, women's social and cultural positions are continuously undergoing a tragic decline. Along this steep course of class differentiation, women, and especially the women of the lower social stratum, are once again becoming the insignificant sacrificial victims and wagers in China's modernization. It seems as if China's historical progress can only complete its course at the expense of the regression of women's culture. An overt oppression and the regression of women's status will perhaps usher in a more self-conscious and profound women's resistance. In this process, will women truly become part of the visible humanity? Or perhaps women's film and television work may emerge as a new marginal culture? I cherish this hope but dare not make an optimistic prediction yet.

Notes

This translation is an edited and shortened version of an unpublished manuscript. I owe many thanks to the generous support of my dear friends Wu Runmei and Zhang Nan.

1 The Marriage Law of the People's Republic of China (*Zhonghua renmin gongheguo hunyin fa*), which abolished arranged marriage and a feudal marriage system characterized by inequality between the sexes and neglect of the welfare of youngsters, was passed in the government's seventh session in 1950. It implemented a new marriage system that guaranteed an individual's right to choose a spouse and protected the welfare of women and children. See *Zhonghua renmin gongheguo hunyin fa* (Marriage law of the People's Republic of China) (Beijing: Renmin chubanshe, 1950).

2 All-China Women's Federation, *Chengshi funü canjia shengchan de jingyan* (The experience of urban women participating in production) (Beijing: Xinhua shudian chubanshe, 1950).

3 Originally proclaimed by Mao Zedong in a speech for China's youth at the Ming Tombs' Reservoir, located 40 kilometers northwest of Beijing. See *Mao Zedong sixiang shengli wansui* (Long live Mao Zedong thought) (Beijing, 1969), p. 243.

4 See Jing Lingzi, *Shihai gouxuan: Wuhan luoti da youxing* (Seeking the mysterious in the ocean of history: Wuhan's great nudist parade) (Beijing: Kunlun chubanshe, 1989).

5 See works by modern women writers such as Lu Yin, Bai Wei, Ding Ling, and Zhang Ailing.

6 Socialism and the Chinese industrial revolution of the 1950s created a great occasion for "the sisters to stand up" and, as corroborated in numerous historical documents and statistical studies, Chinese women on an unprecedented scale entered the course of contemporary Chinese history. See All-China Women's Federation, *Zhongguo nüxing jiefang ziliao xuanbian* (Selected materials on the liberation of women in China) (Beijing: Zhongguo funü chubanshe, 1993).

7 According to these Maoist narratives, all women in Old China were doomed to misery and despair. This narrative strategy did not pertain just to women. It was employed to narrate the common tragic fate of all of the oppressed in Old China. This can be illustrated in the lines of the "Funü jiefang ge" ("Song of liberated women"), a popular song of the fifties and sixties. "The old society was a dark, bitter well ten thousand feet deep. We who have suffered are at the bottom of the well, yet women are even lower yet." The description of the fate of women consequently became a signifier, an apt and profound metaphor for the common fate of all the toiling masses of Old China; once New China was established and the CCP brilliantly illuminated their horizons, their miserable fates were relegated to the historical past. New China's classic film, directed by Zhang Shuihua, *Bai maonü* (*White-Haired Girl*, 1950) exemplifies this historical discourse. In the film, Xi'er, a peasant girl, is compelled to become a bondmaid to repay her father's debt to the local landlord. To escape her master's sexual predation, Xi'er flees to the mountain caverns, where she hides out. Her life is so primitive that she does not see the light of day until the Liberation Army arrives.

8 The delineation between Old and New China is spatially represented by a stone boundary marker in the film *Hongse niangzi jun* (*The Red Detachment of Women*,

1960), directed by Xie Jin. This stone boundary marker divides the "liberated territory" from the "Nationalist territory," as well as starkly dividing women's two disparate historical fates. In the "Nationalist territory," a woman is enslaved, imprisoned, beaten, sold, or captive to a dull-witted husband within an arranged marriage. In the "liberated territory," a woman enjoys emancipation, sexual equality, free love, and takes part in the Communist mission alongside men.

9 In this chapter Dai uses the convention, common among Chinese intellectuals, of distinguishing between a general "modern" epoch and the "contemporary" epoch when she divides Chinese film history into pre-1949 and post-1949 periods. When she employs the conventional phrase "classical revolutionary" with reference to a genre, forms or model, she is referring to the standard finalized in the 1950s for the typical "revolutionary" film protocol.—TRANS.

10 From 1949 to 1955, the base for film production shifted from Shanghai to Changchun (the Changchun Studio was initially called the Dongbei Studio). The majority of the principal filmmakers, as the "liberated areas' revolutionary art workers," lacked experience making feature films. As a result, the postwar forties films were very different from the films first made in New China. Chinese film experienced an important turning point after the well-known French film scholar, Georges Sadoul, upon visiting China, praised Chinese film of the 1940s. Consequently, many of these forties films were re-released and New China's film began to be influenced by the traditional heritage of Chinese film.

11 This can be seen in the Maoist saying, "China's women all have lofty ideals, as they love military attire more than women's clothing." See Mao Zedong, "*Qijue: Wei nü minbing tizhao*" ("A Poem: Signing a Picture for a Female Soldier") in *Zhuxi shici* (The selected poems of chairman Mao) (Beijing: Renmin chubanshe, 1960).

12 See chapters one and two of Dai Jinhua and Meng Yue, *Fuchu lishi dibiao – xiandai funü wenxue yanjiu* (Emerging from the horizon of history: a study of modern women's literature) (Zhengzhou: Henan renmin chubanshe, 1989).

13 This representation and discourse of women can be seen in the classic revolutionary film, *The Red Detachment of Women*. As soon as Qiong Hua and Hong Lian arrive at the Red Army's Red Stone Village after escaping from the Coconut Grove Manor, which is under the hegemonic control of the Nationalists and the evil landlord Nan Batian, the dark evening rain suddenly changes into a clear morning filled with red clouds, and the male clothing Hong Lian is wearing miraculously changes into women's clothing. Shortly thereafter, however, the gray army uniform that women in the detachment wear replaces Hong Lian's female attire.

14 From one perspective, reports on violence against women are a historical fact of the Chinese Civil War and the War of Resistance against Japan.

15 See the Qing Dynasty ballad "Song of Mulan" in Shen Deqian's *Gushi yuan* (Source of ancient verse) (Zhonghua shuju, 1963), pp. 326–7.

16 The translation is from Xu Yuanzhong, *Song of the Immortals: An Anthology of Classical Chinese Poetry* (Beijing: New World Press, 1994), p. 43.—TRANS.

17 Ibid., p. 43.

18 *Dao ma dan* or "mounted female warrior" is one of the female roles or *dan* in Peking opera. Excelling in martial arts, she is dressed in elegant armor and fights mounted on a horse. Her performance includes both singing and dance.

19 *Yang jia jiang* (*Yang Family Generals*) is a multichapter novel whose author is unknown. The story derives from *BeiSong zhizhuan* (Biographies of the northern song).

20 A well-known Peking opera act, also called "Zhan jinshan" ("Battle at Jinshan"), in which the Southern Song's female general, Liang Hongyu, the wife of the Song general Han Shizhong appears. In the Southern Song's fourth year (1130), Liang Hongyu and Han Shizhong blocked the advance of the Jin army. Liang's drumming invigorated the Song army, resulting in a crushing defeat for the Jin army.

21 Two famous Peking operas, *Yang Family Generals* and its sequel. The former is about a bandit's daughter, Mu Guiying, who falls in love with General Yang's son, Yang Zongbao, who had been dispatched to subjugate the bandits. Through her formidable combat abilities, Mu Guiying defeats Yang Zongbao, and they are married within the bandit's fortress. The latter is about Yang Zongbao's return to the Song camp after he marries Mu Guiying. Because he had committed the offense of marrying without his father's permission, he is tied up at the barracks. When Mu Guiying's forces arrive, General Yang has no choice but to release his son and surrender his commander's seal.

22 *Kongque dongnan fei* (*Southeast Fly the Peacocks*) depicts the marriage of the beautiful and clever Liu Lanzhi to Jiao Zhongqing, a petty official in Lujiang prefecture. Although their relationship is strong, Liu is returned to her family at the urging of Jiao's mother. The two swear to uphold their wedding vows, but Liu is married off by her older brother and as a consequence she drowns herself. When Jiao hears of her death he hangs himself out of grief. *Chai tou feng* (*Phoenix Hairpin*) is a well-known verse composition by the Song dynasty poet Lu You. The verse laments his short-lived marriage and his reencounter with his first wife, whom his mother had expelled. See Long Yusheng, ed., *Tang Song mingjia ci xuan* (Anthology of Tang and Song verses) (Shanghai: Shanghai guji chubanshe, 1980), pp. 231–323. *Fusheng liu ji* (*Six Records of a Floating Life*), with four extant chapters, was written by Shen Fu in the Qing dynasty. It autobiographically narrates the relationship between Shen Fu and his cousin Chen Yun, who becomes his wife. Although they have a strong relationship, Shen Fu's mother ostracizes Chen Yun, who has committed an offense; Chen Yun then dies in illness and poverty. Later, Shen Fu's old friend "bestows" a concubine on him and he reenters the "spring dream." See Yu Pingbo, ed., *Fusheng liu ji* (Beijing: Renmin wenxue chubanshe, 1980), p. 38. [For the standard English translation, see Shen Fu, *Six Records of a Floating Life*, trans. Leonard Pratt and Chiang Su-hui (New York: Penguin, 1983)— TRANS.]

23 The silent films Wu Yonggan, *Shennü*, 1934; Sun Ye, *Ye meigui*, 1932; Shen Xiling, *Shizi jietou*, 1937; and Yuan Muzhi, *Malu tianshi*, 1937.

24 Cai Chusheng *Xin nüxing* (*New Women*, 1934).

25 Wang Weiyi and Xu Tao, *Guan bu zhu die chunguang* (*Impossible to Imprison the Light of Spring*, 1948); Hong Shen and Zheng Xiaoqiu, *Ruozhe, ni de mingzi shi nüren* (*Frailty, Thy Name Is Woman!*, 1948); Chen Liting *Yaoyuan de ai* (*Far Away Love*, 1947).

26 Of course, frequently it is only at the moment that this type of male-dominated social order is enfeebled by an external, violent threat that women's literary work obtains a particularly vivid style highlighting the female experience and predicament. After the May Fourth period, women's literature experienced another peak during the war years of the 1940s.

27 Dai is casting the May Fourth era as a Chinese enlightenment, though its modernity project required much reiteration. The intellectuals were the agents of enlightenment amidst threats to Chinese survival. That is how Chinese intellectuals came to select "science and democracy" as their hallmarks.—Trans.

These concepts were first brought out in Jin Guantao and Liu Qingfeng's, "Lishi de chensi – Zhongguo fengjian shehui jiegou ji qi changqi yanxu yuanyin de tantao" (Reflections on history: on the structure of feudal society and the reasons for its longevity), in *Lishi de chensi* (*Reflections on History*) (Sanlian shudian, 1980).

28 This film caused a great disturbance even before its release because it violated the norms of patriarchal society. It led ultimately to the death of Ruan Lingyu. See Zhu Jian, *Wumian yinghou Ruan Lingyu* (Ruan Lingyu, the crownless queen of actresses) (Lanzhou daxue chubanshe, 1997), pp. 203–89.

29 Intriguingly, while this conflict did sacrifice the actress Ruan Lingyu, it never sacrificed the film's male director, Cai Chusheng. As contemporary author Su Su has quite perceptively pointed out, Ruan Lingyu's death is less representative of an abstract conflict between the new woman and the patriarchal/male-dominated culture than of a more concrete conflict between the new women of the May Fourth generation emerging on the horizon of history and those old literati of a bygone generation. See Su Su, *Qian shi jin sheng* (Previous life, this life) (Shanghai: Shanghai wenyi chubanshe, 1997), pp. 76–81.

The behavior of these "perfectly new" new women on the historical scene was actually even more resolute and courageous than their appearance (even depicted in women's own narratives) in discourse. If, as a type of linguistic existence, the new woman confronted the culture's and discourse's extreme barrenness, then it may be supposed that this type of lack, due to the temporary absence of norms and oppression, would at the same time create the opportunity for freedom.

30 Hu Lancheng, *Jinsheng jinshi* (This life time, this cycle) (Taipei: Sansan Books, 1990), vol. 2, pp. 273–306.

31 Ibid., p. 44.—Trans.

32 A phrase used frequently in the Women's Federation and in women's publications. It refers to women's taking on both public, social duties and housework. It could also be translated as "the double burden."—Trans.

33 See Chen Shunxin's preface, "Nüxing zhuyi piping yu zhongguo dangdai wenxue yanjiu", (Feminist criticism and contemporary Chinese literary studies) in *Zhongguo dangdai wenxue de xushi yu xingbie* (Narrative and gender in China's contemporary literature) (Beijing: Beijing daxue chubanshe, 1995), p. 22.

34 Ibid., pp. 87–8.

35 Wang Yan, *Zhan huo zhong de qingchun* (*Youth in the Flames of War*, 1959).

36 Mao Zedong, "Lun lianhe zhengfu", (On the united front) in *Mao Zedong xuanji* (Selected works of Mao Zedong) (Beijing: Renmen chubanshe, 1977), p. 1031.

37 Cui Wei, *Qingchun zhi ge* (Song of Youth), 1959. Actually, the original work does contain a large portion of the author's autobiography. However, when it was written and published, this important fact had still not been noted. In terms of reception, its female autobiographical component in film/fiction was one of the reasons it received a continuously warm reception amongst China's urban audience/readers.

38 See Dai Jinhua, "Qingchun zhi ge: lishi shiyu zhong de chongdu" (Song of youth: an historicized rereading) in *Dianying lilun yu piping shouce* (Handbook to film theory and criticism) (Beijing: Kexue jishu wenxian chubanshe, 1993), pp. 199–217.

39 Mao Zedong, "Zai Zhongguo gongchan dang quanguo xuanchuan gongzuo huiyi shang de jianghua" (A talk at the CCP Conference on National Propaganda) in *Mao Zedong Xuanji* (Selected works of Mao Zedong), vol. 5, p. 406.

40 Mao Zedong, "Datui zichan jieji youpai de changkuang jingong" (Overthrowing the ravage attacks of the rightist petit-bourgeoisie) in *Mao Zedong Xuanji* (Selected works of Mao Zedong), vol. 5, p. 440.

41 Mao Zedong, "Jianding de xiangxin qunzhong de daduo shu", (Resolutely believing the masses) in *Mao Zedong Xuanji* (Selected works of Mao Zedong), vol. 5, p. 492.

42 See Xie Jin, *Tanyilu* (The notes of film art) (Shanghai: Shanghai wenyi chubanshe, 1991), pp. 201–4. After the love relationship between the male and female leads in *The Red Detachment of Women* was revised six times, it was finally completely cut out.

43 According to the official rhetoric after 1979, 1955 was selected as the upper limit in the historical purging of the Mao Zedong era. Otherwise, the purge could violate the CCP's legitimacy.

44 After 1978, the representation and voice of the class-defined working woman within art and culture almost completely disappeared, to be replaced by the urban, intellectual woman.

45 From Bai Xifeng's spoken drama, *Fengyu guren lai* (An old friend) in *Bai Xifeng juzuo xuan* (Selected plays of Bai Xifeng) (Beijing: Zhongguo xiju chubanshe, 1988), p. 137.

46 See Zhen Yefu, *Daijia lun: yi ge shehuixue xin shijiao* (The cost of argument: a new sociological perspective) (Beijing: Sanlian shudian, 1995), pp. 68–75.

47 Dai Jinhua, "Xieta: chongdu disidai" (The slanted tower: rereading the Fourth Generation) in *Dianying lilun yu piping shouce* (Handbook of film theory and criticism), pp. 8–12.

48 See, for example, Chen Kaige, *Huang tudi* (*Yellow Earth*), 1984; Wu Tianming, *Lao jing* (*The Old Well*), 1987; Teng Wenji, *Huanghe yao* (*Ballad of the Yellow River*), 1990; and Hou Yong, *Tian chu xue* (*Blood from Heaven*), 1991.

49 Both "Zhi you yi ge taiyang" (There is only one son), by Zhang Jie, a repre-

sentative woman author of the eighties, and "Shushu de gushi" (Uncle's story), by Wang Anyi, the new era's most outstanding woman writer, engaged the Chinese male intellectuals' predicament and the "dislocation" (*cuowei*) of their gender role in the cultural construction of superiority/inferiority, center/margin, and East/West.

50 Zhang Yimou's *Raise the Red Lantern* provides one of the most interesting examples. Here we encounter two basic ingredients vital to the metaphor of the Orient: the indispensable physical space of Old China (a prisonlike ancient mansion); and an allegorical style of writing symptomatic of the eighties tropes current in the "movement of cultural reflection." By the latter I mean stories about the endless struggle for and succession of power in Chinese society told through the contests among wives and concubines. The most eye-catching element in the film is the visual absence of the main male character. As a sound from beyond the frame, and as a shadow or silhouette, the male master is visually absent. The opulent stylization of the language of shots further serves to exile the master's desirous gaze beyond the story's setting. Therefore, the beautiful and exotic female roles appear to be unobstructed within the "anonymous" gaze of the camera-eye. When this exquisite and graceful image of "oriental beauty" was finally "exhibited" in the "occidental" world, the male protagonist's visual absence was translated into the suspension of the agent of desire. Consequently, the perspective of those "anonymous" shots was turned into an empty seat to be freely occupied by the Euro-American (male) audience. An "orientalized" space, an "orientalized" story, and "oriental" beauties, together formed a "spectacle" (*qiguan*) within the Western (occidental) field of vision. In the classic model of to gaze/be gazed at, male/female, and subject/object, the Fifth Generation filmmakers, embracing a subservient posture, accept their own feminized status within the rules of the game of gender/ethnicity and culture/power.

51 Zhu Ma, ed. *Dianying shouce* (Notebooks on cinema) (Chengdu: Sichuan daxue zhongwen xi, 1980), p. 317.

52 Films based on "female material" made at this time include: Wang Junzheng, *Shanlinzhong touyige nüren* (*The First Woman in the Forest*), 1987; Wang Junzheng, *Nüren-Taxi-Nüren* (*Woman-Taxi-Woman*), 1990; Qin Zhiyu, *Yinxing shu zhi lian* (*Love Affairs at the Ginko Tree*), 1987; Qin Zhiyu, *Zhuli xiaojie* (*Miss Julie*), 1989; Qin Zhiyu, *Dushen nüren* (*Single Women*), 1990; Bao Zhifang, *Jinse de zhijia* (*The Golden Fingernail*), 1988; Wu Zhennian, *Jianu zhenqing* (*A False Woman's True Love*), 1988; Wu Zhennian's television drama *Nürenmen* (*Women*), 1990; Dong Ke'na, *Shui shi disan zhe* (*The Third Party*), 1988; Dong Ke'na, *Nüxing Shijie* (*Woman's World*), 1990; Lu Xiao ya, *Relian* (*Unrequited Love*), 1989; Wang Haowei, *Cunlu dai wo huijia* (*The Path Takes Me Home*), 1990; Wang Haowei, *O, Xiangxue* (*Oh, Sweet Snow*), 1992; Guang Chunlan, *Huoyan shan lai de xiao gushou* (*The Drummer from Flame Mountain*), 1992.

53 From a spoken dialogue in the film *The Seagull*.

54 See chapter 5 of this volume.

Translated by Jonathan Noble

5

"Human, Woman, Demon": A Woman's Predicament

The Subject of Woman

The subject of woman is, it would appear, first and foremost one of silence. The subject of woman is always metaphoric: the "madwoman in the attic," the woman confined and silenced, who has only fiery rage to transform her prison into ruins. Everything about her, including her interpretation, is given her by the Mr. Rochesters, that is, by men. She is labeled a madwoman and thus stripped forever of discursive power, the ability to self-narrate.[1] The subject of woman is also the young woman in the ancient Chinese folk legend, *Beijie hongluo* (Unknotting the Red Bundle Behind Her Back). In a period of state decline, incessant warfare, and imperial dissolution, she has escaped selection as an imperial concubine by not registering her name in the official census, and thus becomes nameless. But to save her aged father from the emperor's threat, she stands before the crowd of people in the Imperial Hall and, hands behind her back, unties a knotted and buttoned red bundle, a "gift" from a powerful enemy-state that, were it to remain untied, would be a declaration of war. Of course, because her action saves the people from disaster, she is chosen to be an imperial consort and brought into the palace anyway, rendered nameless and speechless once more. With a fleeting appearance in male history, she falls forever wordless into the very tragic fate she had attempted to escape. Her deeds and their narration occur "behind the back" of History, embellishments on the beautiful painted screen of the male story, or as its distant and obscure background.[2] The subject of woman is also the shadow of a naked woman rushing through the sleeping dreams of men, silent, never having existed in the past, never to appear in the future. For the Italian writer Italo Calvino, humanity's civilized city is built for her, built to imprison her – a city where she is fated to be forever absent.[3] Chinese and world history and civilization are replete with images of women and discourses about women, but the real bodies and discourses of women are forever "absent in their presence." As in *Jishi yu xugou* (*Documentation and Fabrication*),[4] the novel by contemporary Chinese woman writer Wang Anyi, the endpoint of a pursuit of a matrilinear order may be where the memories of the living and oral legends disappear; extending that pursuit into written language – the extant textual fragments of civilization – reveals only the shadows of male ancestry.

So the subject of woman is once again about the subject of self-expression. If we say there exists a female memory that is severed, suffocated in History/male discourse, then a feminist cultural struggle is that which intends to give voice to this silent memory, to give it expression. To be sure, in mountainous south China there once was a "women's writing" (*nüshu*), a written language that belonged to a sisterhood. An as yet unauthenticated legend of this script tells of an "imperial consort" who, having had the "fortune" to be selected to enter the palace, and to tell her sisters who remained outside about its complexities, its jungle of prohibitions, and the many ways women in it suffered, created a form of writing that only women could write and recognize.[5] This ancient, meandering form of writing, which existed beyond male History – official and unofficial historiography – was finally "discovered" in contemporary China and banned. The deaths of the last old women able to write and recite passages verbatim in this language mean that "women's writing" is quickly receding into the mists of time; it is a miracle that now exists in memories of a female world and in the documents of literati and male scholars. It is the "golden voice" of the various sisterhood legends and speech patterns only women were alleged to have had. In the struggle for discursive possibility, women living in civilized society have often encountered the "plight of Hua Mulan,"[6] for we have no chance of creating a new heaven, an(other) linguistic system, within patriarchal culture.[7] This is the predicament of a female discourse and narration, the very predicament of female existence. Cultural tradition places women in a city of mirrors. For women to be women in the mirrored city is to be forever off-balance, wounded, mired in distress. In the mirrored city, "real women" appear on stage either in men's costume and speaking in men's voices or they are "returned to a former female self" and so rendered forever silent. In terms of expression, a women's "reality" does not exist: for the reality of women cannot be narrated through male, phallocentric, and logocentric discourse; and a female reality cannot be an essence, normative and pure. The predicament of women originates in the prison of language and the prison of norms, in the difficulty of self-recognition, in besiegement and the perplexity of these multiple mirrored images. Female existence is often a kind of mirrored existence: not the perplexity that comes of narcissism, nor the psychological trauma suffered in tragedy, but a kind of coercion, an intense pressure, a civilized violence that transforms women's flesh-and-blood bodies into butterflies pinned to death.

It is in this sense that Huang Shuqin's *Human, Woman, Demon* becomes an exceptionally interesting feminist text. In many senses, it is to date the first and only "feminist film" in China. It concerns narration and silence; and it is the story of a real woman, as well as a metaphor about women, especially the historical fate of modern women.[8] She is a woman who rejects and attempts to escape from the fate of women, a successful woman who succeeds because she performs the role of a man; but, in the end, she is still a woman and thus beyond salvation. The director, Huang Shuqin, clearly had no intention of making an experimental feminist film. Nor did she ever display any self-consciousness about feminist film per se during the process of producing the film. She accepted an essentialist, irrefutable, "common-sense" view of gender: that a woman's happiness comes exclusively from marriage, which is the "natural product" of heterosexual love. Yet, at the same time, every scene and every detail of the film is infused with a wrenching pain intuited from the experience of being female and an intensely condensed, profound empathy for the real fate of Pei Yanling, an actual woman artist, thus questioning essentialist gender expression and the hypocritical and fragile sexual landscape of patriarchal society. The film is neither a self-conscious pose from the margins nor an effort at resistance. It is a window that has been opened in a bricked-up wall; and a new kind of landscape through the opening can be glimpsed through the aperture – the landscape of women.⁹ The protagonist, Qiuyun, is in no way a female rebel. She is not, nor can she be, a "madwoman in the attic." She just goes after what she wants, stubbornly and irrepressibly. Hers is not a mad cry but a slight, mournful laugh, lacking any modicum of self-pity, filled with silent compassion. This is the self-portrait of contemporary Chinese women. Theirs is both a longing and a dream born in patience: the desire for salvation, but with a profound understanding that salvation will not fall into their laps. In a sense, it is a retelling and a reenactment of the Hua Mulan story.

Choice and Lack

Human, Woman, Demon opens with a scene that is at once bewitching and nightmarish. After the first frame, three make-up jars filled with red, white, and black greasepaint gradually appear in a close-up shot. In the dressing-room mirror the attractive, handsome face of a young woman, Qiuyun, enters the frame. She removes her milky-white jacket, binds up her head of lovely hair, and with a practiced hand begins to paint her face with a make-up brush. Each tiny stroke of the brush covers the face of the woman and replaces it with a painted visage of machismo and martial valor. At every twitch of its features, this face reveals a wondrous grotesqueness. The dresser applies the various layers of the costume, and gradually the woman's delicate shape disappears beneath a long red gown. When the headdress and beard are placed on her, this woman no longer exists. She has been replaced by Zhong Kui, a wondrous, ugly, ultimately male figure, fierce and intense, shrouded in silent grief and an aura of grandeur and might. As this Zhong Kui sits down before the mirror, we see the reflections of many Zhong Kuis; as though perplexed, Zhong Kui leans forward for a closer look and now sees in the mirror numerous Qiuyuns wearing milky-white jackets. As the camera slowly pulls back, we see Qiuyun seated alone at the mirror looking intently at the Zhong Kui in the mirror; then we see a seated Zhong Kui staring at a reflected Qiuyun. Qiuyun and Zhong Kui alternate several times before the mirror. They are both within the mirror, but are they stepping into a hall of mirrors, or falling into a nightmarish world: woman? man? true self? role? human? non-human? demon? Clearly a moment of descent into the confusion of the mirrored images, this is not merely the intoxicating experience of an artist becoming her role, it is the quandary of a modern woman who must perform, indeed can only perform. The tragic question "Who am I?" seizes the moment, but the "I" or subject speaking, asking the question, is specifically a woman whose difficulty with recognizing her gendered identity and social role is what defines her. This is not the manifestation of a split in a frenzied psyche, nor the consuming conflict in a disturbed mind between self-love and self-hate. "I" registers perplexity rather than shock; a prolonged, hidden suffering rather than madness. Indeed, the opening scene of *Human, Woman, Demon* presents a phantasmagoric situation that constitutes nothing less than a metaphoric statement about the circumstances of modern woman's existence. From the film's first moment, definitive notions of gender and the gender landscape have already broken down to reveal interlocking fissures.

Human, Woman, Demon is a narrative of growing up. It is the tale of a woman artist's vocation. In thrall to an uncontrollable desire, Qiuyun immerses herself so deeply in the theater that she must rend her life and cast aside all attachments in order to perfect her performance and become her "role." At the level of meaning this is a woman's tale. As the narrative of a "real" or "normal" woman, Qiuyun's life is more a despairing adherence to or revision of the patriarchal gender order than a transgression of or affront to it. Because of this she becomes a successful, though unfortunate, woman who never bemoans her fate. Scripting and interpreting Qiuyun's life, Huang Shuqin certainly does not resort to the current nostrum in contemporary China that, for a woman, career and life (in blunter terms, marriage) are doomed to incompatibility; nor does she represent an allegedly female choice between professional success or personal happiness. If we say that a "woman is not the moon, and does not rely on the radiance of man's reflection to illuminate herself," then in this film, in Qiuyun's career, in her universe, a male sun has never shone.[10] Qiuyun's narrative of escape is a story of refusal; to avoid becoming the kind of "good woman" that exists only in fantasies, she seeks to escape the fate of women. Yet because of this she must also refuse the path of a

traditional woman. Indeed, she even refuses to play a woman character on stage.

A classic Freudian "primal scene" occurs during Qiuyun's first
escape.[11] The headstrong little girl ends a game of "marrying the
bride" by announcing, "I won't be a bride, not for any of you!" During
Qiuyun's flight from the pursuing boys she discovers her mother and
another man, clearly not her "father" (in actual fact this man turns out
to be Qiuyun's biological father), making love in a haystack. Shrieking,
she flees once again. This scene is not a simple female statement or
self-narration of a constituting, traumatic life experience, though it
certainly smashes any idealized images of a happy nuclear family that
Qiuyun may be harboring. Self-narration follows in the consequent
conflict with the boys. If we accept this primal scene as indeed constituting the opening of a kind of tragic female life, it is a wholly social
one. It is Qiuyun's first encounter with and escape from the reality of
women. It is also her first naming as a woman and her mother's
daughter, which will rivet her to the historical and social cross she has
to bear. This sort of fate brings with it humiliation and the possibility
that at any time she might be banished by the Ur-society. As a social
woman, what constitutes Qiuyun's traumatic life experience is certainly not the scene of her mother's lovemaking, but the scenario of
her conflict with the boys. These boys who once adoringly surrounded
her suddenly become a band of fiends. Instinctually, she turns for
help to a male, the "little man" Erwa, who until this point in her life
has always served as a protector and authority, and is her close childhood playmate. Traumatically for Qiuyun, after only a moment's
hesitation Erwa joins the ranks of the "enemy." This does not just hurt
Qiuyun, it is a banishment: she despairs. Then she fights back, and "of
course" she loses. Just as earlier she began to understand woman, now
she also comprehends man. This moment of cruel play devastates all
her notions of an idealized world: if, as common sense has it, man
equals power, then for a woman man signifies protection, as well as
possible devastation or harm. The question hinges on circumstantial
social and historical conventions: a woman cannot expect to unite
with men when she opposes society for the sake of her sex. Unfolding
before this little girl is the truth of this metanarrative.

The first time Qiuyun takes flight in shock and terror, but the second time she chooses for herself, refusing to play women characters in order to evade women's fate. Qiuyun's adopted father vehemently opposes her decision to become an actress. The profession makes him anxious, and he warns her about what happens to girls and women in it: "How can girls learn performance, what good comes from women actors going on stage! Even if you avoid the bad ones who want to take advantage of you, you'll eventually turn into the sort of person that your mother is." Apparently, then, Qiuyun can only either be a "good woman," and consequently humiliated and hurt, or she can "degenerate" into a "bad woman," and be humiliated, spurned, and banished. Here, to be a woman is to play a tragic role from which one cannot escape. And though her father's advice is steeped in sympathy, it constitutes yet another metanarrative of womanhood: it denies happiness to the "good woman," salvation to the "bad," and vitiates all other possibilities beyond these two constituents of the double bind. But Qiuyun assesses the advice and makes her choice: "Then I won't play women's roles, I'll play men." An intriguing image in this scene is that of Qiuyun, exhausted, lying on a haystack, with nothing on but a red undershirt; a little boy enters the frame and peers curiously at her motionless figure. At this point, the edge of the frame cuts off the boy's torso, turning his naked lower body into a sexual index. And yet, this is not a reference to Freudian phallic worship or a feminine complex of "lack," but rather conveys a simple factual statement: Qiuyun can escape a woman's fate and refuse to play the female role, but this choice cannot change her sex. She is simply choosing another, more difficult, thorny path, a path of no return with "no regrets whatever one encounters, even death." A woman cannot escape the fate of women: this is a kind of social fatalism.

The ingenuity (or textual trickery) of metanarrative's construction of women lies precisely in the ways these stories end. Every love story must conclude with a wedding ceremony: "The couple bow to each other and enter the nuptial chamber." Music fills the air. The curtain slowly falls. Or the Prince and Snow White (or Cinderella, or Thumbelina) have a grand wedding and live happily ever after. The potential story of the marriage lies forever in the obscurity of the extra-diegetic.[12] A Hua Mulan tale always terminates after the lines "I replace my martial attire with the garments of my former days,"[13] and then the male (real or performative) world and the female world are situated in two separate spaces, two temporalities. In classical meta-narrative, even in the many Hua Mulan stories, there is no pain or confusion. The world of *Human, Woman, Demon*, a feminist film, how-ever, is never clear or easy. Although little Qiuyun refuses female roles – she renounces women's attire and throws herself into the itin-erant life of the artist, dressed as a stubborn boy – despite even a series of humiliating misrecognitions (for instance, the tragicomedy of being mistaken for a boy as she emerges from the women's public wash-room), she will grow up and become a young woman, will love, and desire to be loved. Qiuyun longs to be recognized and named as a woman; recognition and naming signify an affirmation of the life and value of a woman (with Huang Shuqin this will always follow the clear and immobile pattern of love and marriage). When Qiuyun finally gains this confirmation ("You are a good-looking girl, very feminine") from Maestro Zhang (the only man, besides her adopted father, who, if he doesn't dazzle her, at least "discovers" her sex and feels tender toward her), she stages her third refusal and escape. Recognition and naming still imply erotic love (as when Zhang says, "I feel as though I will never tire of gazing at you"). This scene also takes place at night among the haystacks, and once again Qiuyun flees in a state of shock and terror. In a point of view shot (POV), haystacks like flickering ghostly shadows seem to rush toward her and press down on her from above.[14] She has refused; she is terrified and loath to repeat her mother's social fate. Yet this time she will grasp that the "scarlet letter" of shame her mother (women) wore is also, contrarily, accompanied by its own happiness and rewards. To be a "normal" woman yet to refuse women's fate means to accept the lack in women's lives.

In *Human, Woman, Demon*, Qiuyun's actions as a performer exact a price beyond the stage. Yet there is still more to this. She can refuse the sexual advances of Maestro Zhang and still have no means of escape: as a woman, she encounters social punishment not just for what she does, but for what she does not do. She is again named as a woman, the daughter of her impure, shameful mother. As a result of Zhang's advances and her retreat Qiuyun becomes homeless. The intense atmosphere of the stage, the public display under dazzling bright lights, comes with a price: loneliness offstage and banishment to a state of voicelessness. The punishment the Ur-society beyond the stage inflicts even insinuates its way onto the stage. When Qiuyun, numb and empty, performs the Peking opera *San cha kou* (*Three-Forked Road*) to the sound of gongs and cymbals, a parallel montage shows Maestro Zhang quietly slipping away into the dark of the night, his family in tow, leaving her forever.[15] In a close-up shot a nail stands upright on the stage table. Backstage – in the middle ground between the world of performance and the real world – countless (male) faces concealed under make-up glance expectantly at each other, a shot that defines the nail as a punishment meted out by a meta-societal conspiracy. As she brings her hand down hard on the table top the nail pierces Qiuyun's palm. She completes her performance, bearing the pain without tears, and the mass of painted faces surround her as if to show concern, but in fact to enjoy, to confirm the punishment. In a close-up shot, the eyebrow of a mask drawn on the forehead of another painted face moves in a peculiarly lively and wicked-looking fashion. Suddenly, all the painted faces, their task fulfilled, vanish, leaving Qiuyun to suffer the cruel form of discipline in wordless banishment. Nearly insane, she grabs the red and black greasepaint and smears it on her face; she stands upon the table, unable to cry, shouting hoarsely toward the oppressively low ceiling and waving her arms in utter despair. Through the entire scene the swinging ceiling lamp creates a sense of confusion and desolation. This is truly a scene from the lives of modern women who choose the path of social achievement. Punishment still exists. It may no longer involve the extreme cruelties of the past, the public parades or forced drownings: it is just a nail, but a nail that pierces your spirit as it pierces your flesh.

In another rhetorical cinematic strategy, Huang Shuqin has an idiot serve as a witness to each of the tragic scenes involving Qiuyun: the conflict between Qiuyun and Erwa; Qiuyun being dragged out of the women's washroom; Maestro Zhang sitting desolately in the waiting room of the train station. The idiot is masculine, a metaphor of the historical unconscious (this is to some degree the same rhetorical [textual?] strategy used in 1980s roots literature and the Fourth and Fifth Generations of Chinese filmmakers).[16] He is always laughing aloud, jostled in a crowd, unmoved and ignorant of all the "small" tragedies visited on Qiuyun.

Qiuyun succeeds, thanks to her wondrous masculine image. It is not, of course, what her father had hoped for when he told her, "All you need to do is become popular, a famous actor, then everything will sort itself out." The price of Qiuyun's success is that she will forever lack a female life. In plot terms, Qiuyun marries and becomes a mother. On the discursive, textual level, however, Qiuyun's father and husband – these two key men in her "normal" female personal life history – are absent. Her "father" is not her biological father. The biological father appears on screen only as the back of a head; he never faces the audience or Qiuyun, has never been a father to her or been named as such. Her husband, appearing only in a wedding photo at the very margin of the screen – an image within an image, an imaginary signifier in all senses, absent in his very presence – serves an indispensable discursive function in the debt collector's report about "Qiuyun's happy family." The husband never appears onscreen, though he is the father of Qiuyun's two children. Apparently he never really "exists" in her life apart from being an obstacle: "if she acts male parts, he minds the ugliness, when she acts female parts, he worries about her"; also, his chronic gambling burdens her with debt.

To be a woman, to fulfill a role, implies that one must become the role. Acting on the stage of life means acting the part of a woman, since in life the stage lights never go off. When Qiuyun performs her success, she still must play-act the happy and perfect woman, assuming all the heavy burdens and losses of womanhood. In this sense the film reconfigures and deconstructs the Hua Mulan story.

The Performance and Loss of Salvation

In many ways, Qiuyun is both a female success and failure. Even as she expresses herself, she is silent. Performing onstage is obviously a form of linguistic agency: playing men, she expresses herself and is successful; and yet while playing men she uses the male image of presence to create the very absence of her femininity. She pays the price of the absence of a female discursive subjectivity when she expresses herself as a woman.

Qiuyun does not perform masculinity in any ordinary sense; rather she brings to life ideal maleness as it is encoded in the old world, traditional China. Her first male role is Zhao Yun from *Changban po* (*Changban Slope*), who is a hero alone in a sea of armies, the metadiscursive protector and savior of the weak – a woman and child, Madame Mi and Ah Dou – in the classical narratives.[17] Zhao Yun in his shining armor is an ageless icon of youth from traditional Chinese culture. Subsequently, Qiuyun also plays the parts of Zhuge Liang, a symbol of male intelligence and military strategy, and Guan Gong, who represents perfect male virtue and embodies Confucian morality and righteousness.[18] This expressive agency offers Qiuyun a kind of distorted female discursive subjectivity. It reiterates classical male discourse and contributes a roundabout enunciation of female desires, while at the same time gently mocking patriarchal discourse. A male image performed through a female subject, an image that exists as the object of female desires, itself constructs a paradox, a peculiar form of irony. This is a circumstance in which a lack is fated to develop because of an incommensurability between the subject and an object. The only exception in *Human, Woman, Demon* is a scene in which Maestro Zhang performs Gao Chong, like Zhao Yun, a traditional Chinese icon of youth, from the opera *Tiao huache* (*Overturning Chariots*).[19] Qiuyun and the young women in comic female *caidan* attire (that is, the costume traditionally worn by those playing yang female roles in Peking opera) are standing in the wings watching. When he exits, the young women surround him and, for the first time, Qiuyun evinces a certain listlessness as she slowly removes the grey beard she is wearing in her role as Xiao En.[20] In the next scene, she is seated before the dressing-room mirror putting flowers in her hair; dressed as a *caidan* she is the feminine complement to Gao Chong. This is not merely an illusory love, but the final wish of a disgraced youth.

Yet what *Human, Woman, Demon* relates is not in the end a story of desire. The themes of the narrative are women and the salvation of women. The film contains another network of levels: the story within the story, the staged Peking opera *Zhong Kui jia mei* (*Zhong Kui Gives His Sister Away in Marriage*). This opera appears at every important moment in Qiuyun's life. Zhong Kui and Qiuyun are not two subjects, between whom there is a misrecognition, a blurring, a mirrored confusion of role and performer, but rather they form a relation of subject and object that will be forever marked by mutual lack, because the role and the performer cannot coexist. As a minor god in the pantheon of traditional Chinese secular mythology, the Zhong Kui of legend is exceptionally talented and passes the civil service examinations with first-place honors. He is expelled, however, because of his extraordinarily ugly appearance; then and there he slits his throat (or smashes his head upon the steps, in another version) and dies. Following his demise, the Jade Emperor honors Zhong Kui with the title "General Who Chops Down Evil Spirits," and gives him a retinue of three thousand soldiers who specialize in killing the evil spirits who haunt the human world.[21] Zhong Kui is a popular figure who grew out of folk legend, one of the pantheon of religious spirits in a nation where people were not meticulous about worship and taboos. Paintings, dramas, and fiction concerning this figure center on two core plot lines: catching ghosts and giving his sister away in marriage. The latter plot relates how before his death Zhong Kui had promised his younger sister to the scholar Du Ping. Even after his death and apotheosis, Zhong Kui does not forget his sister's marriage, since in feudal times a woman with no elder brother or father could look forward to a life of spinsterhood. So he prepares a wedding orchestra of reed pipes, flutes, and drums, and on New Year's Eve he returns again to the human world to marry his sister to Du Ping. In the film's system of signification, Zhong Kui serves as an idealized protector and savior of women. "I have been waiting for you since I was small, waiting for you to beat away the ghosts and save me," Qiuyun, the narrator in the film, declaims. "My perfect Zhong Kui has only been able to fulfill one task, his role as go-between. Do not mind Zhong Kui's ghostly appearance. The fate of women is enormously important to him and so he must find a good man for his sister." That is Qiuyun's dream, neither abnormal nor extravagant – the dream of an average yet uncommon woman.

The cinematic rendition of *Zhong Kui* adds not only a wondrous, dreamy hue to the film but, more significantly, injects into the original story a tragic, desolate quality that it had lacked. To the clamor of gongs and drums, in a cascade of color, with a performance that fuses poetry and dance, Zhong Kui appears to ruminate in solitude on his extraordinary loneliness and despondency. An allegorical element common to Chinese art films of the 1980s, this is obviously an index of the nation's existential state as well as a metaphoric image of the existential condition of contemporary women, or so-called liberated, successful women. In the signifying structure of the film, Zhong Kui becomes the senior figure in which Qiuyun-cum-woman lodges her expectations; but he is *not* an object of desire. The male and female protagonists in *Zhong Kui* are a brother and his younger sister. His status as the older brother prohibits him from being her image of desire; also he is an exceptionally ugly man and so not a possible subject of female desire, broadly speaking. At the same time, he is a famous ghost, a non-hu(man). If we say that he nonetheless appears in the guise of a man, then it is as an incomplete man. Zhong Kui is nonetheless still an idealized male in the story of Qiuyun, a "most perfect man" in a dream that haunts her throughout her life.[22] Perhaps the purpose of the text's web of meaning is to suggest that for the traditional Chinese woman the ideal male image, her "most perfect man," is always a father or brother and never a handsome prince on a white horse. This ideal man can protect her in the face of trials and humiliations. He shows concern for her happiness and will indeed complete it. There is no romantic sentiment here, only tenderness and intimacy. It is the Chinese woman's longing for a feeling of security, belonging, salvation.

One explanation to be drawn from the predicament of modern women disclosed in *Human, Woman, Demon* is that, despite being free in name, even liberated, Qiuyun still names her nameless suffering after the tragedy of Lin Daiyu: "So piteous that my parents died early and I have no one to take responsibility for me."[23] Yet clearly, though Qiuyun is no stubborn rebel, she certainly does not long to have her fate determined by "parental commands and the words of a go-between." Apart from representing the cultural unconscious of Chinese women's devotion to natal kinship ties, Zhong Kui, as the dream figure of women's salvation, actually serves no more than an empty and hopeless ritual of naming, an obscure utopia about salvation. As the performance of man, Zhong Kui is nothing less than an empty signifier inscribed with the nameless suffering of contemporary women, their indefinable situation, the uncertainty that comes from not belonging anywhere, a longing for happiness and salvation. Only the specter of an elder brother, a ghost, a non-hu(man) can fill the role of woman's benefactor: and when this non-hu(man) compels a woman to perform him, we can see how the prospect of the patriarchal order not only splinters, but is itself revealed to have been already as fragile and insubstantial as the background stage scenery.

A stage performance of *Zhong Kui* appears first during the film's initial major narrative sequence and constitutes a part of the idealized, harmonious images of family surrounding Qiuyun then. It is New Year's Eve, at an outdoor village arena. Onstage, Qiuyun's mother and father are performing *Zhong Kui.* In the wings, Qiuyun and Erwa stand entranced at the performance. Everything is jubilant and auspicious. Only when the camera zooms in on a Chinese adage written on rice paper and pasted on a column, "Husband and wife, a sham marriage from the start," do we begin to detect a fissure in this scene of old-world perfection. The second time *Zhong Kui* is performed in the film the jubilant mood has been washed away, leaving nothing but wreckage. When Qiuyun's father as Zhong Kui returns to the human world and knocks on the door of his old home, calling out, "Sister, open the door," no one reappears onstage, indeed backstage is in a state of total chaos. Tragicomically, the elder brother, the savior, finally arrives, to find that his object for redemption has already fled with her lover. The Zhong Kui onstage, Qiuyun's father, despondently fends off the fritters, fruit peels, and old shoes that the audience hurl at him while he attempts to continue the performance single-handedly. From the wings, Qiuyun witnesses her father's pathetic plight and cries out loud. Her mother/Zhong Kui's sister cannot be located, nor is any trace of Erwa to be found.

The third enactment of the same scene unfolds offstage as Qiuyun encounters her former playmates, the group of boys, beside the little bridge over the stream. This time, in a cruel comic imitation of the scene titled "Zhong Kui Gives His Sister Away in Marriage," the boys force little Qiuyun onto the planks that cross the stream, then shake the boards and splash her with water, chanting in unison, "Sister, open the door. I am your brother Zhong Kui returned." When Qiuyun timidly calls on Erwa for help, the boys sing, "Sister, open the door. I am your brother Erwa returned." Erwa responds: "Who's your brother! Go look for your bastard father." And then the boys begin cheering, "Go look for your bastard father." Absent from the scene is precisely that elder brother, Zhong Kui, who brings salvation, safety, a loving heart. This is also the scene in which, as Erwa forces little Qiuyun to the ground, her despairing, pleading eyes drift off into an indistinct distance. And then in Qiuyun's POV shot the story within the story appears, in a wondrous scene from *Zhong Kui*. Sword raised, breathing flames in the darkness, Zhong Kui severs the heads of the demons and materializes as Qiuyun's idealized redeemer for the first time in the film.

In the operatic story within the story, a key narrative strategy is the perennial absence of Zhong Kui's sister. Neither the meeting of the brother and sister nor the marriage ever actually occurs. A joyous occasion – the wedding ceremony and the event of marrying off the sister – is forever deferred beyond the diegesis. Salvation never occurs; completion is never achieved. The first time Zhong Kui appears in a scene within the film proper is after Qiuyun has performed "Three Forked Roads" and the conspiratorial and punitive nail has pierced her palm. As she screams hoarsely with tearless despair, Zhong Kui appears backstage, lit in a ray of bright, strange light. After striding toward her half-closed dressing-room door he peers inside and in a desolate timbre sings: "I've arrived at my home, the house so very cold. I want to knock on the door, but fear startling my sister. Tears flow and swallow up my words." In a close-up, tears of passion well out of Zhong Kui's eyes. In the dressing room, Qiuyun seems momentarily to take the position of Zhong Kui's sister. Yet the male costume she is wearing and the red and black paint she has smeared on her face situate her between these two figures, Zhong Kui and the sister beckoning him. In the real-life scenario, Zhong Kui – absent male savior – and his younger sister from the staged scene or story within the story – absent object of salvation – point simultaneously to the destruction and the redemption of these ancient gender roles.

In Qiuyun's life, her father and Maestro Zhang are obviously characters constructed as Zhong Kui foils. Though they serve the roles of father and elder brother, the text's narrative structure makes them appear in a certain sense incompletely male. Long before Qiuyun's mother escaped, her marriage to Qiuyun's father had become a sham; he isn't even Qiuyun's biological father. When Qiuyun discovers her mother making love with the back of a head in the haystack and rushes back to the old temple where the opera troupe is billeted, a close-up shot shows Qiuyun's "father" lying alone on his bed facing the wall. In what is clearly a POV shot, the camera moves across to shoot the feminine, bared arms of a figure in a dilapidated wall mural; the scene articulates the desire of a sexually frustrated man. He has raised Qiuyun to maturity and in the end lets her go because her decision to become an actress is the only avenue toward completion. Maestro Zhang nearly replicates the actions of Qiuyun's father. On two occasions he mistakes Qiuyun for a woman, thereby projecting the gender misrecognition of Ur-society, and, in so doing, he protects her right to "be a woman." Thus, he too must eventually give her up. Her father sacrifices his only relative for the sake of her future; Maestro Zhang gives up his position as the leading actor of the martial role and leaves it for Qiuyun as an empty space, a gift. Like Qiuyun's father, Maestro Zhang relinquishes the very thing in which he has vested his every emotion. Yet all these men can complete for her is her career, never her happiness. This loss or absence of the male sex – subject and savior in the classical gender discourse – will indubitably rupture the traditional female world. A woman planning to repair this fractured image can only do so in performance, playing an ideal male image; but to play this role implies that she cannot simultaneously be a female subject who occupies an object position. A modern woman who must save herself but cannot falls into the empty fissure that opens up between acting and the absence of a self, female expression and silence, the glittering light of the new world and the complete dilapidation of the old. Qiuyun/woman and the male savior Zhong Kui/man can only, as in the film's prologue, gaze at each other from within and without the mirror.

In the film's final sequence, Qiuyun and her "father" meet again. The room is alight with countless candles, casting a rich, warm glow. Almost happy, Qiuyun imagines: "In tomorrow's performance, you play Zhong Kui and I'll play his sister. You marry me off." It is the last time that Qiuyun will ever seek to repair an ideal image of gender difference. By playing Zhong Kui's sister she seeks to fill up this always absent, empty position; she relies on her father to name her a happy woman onstage. Yet this nomination reappears immediately, though differently, by way of the naming process of the Ur-society; and it indicates disappointment, points out that women have not moved out of their position as the "second sex." While father and daughter are steeped in their happiness, a dark, crooked shadow enters screen left, finally enveloping Qiuyun's entire body. It turns out to be Old Lady Wang, who helped in Qiuyun's birth: "When you were born the only thing visible was your big mouth, crying with all your might, as though in song. Your father thought you were a boy. But I saw you were lacking that little thing and so I knew you were a girl." In the Ur-society's naming, woman is still the incomplete gender. So Qiuyun, a modern, even successful woman, can only harbor one simple, utopian desire: "Actually, I have always felt a woman should marry a good man." The hope of salvation is still vested in a man, though the man is incomplete, a proto-man. The metadiscourse is still classical: the woman "is returned to where she belongs."[24] The predicament of a modern woman appears in the film, but at the same time the film uses a classical discourse to deconstruct classical images of gender.

At the end of the film, the narrator finally allows Zhong Kui to face Qiuyun onstage. In unison they speak: "I've come here to marry you off" and "I'm already married to the stage." "Any regrets?" Zhong Kui asks. Qiuyun answers, "No." As a modern woman unwilling to adhere to traditional gender roles, she will not take the "returning" course. Is she regretless? Certainly, though not without a sense of loss. If we say that Zhong Kui's last performance finally completes the scenario, bringing the (pseudo) male savior and the saved woman together visually, then it is interesting that the two figures face to face on screen are actually both women: the actress playing Qiuyun is Xu Shouli; and Pei Yanling, who performs all the Zhong Kui scenes, was in fact the model for Qiuyun. Once again, contrary to expectation, narrative completes the women's story, completes the expression of incompletable women.

Human, Woman, Demon is by no means a radical feminist film that derives pleasure in destruction. It recounts the story of a woman in what Zhang Ailing has called the Chinese style of simplicity and splendor, and this reveals the female predicament of being between the devil and the deep blue sea. In the ruptures and fissures of the metanarratives of the past, windows open up in walls to expose a world and a human life in the female perspective. Cinematically, the other's salvation of woman does not materialize, nor can it. Yet perhaps self-redemption for a woman lies in ripping apart historical discourse, to allow the real process of her memory to take shape.

Notes

1 See Charlotte Brontë's *Jane Eyre*. See also Sandra M. Gilbert and Susan Gubar, eds, *The Madwoman in the Attic: The Woman Writer and the Nineteenth-Century Literary Imagination* (New Haven, Conn.: Yale University Press, 1979). The Chinese version is *Nüquanzhuyi wenxue lilun* (Feminist literary theory), trans. Hu Min, Chen Caixia, and Lin Shuming (Changsha: Hunan wenyi chubanshe, 1989), pp.113–25.

2 *Beijie hongluo* (Unknotting the red bundle behind her back) is a well-known opera performed in various regional theatrical traditions. [Looking for an excuse to attack, an enemy of the Song sends them a bundle tied together with a series of impossibly complex buttons and knots, demanding that it be untied by someone behind their backs or they will invade. A minister is ordered by the emperor to find someone to fulfill the task, or his head will be chopped off. Unable to find anyone, his daughter finally comes forth to save his neck. Her name had never been officially registered because her father had wanted to spare her from being selected as a concubine for an immoral emperor. The daughter succeeds in unraveling the bundle and saving the empire, but in the process she gains a name and is selected as an imperial consort.—Trans.]

3 From Italo Calvino's *Invisible Cities*, cited and discussed in Teresa de Lauretis, *Alice Doesn't: Feminism, Semiotics, Cinema* (Bloomington, Ind.: Indiana University Press, 1984), pp. 12–56. Dai is clearly indebted to de Lauretis, who writes: "Calvino's text is thus an accurate representation of the paradoxical status of women in Western discourse: while culture originates from woman and is founded on the dream of her captivity, women are all but absent from history and cultural process" (p. 13). The Chinese translation is "Cong mengzhong nü tanqi" ("Opening the discussion with woman in a dream"), trans. Wang Xiaowen, in *Dangdai dianying* (Contemporary film), vol. 4, 1988, p.13.— Trans

4 Wang Anyi, *Jishi yu xugou – chuangzao shijie fangfa zhi yi zhong* (Documentation and fabrication: one way of creating the world) (Beijing: Renmin wenxue chubanshe, 1993). [This book is in the form of an autobiography that is at once factual and fictional.—Trans.]

5 See Zhao Liming, "Xu" (Preface) in Zhao, ed., *Zhongguo nüshu jicheng: yi zhong qite de nüxing wenzi ziliao zonghui* (Encyclopedia of Chinese women's writing: a compendium of materials on a unique form of women's writing) (Beijing: Qinghua daxue chubanshe, 1992), pp. 15–17. [Dai Jinhua relates here only one of the several legends about the origins of this writing system.—Trans.]

6 When her father is ill and unable to serve the emperor in his war against the invading barbarians, Hua Mulan disguises herself as a man and battles in his place

for twelve years. After the war has been won, she returns home and dons her female attire. See Julia Kristeva, *About Chinese Women* (New York: Marion Boyars, 1974), p. 93.

7 For related discussion, see Laura Mulvey, "Visual Pleasure and Narrative Cinema," *Narrative, Apparatus, Ideology: A Film Reader* (New York: Columbia University Press, 1986), pp. 198–209. [Dai Jinhua may have in mind Mulvey's discussion of psychoanalysis and its relevance to feminist criticism. The question for Mulvey is how to fight patriarchy "while still caught within the language of patriarchy. There is no way in which we can produce an alternative out of the blue, but we can begin to make a break by examining patriarchy with the tools it provides" (p. 199). For the Chinese text, see the translation by Zhou Chuanji in *Yingshi wenhua* (Visual Culture), vol. 1, 1988.—Trans.]

8 The prototype for the story comes from the real-life experiences of the female artist Pei Yanling (who performs Zhong Kui in the film). See Dai Jinhua and Mayfair Yang's interview with Huang Shuqin in *positions: east asia cultures critique*, vol. 3, no. 3, 1995. For the Chinese original, see "Zhuiwen ziwo" (Self-queries) in *Dianying yishu* (Cinematic art), vol. 5, 1993.

9 From notes taken at a lecture by the director Huang Shuqin at a conference organized by the film department at UCLA on 2 April 1995. Huang Shuqin said that she hoped her own films would express a female perspective, as if opening an east-facing window in a house that ordinarily only had windows facing north and south, revealing perhaps some different scenery.

10 The play *Fengyu guren lai* (A friend arrives in a storm), by the woman playwright Bai Xifeng, describes the choices made by a mother and daughter in their life experiences as women intellectuals and the conflict between their professions and loves. When the play was performed in Beijing in the early 1980s, it gave rise among audience members of both sexes to very heated reactions and one of its lines of dialogue ("woman is not the moon, and does not rely on the radiance of man's reflection to illuminate herself") became for a time a popular turn of phrase among urban women. In a certain sense, "A friend arrives in a storm" was a rather early self-conscious feminist expression of opposition in the post-Mao period. See *Bai Xifeng juzuo xuan* (Selected plays of Bai Xifeng) (Beijing: Zhongguo xiju chubanshe, 1988).

11 Freud's "primal scene" is the witnessing of or fantasy about parents copulating.

12 "Diegesis" is commonly used in film criticism to refer to the world created by a film's narrative.—Trans.

13 See the *yuefu* "Mulan shi" ("The ballad of Mulan"): "Ten thousand leagues she marched to the borderland, flying over mountains and through passes. War drums echoed through the bitter cold, the winter light shone on coats of mail. Great generals of many battles perish, foot soldiers return after years of battle. . . . I open the east gate and sit on my bed in the western chamber. I replace my martial attire with the garments of my former days. By the window I do my hair, before the mirror I place a yellow flower there. She went out and greeted her comrades,

who were all shocked, for they knew not the one with whom they had traveled for twelve years was the woman Mulan." From Shen Deqian, ed. *Gushi yuan* (Ancient poems) (Beijing: Zhonghua shuju, 1963), pp. 326–7.

14 A point of view (POV) shot is taken from the perspective of a particular character.—Trans.

15 *Sancha kou* (Three-forked road) is a famous Peking opera derived from the long *pingshu* narrative *Yang jia jiang* (Yang family generals). It recounts the story of General Yang Jianye of the Song dynasty leading his troops to Liao; because the rations don't make it to the front, he loses the battle and commits suicide. The Yang family sends a general to find out where Yang Jianye's body was buried. The general puts up for the night in a small inn in foreign territory. Xiao Er from the inn is a Song loyalist who mistakes the Song general for a foreign general, while the Song general mistakes Xiao Er for a Liao spy. As a result of this misunderstanding, they begin to fight each other. In the end, the misunderstanding is cleared up. This was originally a comic martial opera but was later performed as a serious martial opera.

16 As part of the movement of cultural reflection in the early and mid 1980s, roots literature and Fourth and Fifth Generation films often used the idiot as a metaphor for the ignorance of traditional Chinese culture or for the historical unconscious. The most typical of these are Han Shaogong's novella "Ba, ba, ba" ("Dad, dad, dad") and the Fifth Generation filmmaker Zhang Zeming's *Juexiang* (*Swan's Song*).

17 *Changban po* (Changban slope) is a well-known Peking opera derived from the classic novel *Sanguo yanyi* (Three kingdoms) by Luo Guanzhong. The story is about Zhao Yun, a great general under the command of Liu Bei, who as a youthful hero fought a bitter, solitary battle at Changban Slope against the great army of Cao Cao to protect Liu Bei's wife, Madame Mi, and their son, Ah Dou; hence, the famous act "Saving Ah Dou at Changban Slope."

18 In the film, Qiuyun performs Zhuge Liang and Guan Gong (Guan Yu) in the two famous Peking operas *Qunying hui* (A meeting of heroes) and *Huarong dao* (The Huarong road), respectively, both of which are derived from *Three Kingdoms*.

19 A famous martial piece from the Peking opera repertoire. The story takes its material from the classic Chinese novel, *Shuo Yue quan zhuan* (The biography of Yue Fei). The Southern Song general Yue Fei leads his troops to battle against the invading Jin army. The Jin obstruct them with an articulated armored vehicle (also called a pulley car, *hua che*). The Song general Gao Chong breaks through their formation alone and pushes over their pulley cars with his long spear; when he tries to push over the tenth one, his horse collapses and he is crushed to death by the pulley car.

20 Xiao En is a principal character in the famous Peking opera *Da yu sha jia* (Fisherman's revenge), which is derived from the classic Chinese novel *Shui hu hou zhuan* (The water margin revisited), one of the many sequels to *Shui hu zhuan* (The water margin). The story takes place after the heroes of Mount Liang Marsh have been given amnesty by the court. The former hero of the marsh, Xiao En, takes his

daughter home with him to earn his living as a fisherman, but corrupt officials press them with heavy taxes, leaving them no way out but to kill the officials and rebel again.

21 See the section on Zhong Kui (no. 49) in Ma Shutian, "Daojiao zhu shen" (Daoist gods), *Huaxia zhushen* (Gods of China) (Beijing: Yanshan chubanshe, 1990), pp. 265–79. The entry on Zhong Kui in Zong Li and Liu Qun, *Zhongguo minjian zhushen* (Chinese folk gods) (Shijiazhuang: Hebei renmin chubanshe, 1986), pp. 231–41, cites the Song dynasty writer Shen Kuo's *Mengxi bitan* and many other classical collections of anecdotes which recount the legend of the Tang artist Wu Daozi painting for the Tang emperor Xuanzang a picture of Zhong Kui catching ghosts. The legend has it that, upon returning to the palace from Li Mountain, the emperor falls ill and cannot be cured for a long time. One night he has a dream in which he sees two ghosts, one big, one small. The small ghost steals the imperial concubine Yang Guifei's purple perfume bag and the emperor's jade flute, circles the hall, and flees. The big ghost, wearing a hat and blue clothes (sometimes, he has a black face that is completely bearded, a tattered hat, and a blue gown), grabs the small ghost and first digs out its eyes, then splits him in half and swallows him. The emperor asks the big ghost who he is and he responds, "Zhong Kui." When the emperor awakens, he is cured; so he orders Wu Daozi to paint Zhong Kui as a door god.

22 In the film, Qiuyun hangs Zhong Kui's painted face in her home and pays no heed to her husband's and friends' opposition to her determination to perform Zhong Kui; she tells her child, "your mother wants to perform a most perfect man."

23 See chapter thirty-two (in which "Bao Yu demonstrates confusion of mind by making his declaration to the wrong person; and Golden shows an unconquerable spirit by ending her humiliation in death") of Cao Xueqin's *Hong lou meng* (Dream of the red chamber) (Beijing: Renmin wenxue chubanshe, 1957), pp. 331–2: "Upon hearing these words Daiyu didn't know whether to be happy, alarmed, regretful, or sorrowful. . . . Sorrowful because though there are things of burning importance to be said, without a father or a mother I have no one to say them for me." For an English translation, see *Story of the Stone*, 5 vols., trans. David Hawkes and John Minford (Harmondsworth: Penguin, 1977).

24 In ancient Chinese, a woman who lives with her husband's family is said to "return." To marry a woman off is also called "returning." In the "Nanshan" chapter of the "Guofeng" section of *Shijing* (*The Book of Odes*) there is a poem which reads in part: "The road to Lu is easy and broad, / For this lady from Qi on her wedding day (*gui*)." *Yijing* (The book of changes) contains the hexagram "*Guimei*" (Returning bride).

Translated by Kirk Denton

6

Redemption and Consumption: Depicting Culture in the 1990s

Cultural Mao Zedong

Of the social and cultural phenomena at the end of the 1980s and the beginning of the 1990s, the one that most caught people's attention had to have been "Mao Zedong fever." This undoubtedly marked the first appearance of the mutual coexistence of the ideological state apparatus and an emerging public space, two opposite entities that cannot but deconstruct each other through several coexisting but conflicting sociocultural symptoms: for instance, the reaffirmation but consumption of prohibitions; the reiteration of mainstream discourse but a voyeuristic desire to pry into political secrets. In other words, we could say that an interesting public space emerged as an informal forum for multiple discourses. In some sense, while Mao Zedong fever reached a peak in 1990 and declined somewhat thereafter, it continued uninterrupted until it achieved yet a new climax on a grand scale during the organized activities of the 1993 centenary commemorations. It is in just this specific public space that Mao Zedong fever, emerging from several centers via multiple media, actually constructed an inscription of the cultural Mao Zedong. This was a reconstruction and a parody, an employment and a consumption of ideology.

In fact, even though it was a classic method for employing mainstream discourse, the image of Mao Zedong appeared not only as simply the reproduction of classic revolutionary narrative, or as some may say "the national narrative" of the initial "traumatic circumstances" representing the nation-state, but also as a new narrative tactic, a retelling and reconstruction of the classic narrative discourse of divinity and revolution in the midst of deviation and dislocation. Such were the circumstances not only in the major revolutionary epics of the 1990s, also known to some as the main melody films – such as *Kaitian pidi* (*The Birth of New China*), *Da juezhan* (*Decisive Battles*), *Kaiguo dadian* (*Founding the Nation*), and *Chongqing tanpan* (*Negotiations in Chongqing*) – but also in numerous feature film and television mini-series featuring Mao Zedong as the main character and using biographical materials. In a certain sense, Mao Zedong fever, both as the narrative about the Great Leader, the narrative of revolutionary history, and as the symptom of an emergent public space arising from the social stratum of urban residents, was not a discursive system of mutually opposed conflicts, or the struggle and opposition among cultural and discursive powers between center and margin. The fact is that by the end of the 1980s, even before mainstream discourse and revolutionary canonical narrative returned to its reliance on Mao Zedong's image, a hint of Mao Zedong fever had already appeared within urban society.

In what seemed to be a new fashion or fad, portraits of Mao Zedong (and occasionally portraits of Zhou Enlai), which had been standard emblems of the divine, appeared as dangling decorations on the windshields of cars, vans, and taxis, replacing fuzzy toys, bottles of air freshener (which as something "foreign" supposedly created a Western atmosphere), and inverted lucky *daofu* pendants (the traditional talisman for a safe journey). Then the same illustrations were used to decorate leather beeper pouches, watch faces, and windproof lighters. This was quite in vogue for a time. However, this did not simply express some form of discontent or attitude of political protest, as some overseas commentators have claimed. Rather, in a certain sense, the promise of the fulfillment of the Four Modernizations at the end of the 1970s and the beginning of the 1980s had once again ushered in a Great Leap Forward or fervid, utopian expectation. And for the entire decade of the 1980s the hot-air balloon of optimism and idealism continued to rise with ever increasing speed. When the gulf between imagination and reality became obvious at the beginning of the 1990s, it undoubtedly brought with it strong disappointment and discontent; at the same time, the continuous public exposure of high-level corruption deepened this sense of loss and dissatisfaction.

Therefore, the onset and peak of Mao Zedong fever has indeed had political and real significance for the reiteration of canonical myth in the new social context. It signifies an imaginary redemption and a nostalgic return to the past. For it is simultaneously an important social and cultural symptom, revealing to people the state of mind of the society of mainland China during its transformation; a recollection, not without sincere feeling, of people's faith in authority before the onset of gradual pluralization and the evaporation of the center; a look back at an age of idealism, neither without cynicism nor without sentimentality, before the great tide of pragmatism and commerce, and the imminent victory of consumerism; a call to heroes and myths from the people in an age that "needed heroes"; and the last surge of lingering patriotism from a nation losing divinity and taboos, reluctant to part with a last symbol of the sacred and the untouchable. It now and again conveys in the process of rewriting a desire for redemptive memory. Or, more accurately, the popular swelling of Mao Zedong fever signifies the people's longing for a sense of trust and "security" in society, the memory of an age that, while not prosperous, still (at least in theory and imagination) neither knew hunger nor felt threatened.

However, what the majority of commentators either ignore or overlook is precisely the medium of Mao Zedong's image at the onset of Mao Zedong fever. Obviously, cars, beepers, and windproof lighters at the time were symbols of fashion, signifiers of consumerism. Therefore, it was more the revelation of a political unconscious than some kind of clearly conscious political behavior: the displacement and identification of political power with consumerism. Here, we are witnessing the trend of the consumption and normalization of ideology carried out in a form that was irreverent and profane, that dissolved the sacred and the untouchable.

By the end of the 1980s and the beginning of the 1990s, among thousands and tens of thousands of publications and audiovisual products, the hottest of hot topics was Quan Yanchi's book, *Zou xia shentan de Mao Zedong* (*Mao Zedong Off the Altar*), which was ostensibly the memoirs of Li Yinqiao, who for so many years followed Chairman Mao as the commander of his bodyguard. There were several other largely similar popular publications: *Zou xiang shentan de Mao Zedong* (*Mao Zedong Ascending the Altar*); *Hongqiang nei wai* (*Inside Beidaihe*); *Lingxiu lei* (*Tears of the Leader*); *Weishizhang tan Mao Zedong* (*The Commander of the Bodyguard Talks About Mao Zedong*). One hundred thousand copies of *Mao Zedong Off the Altar* were distributed for the first edition alone, and it continued as a best seller through subsequent editions over the next four or five years (and that's not counting, for the moment, pirate editions and revisions). What is interesting is that it was not only an outstanding best seller, but also in some senses sounded the keynote of Mao Zedong fever and constituted a set of observations for this important social and cultural phenomenon. And this work, which so many millions struggled to buy and wept over, actually became the most successful example in the change of mainstream discourse and discursive tactics, both intentionally and unintentionally.

"Off the altar" is literally what this bout of "Mao Zedong fever" signifies. If we follow the interpretation of Song Yifu and Zhang Zhanbin, who take the Mao Zedong fever of the 1950s as the beginning of the deification movement and the Mao Zedong fever of the 1960s as its frenzied pinnacle, then the Mao Zedong fever at the end of the 1980s and beginning of the 1990s was the process of narrating or renarrating a "de-apotheosis."[1] Even though previously there had been titles that took similar forms, such as *Gensui Mao Zhuxi changzheng* (*Following Chairman Mao on the Long March*), it was in *Mao Zedong Off the Altar* that descriptions of Mao's daily life appeared for the first time: we see him as a husband and a father, performing the normal activities of eating and drinking. Here, he is a great man, but one of flesh and blood, whose temperament and logic are informed by his emotions; a man who, because his spirit transcended ordinary people's, had to accept more and greater suffering; a man made so lonely by his greatness that he was even beyond help. Many of the great historical events of New China are therefore endowed in this book with individualized and personalized motives and explanations: he is the leader of myriads, yet still with all the feelings of an ordinary person.

People would thus revive and rewrite their sense of veneration for Mao Zedong in an entirely new mood of compassion and forgiveness generated by their experience of reading this book. As a result, *Mao Zedong Off the Altar* became required source reading for nearly all the contemporary historical large-scale revolutionary epics, biographical films, and television series on Mao Zedong, and nearly every film and television production of this kind had to contain situations and details taken from the book. In a narrative tone of emotiveness and individualization, which was handled in a relatively low key, the rewritten historical scenes repeatedly demanded of readers and audiences (the People?) a sense of understanding, forgiveness, and shared responsibility.

In a sense, *Mao Zedong Off the Altar* not only supplied many main melody films with new source materials, new narrative strategies, and a new tone and approach, it also became an indispensable reference for all those engaged in the subsequent boom of writing, publishing, and marketing best sellers on Mao Zedong. Books like *Mao Zedong zhuan* (*The Biography of Mao Zedong*), *Wo yan zhong de Mao Zedong* (*Mao Zedong in My Eyes*), *Shenghuo zhong de Mao Zedong* (*Mao Zedong in Life*), 1946–1976 *Mao Zedong shenghuo shilu* (*Chronicle of the Life of Mao Zedong, 1946–1976*), *Mao Zedong de ernü'men* (*Sons and Daughters of Mao Zedong*), *Mao Zedong yishi* (*Anecdotes of Mao Zedong*), *Mao Zedong yiwen lu* (*A Record of Anecdotes About Mao Zedong*), and *Zoujin Mao Zedong* (*Mao Zedong Up Close*) were all best sellers whose first editions sold anywhere from tens of thousands to hundreds of thousands of copies, filling bookstores and bookstalls in every major city. Simultaneously, along with Mao Zedong fever, the songs of the 1960s and its Cultural Revolution regained popularity, performed by popular singers with electronic accompaniment. Taking their theme from "I Cherish You, *Mao Zedong off the Altar*" (performed by Zhang Mi and Yang Zongqiang), audiovisual publishers throughout the nation published hundreds of audiocassettes and CDs with odes to Mao Zedong and songs of his quotations.[2] This music was truly popular and could be heard on cable broadcasts with classical trumpets, on the radio, and on television; in concerts of every description, in variety programs, in karaoke clubs and KTV booths; and even at home, thanks to the craze for home karaoke. At open-air dance floors, in expensive, elegant dance spots, for youth, it was a new and different fad, and for middle-aged and older people, it was a fond and familiar, personal memory that spanned forty years. When in 1993 the French pianist Richard Clayderman visited China and performed in Beijing at the Capital Stadium, filled to its capacity of tens of thousands, his pastiche style, a style of performance that was simultaneously both extremely elegant and comic, and his rendition of the exquisite, moving "Autumn Whisper," known throughout China, certainly drew an enthusiastic response from the youthful audience, but only when the melody of "Reddest of Suns, Mao Zedong Is Dearest to Me" was heard did the entire stadium truly erupt.

The dominant discourse of authority, in the process of narrating a "de-apotheosization" that centered on *Mao Zedong Off the Altar*, tried to conform, through new narrative strategies and tone, to "the time in which the myth is told [retold]".[3] Among news features on these burning issues, two hot topics that created a sensation revealed another significance that people had overlooked. One was the news feature that every entertainment and gossip publication vied to print and reprint about a certain actor whose particular appearance allowed him to specialize in portrayals of Mao and who was demanding high fees to appear on evening arts and literary shows and then cheating on his taxes.[4] The other was the subsequent report that the daughter of Li Jiefu, an important and famous composer of the 1960s and 1970s, was suing several audiovisual publishers for pirating Li's work and violating his copyright and right of acknowledgment. This case was decided in favor of the plaintiff and concluded with two of the companies publicly apologizing and paying damages. As a suit over copyright and right of acknowledgment to a cultural product that during the 1960s and 1970s had been a powerful instrument of political propaganda and ideology, this peeled away the inertial imagination and cognitive mode that held music to be the spiritual wealth commonly owned by society, and it laid bare the music's value as privately owned property.

These two news features revealed that behind Mao Zedong fever lurked the reality of a consumer culture and of cultural consumption. In a certain sense, from the first peak of Mao Zedong fever in 1990 to the present, this is a fact that was all too clear. The vulgar Mao Zedong badge, once taken by people as the product of ignorance and authoritarianism, now became a personal collector's item of great value and was also reproduced and sold. All sorts of "precious red books" of that era – *The Quotations of Chairman Mao*, the four-volumes-in-one pocket edition of Mao Zedong's *Selected Works*, and Mao's portrait – went for unheard-of prices in places frequented by foreign tourists and travelers. Cultural Revolution postage stamps were traded up in value by stamp collectors until they reached phenomenal prices. Even various kinds of mimeographed circulars from the Cultural Revolution were snapped up like rare valuables. If we say that the birth of Mao Zedong fever had its profound and pluralistic social, cultural, and psychological components, then its proliferation contained a relationship of supply and demand in the consumption of contemporary Chinese political exhibitionism and voyeurism.

It truly was a process of ideological production and reproduction, determining a consumer-culture fad with the most Chinese of characteristics. Mainstream discourse and consumer culture clashed with each other, relied on each other, mutually deconstructed each other, and constantly merged with each other. If we say that the process of "de-apotheosization" on which the mainstream narrative of the 1990s relied repeatedly tried to fashion a new cultural conformity by converting divinity, worship, and dread or loathing into understanding, compassion, and forgiveness, then the flaw in this strategy was that these feelings removed the last traces of divinity from the idol. If we say that "ruined temples are still shrines, toppled idols are still divinities," then the sensational Mao Zedong fever, which consumed prohibitions, memory, and ideology, also eliminated the canyon between "the loftiness of the palace" and "the vastness of the realm," between the transcendence of the divine and the mundane world of the urban residents. Perhaps it could be said that this is something special to mainland China: sunset and dawn overlapping each other, the conclusion and the beginning of yet another age.

The gala artistic performance held on 26 December 1993 by China Central Television at Mao Zedong's hometown, Shaoshan, to commemorate the one hundredth anniversary of his birth seems to be an interesting case in point. The first half of the performance was a series of odes to Mao Zedong from the 1960s and 1970s, sung by a grand chorus – majestic, powerful, manifesting again and again the magnificence and fascination of socialist choral art. Yet in a child's solo written especially for the occasion, the following lines appear: "I asked Mama, 'Who is he?' / Mama said: 'He is the clouds in the sky; / He is the lamp on the wall; / He is the brave old eagle in the mountains; / He is the busy bee.'" In the pluralistic yet shared writing of the Cultural Mao Zedong, a social and cultural transformation, an entirely new shift of power and change of direction, is taking place.

The Reappearance of the Original Picture

Among the many social and cultural phenomena in the consumption of memory and ideology, those unique products of the Cultural Revolution era – the community, culture, and writings of educated youth, and the transformations and shifts in the discourse about educated youth – form yet another rich set of symptoms in culture and the consumption of culture.

In one sense, the term *educated youth literature* that flourished in the mid and late 1980s does not just refer to a particular group of writers or a particular set of narrated events, but also to a narrative mode of multiple sutures, an extremely particular cultural space penetrated by a pluralistically determined discourse. It was unadorned confession and also a spiritual mask, an exhibition of wounds and a display of spiritual wealth. It was a written record of the special memories of a generation, whether expurgated, unadorned, or fictionalized. At the same time, it was "seeking roots," pursuing and questioning the sorrow and despair in the national cultural memory. It was a movement in which avant-garde literature occasionally participated, and it occupied a space that women's writing often entered. Like the movement for cultural reflection, it was actually the cultural extension of stillborn political reflection, its transformation into metaphor. Educated youth literature unquestionably continued, in the wake of the "literature of the wounded" and "reflection literature," to assume directly the ponderous and onerous memory of the politics of the Cultural Revolution/reality.

However, unlike the "literature of the wounded" and "reflection literature," the specially designated space of educated youth literature contains profoundly complex emotions and declarations. It is more like endlessly coiling memories and recollections than yet another accusation; more like a record of dreams and glory than penitence; more an inability either to resign itself or to control its own feelings than a deep reflection on history. Consequently, educated youth literature appears to be a special case, with a special license to link memories of the Cultural Revolution, the Red Guards Movement, and the rustication movement of educated youth "up to the mountains and down to the countryside" with mainstream ideology, forming subtle shifts and convergences. In fact, from "Lüye" ("Green Night") to "Da linmang" ("Forest Primeval"), from "Zhe shi yipian shenqi de tudi" ("This Is a Piece of Miraculous Earth") to *Jin muchang* (*Golden Pastures*) and even to "Maijie duo" ("Haystacks") and "Gang shang de shiji" ("A Century on Duty"), from first to last, educated youth literature, whether typical or less typical, had a basic tone: of remorse during one's youth (yet with no regrets for one's youth), of sorrow and pain, of high spirits or of guilty reflection, all of which were out of place with the unofficial post-revolutionary mainstream discourse, which thoroughly repudiated the Cultural Revolution.[5] However, educated youth literature could form such a special category, obtain such special license, precisely because it held on doggedly, passionately, and irrationally to a fervor for idealism and for a heroism that does not regret having suffered terrible wounds. Unquestionably, this is the spirit and the fundamental narrative tone that won (and today still wins) the strong approval of official mainstream ideology. In fact, as far as educated youth literature goes, it is less a refusal to purge the era of the Cultural Revolution than a refusal to purge the memories of the writers' own youth.

Milan Kundera described the cultural situation of Eastern Europe during the 1960s as one in which "a generation erased their own youth," but what happened in mainland China during the 1980s would seem to be the exact opposite.[6] To a generation of people who spent their youth during the ten years of the Cultural Revolution, slogans like "Make the Gang of Four Give Back Our Youth" sounded too glib, while "Subtract Ten Years from Our Age," tantamount to purging or negating their own extraordinary youth, was too cruel. If what the masses of the 1980s were longing for was a discourse that imagined an awakening from a nightmare to the morning, a farewell to what had suddenly become an unbearable memory of history, and a fantasy in which, while laughing heartily in order to forget, they consolidated a new beginning or new life; if the "literature of the wounded" that stirred up such an incessantly fervid reaction attempted, through fictive heroes and tender sentiments, to rescue the individual person from history; then what educated youth literature sought was to redeem the self from the calamity, the pillaging, the evil that was history: it was the memory of youth as substitute. Consequently, the writers tried with near desperation to rip away the memory of their youth from history and the discourse of history. Undoubtedly, it was all in vain. The intensity of a thoroughly scarred idealism unexpectedly caused the generation of educated youth and the literature of educated youth not only to converge with classic mainstream discourse, but also to echo the idealism of suffering of the 1950s generation. Yet, it was in just this process of stripping off, within the memory of youth – or rather in the process of redeeming for a generation the value of the self from despair – that the accounts of heroism and idealism gradually intruded into the discourse of individualism, even though constrained by the circumstances, the reality, and the terms of collectivism.

By the late 1980s, educated youth literature and the representation of educated youth became a field of pluralistic discourse in the course of its gradual dissemination into the cultural space crossed by multiple discourses. One faction finally entered mainstream discourse to become an important part of it. Another faction, in the increasingly apparent culture and reality of utilitarianism, became, on account of the dogged persistence of their faith and the purity and fragility of their idealism, the declarations of so-called losers and outcasts. The most extreme among these adopted a fanatical fervor for cultural heroism and, during constant encounters with and displacements of mainstream discourse, gradually became marginalized. In fact, during the decade of the 1980s, the generation that had thrown itself into the educated youth movement ("up to the hills and down to the countryside") through various channels (principally the restored university-entrance examination system), mounted the political and economic stage and gradually came to control Chinese society; and it was people of this generation who became the principal cadres and the core of elite culture during the 1980s. Here the discourse about the "Third Generation" and "Fourth Generation" constantly developed and proliferated, actually becoming something akin to the practice of legitimating ideology.[7]

A work of this period that was situated between fact and fiction, Lao Gui's *Xuese huanghun* (*Blood-Red Sunset*, 1987), unexpectedly became a sign of the break between the culture of the 1980s and that of the 1990s and at the same time constituted a floating bridge linking these newly separated shores. The narrative tone of the work (a biography approaching the style of a diary) and the identification of the narrator with the other characters, uniting them, gives *Blood-Red Sunset* a special characteristic that makes it seem a naked, severe, nearly savage original picture reappearing. Manifested in this reappearing picture of the years of the Cultural Revolution and educated youth are the jumbled substances and stuff specific to that discourse of idealism, as well as the cruelty and violence that by necessity it contains; the mauling of heroism and its failure to encounter reality; and the desperate resistance and struggle of individualism, but only for the sake of the approval of and admittance to the collective. One walks away, only to find oneself returning again and again to the entirely outrageous circumstances encountered by a generation. But all this appears openly, without concealment, only in a personal, individual memory that is unreflective or rather that refuses reflection and remorse. In a certain sense, this work, which appeared only after repeated delays, provided a master copy for many of the educated youth writings. It was like an original picture whose color had peeled away and then was made to reappear – the familiar, the gorgeous, the famed picture-scroll. It was obviously unlike the "literature of the wounded," "reflection literature," and "root-searching literature." It was only the discourse of an individual – merely a naked, or rather an utterly sincere, statement of idealistic purity and devout sincerity (unexpectedly completing the transformation from the social ideal of heroism to cultural heroism) – calling on the collective/society to give belated recognition to the heroic conduct of the individual who has endured humiliation and exile. It would seem to be the necessary compensation for the persistence and the insistence of some youthful feelings.

The "Value" of Memory

It is both interesting and important to note that when *Blood-Red Sunset* was most popular, going through one printing after another, what it aroused was not shock over the work's blind lack of reflectiveness, its refusal of remorse, or its fanaticism. Instead, a heat wave of powerful nostalgia and lingering affection was suddenly stirred up by the reappearance of an original picture. In fact, *Blood-Red Sunset* evoked the memory of a generation and its longing for "the rectification of the name" more directly than any of the previous educated youth writings or discourses on the "Third Generation" and the "Fourth Generation." Consequently, next to another impassioned scene at Tiananmen Square, and alongside the furor over the Exhibition of Modern Art, a large-scale display of illustrations and objects entitled My Soul Belongs to the Black Earth opened solemnly at the Museum of History, next to Tiananmen Square. It was a time and place that, not by coincidence, indicated plainly that a generation persisted in maintaining the memory and the record of its youth, when it had stubbornly and tortuously tried to enter the moment and the circuit of history. The same theme of refusing remorse – "no remorse for one's youth" – again and again resoundingly echoed the main melody of the "battle of the century," which was tragically moving and blindly carried to extremes. The subsequent reminiscences and songs about the black earth, the yellow earth, and the red earth, which continued throughout the 1980s and into the 1990s, and the large number of memoirs, reportage, and "historically faithful" writings on the educated youth movement following *Blood-Red Sunset* and the exhibition My Soul Belongs to the Black Earth created a new kind of best-selling book and best-selling author. Among those that attracted people's attention were *Da Caoyan qi shi lu* (*Revelations of the Grasslands*), *Zhongguo zhiqing chao* (*The Tide of Chinese Educated Youth*), *Zhongguo zhiqing buluo* (*The Tribe of Chinese Educated Youth*), *Fengchao dangluo 1955–1979 nian: Zhongguo zhishi qing nian shangshan xiaxiang yun dong shi* (*Through Storm and Stress: The History of the Chinese Educated Youth Movement*), and several dozen other titles.

As a new cultural symptom, from beginning to end there persisted in educated youth literature a profound debate and conflict between "youth unrepentant" – a memory of youth, a confirmation of self and history, an ideologically legalized practice promoted by the power of what was already deemed correct and socially dominant – and "the memory of blood and tears," the reflective, accusatory practices of elitist culture that placed doubt on history. Obviously, however, the latter was rapidly reduced to an inferior position, as the former was supported not merely by some form of mainstream discourse, but was also tacitly based on the macropolitical economy of utilitarianism and the economic and political power of those who adopted such a position. At the same time, converging with the main trend in the reportage literature of the late 1980s, educated youth literature responded to a special voyeuristic demand on the Chinese mainland for the disclosure of political secrets and thus became a harbinger of the consumerist culture that was about to erupt. However, it was the writers of the historical accusation form (or rather, the appropriators of the signs of that position) who successfully converted the history of educated youth into one of the best vehicles for violence and even sex. Accompanying this was a fad for educated youth returning to the countryside, which for a time surged until it nearly became a cult. It is evident that this was not a returning in the same sense as those recorded in *Nanfang de an* (*The Southern Coast*) or *Xinling shi* (*Spiritual History*),[8] but was more like a self-confirmation in the sense of revisiting home after one has left and become a success, or like the popularity of a new type of item on travel itineraries. Here, consumer culture repeatedly demonstrated its ability to adopt the ways of consumer ideology.

Nostalgia as a cultural symptom and a social fashion among educated youth and veterans of the rural commune teams, together with the reappearing memories of youth, was directly transformed, in the Beijing of the 1990s, into a mode of consumption and consumer fashion in the wave of consumer culture. Early in the 1990s, at various thriving locations in Beijing, there appeared middle- and high-priced taverns and restaurants with names like Black Earth, Sun Flower Village, and the Inn of the Former Rural Team Workers. The ingenious proprietors of these establishments set up several rural-style brick beds (*kang*), had the customers sit cross-legged on them, and served the sort of fare never before admitted to elegant establishments – potato-noodle pork stew, corn-flour cakes, cornmeal congee, "ants climbing a tree," and peppery "tiger food" – while of course including a wide variety of dishes from the exquisite and elegant northeastern--style cuisine. Even the plainest dishes from backwater counties had an impressive price. Opening nights at Black Earth, Sun Flower Village, and the others were lively, impressive events, and as jammed as a marketplace. These establishments not only created a new fad and new social meeting spots that were the height of popularity and fashion but, in the aftermath of the popularity of Shandong, Cantonese, and Sichuan food, they also actually established the reputation and popularity of northeastern food. A notice pasted up everywhere soliciting people to compose scrolls of antithetical couplets for the Inn of the Former Rural Team Workers read: "The ideal spot for the nostalgia and dreams of those who once worked in rural production teams."

When the former educated youth (or rather, the "successful" among them) found a meeting place for "nostalgia and dreams," what they got was no longer the reappearance of the original picture or the time of their memories, but signs that had been duplicated and sold, ceremony and flavor, a mode of consumption, and nothing more. A "memory" with the price clearly marked. There is an interesting display at the Black Earth restaurant, where they have set aside a wall for people who spent time in the Great Northern Wilderness of the northeast to stick up their calling cards. Certainly there are a lot of names from all walks of life, but the majority have positions and titles – chairman of the board, general manager, and so on – at numerous and as yet unfamiliar companies in trade, real estate, advertising, and so forth. Consequently, the historical memory of life on the black earth, which is not devoid of the inspirational, is juxtaposed with modern, urban modes of communication; the fervent, heartfelt experience of nostalgia and recollection, with realistic utilitarian goals; the imaginary return to a youth for which one has no regrets, with the display and authentication of being on the road of struggle/to success (for which money and consumption are the absolute and only standards): these elements are not without a postmodern significance, sutured or brought together in one pastiche. A new culture and reality of utilitarianism and consumerism has transcended even the transformation from the spirit of the Great Northern Wilderness to the miracle of tea in big bowls.[9]

Winning popularity throughout urban and rural China at this time, Li Chunbo's song "Xiaofang" appears to be an even more interesting example of the rise and development of a deep social and cultural shift. As a "post-educated-youth" song, the straightforward lyrics and simple tune of "Xiaofang" imitate and revise the educated-youth songs. Eliminating the fervor, the grief, and the despair of those years,

"Xiaofang" is easygoing but not insincere, simplistic perhaps but not without heartfelt sentiments. Obviously this is not the reappearance of an original picture, but more a matter of taste and consumption on the order of Black Earth and Sun Flower Village. Rather than any actual, painful memory, it is more accurately described as a sense of security, approaching even superiority and extravagance, that comes from being at some remove. However, what is more interesting is that this song, created with popularity/consumption in mind, actually was extremely popular nationwide for some time, but not for the reasons that its creators expected nor in the way that they expected.

The original intent was, through "a girl named Xiaofang," to enter the cult of consuming memory and look back on the years of one's youth from a position of security and superiority: "Thank you for the love you've given me. I'll never forget it in this life. Thank you for the tenderness you've shown me. It helped me through those years." But unexpectedly the people who were taken with the straightforward, simple, but genuine "Xiaofang," who were moved by the song's natural, young village girl with braids, turned out to be the peasants who were leaving their villages and flooding into the cities at the end of the 1980s and the beginning of the 1990s, along with a new generation of urbanites who had no more than an imaginary experience of rural China. It was among these newly arrived people who were on the margins of urban society and among these urban youth that "Xiaofang" received its greatest welcome. Easy-going recollections of distant days long gone were replaced by feelings that were being generated on the spot. The narration, which did not require any memories, and the traditional image of a young girl, together with a love affair of the sort that abounds in pop music, simultaneously gratified the cultural demands of the marginal populace of the cities and filled some unmet psychological need among urban youth. Then too the straightforward lyrics and the simple melody gave the song a distinctive flavor, which responded to the longings of somewhat cynical minds to recover naturalness and sincerity. No one thought of lyrics like "It helped me through those years" as having any specific reference.

Subsequently, another successful song by Li Chunbo, "A Letter Home," which was created for these specific consumer demands, no longer relied on memory or an imaginary pretext and was composed of common, even daily, circumstances, as in an ordinary letter home. Retaining not even the simplest rhyme scheme, in this instance Li directly employed the most commonplace language and formulas, such as "I send you best regards," so that for the urban workers and their kind, it evoked the immediate circumstances and sensations they had experienced, while to urban youth, what it conveyed was sarcastic, bored, and bold. No longer burdened by such transcendent aims as providing unsettling recollections, reflections, and the rectification of names, or "letting history inform the future," all that was left was the emergence and the construction of a new mental mood or state. Subsequently, Li Chunbo's songs and others, such as Ai Jing's "My 1997," formed an important new type of indigenous popular music: urban folksongs.[10] The city and consumption began to replace the consumption of ideology and memory, and their gradually familiar forms occupied the new cultural space. It was an era that died out as quickly as it was born. Again and again, in the forms of their consumption and entertainment, people deconstructed the prohibited and the sacred, consuming memory and ideology. A future that is no longer an unbearable burden must have lifted people's spirits, and the prospect that it will no longer be limited to the expression of official views is a relief. Yet does an era completely shorn of taboos and reverence present an optimistic picture? I still have only the authority and capacity to describe.

Notes

This essay first appeared in *positions: east asia cultures critique*, vol. 4, no. 1, 1991, and appears here by permission of Duke University Press.

1 Song Yifu and Zhang Zhanbin, *Zhongguo: Mao Zedong re* (China: Mao Zedong fever) (Datong: Beiyue wenyi chubanshe, 1991).

2 By March 1992 there were twelve audiocassette titles on Mao Zedong that were major best sellers. [The Chinese text lists the twelve titles and their publishers. —TRANS.]

3 American film theorist Brian Henderson comments on the meaning of narrative works: "Finally the operation of a myth . . . always has to do with the time in which the myth is told, not with the time that it tells of." See Brian Henderson, "The Searchers: An American Dilemma," in Bill Nichols, ed., *Movies and Methods: An Anthology* (Berkeley and Los Angeles: University of California Press, 1976), p. 434;

and Dai Jinhua, trans., "*Sousuozhe – yige Meiguo de kunjing*," *Dangdai dianying* (Contemporary film), no. 4, 1987, p. 68.

4 The actor referred to is Gu Yue, celebrated for his portrayals of Mao Zedong.—TRANS.

5 See Zhang Chengzhi, "Lüye" (Green night), *Shiyue* (October), no. 2, 1982; Zhang Chengzhi "Jin muchang" (Golden pastures), *Kunlun*, no. 2, 1987; Kong Jiesheng, "Da linmang" (Forest primeval), *Shiyue*, no. 6, 1986; Liang Xiaosheng, "Zhe shi yipian Shenqi de tudi" (This is a piece of miraculous earth), *Beifang wenxue* (Northern literature), no. 8, 1982; Tie Ning, "Maijie duo" (Haystacks), *Shouhuo* (Harvest), no. 5, 1986; Wang Anyi, "Gang shang de shiji" (A century on duty), *Zhongshan* (Bell mountain), no. 1, 1989.

6 Milan Kundera, *The Book of Laughter and Forgetting*, trans. Michael Henry Heim (Harmondsworth: Penguin Books, 1981). The novel begins by describing multiple acts of private and public "erasure" of the past in Czechoslovakia following the Soviet invasion in 1968.

7 The terms "Third Generation" and "Fourth Generation" appear in several late 1980s sources. The Third Generation refers to people who reached maturity between the late 1940s and the late 1950s; and the Fourth Generation, during the 1960s and the early 1970s. Alternatively, the Third Generation refers to those who were in university or senior middle school and joined the Red Guards at the outset of the Cultural Revolution; while the Fourth Generation refers to those who came of age as reeducated youth during the succeeding ten years.—TRANS.

8 Kong Jiesheng, *Nanfang de an* (The southern coast), *Shiyue* (October) no. 2, 1982; Zhang Chengzhi, *Xinling shi* (Spiritual history) (Guangzhou: Huacheng chubanshe, 1992). [These are accounts of how men's identities have been reshaped by living in remote locations of Hainan and southern Ningxia.—TRANS.]

9 During the 1980s a story was promulgated about a group of reeducated youths who returned to the city from a construction corps in the northeast and began selling large bowls of tea on the street for a few pennies, eventually moving up to large-scale enterprises.

10 Ai Jing's "My 1997" is another interesting example. Adopting an extremely colloquial language and folk style, it situates the recovery of Hong Kong in 1997, which is sometimes referred to as "the big deadline," within the realm of Ai Jing's own personal fortunes, so that it no longer appears as a historical moment: "Hurry up, 1997," merely so that "I can go to Hong Kong, too."

Translated by Edward Gunn

7

National Identity in the Hall of Mirrors

"Literature of the Chinese Diaspora" and Best Sellers

In the early 1990s a popular genre commonly called *liuxuesheng wenxue* (literature of the diaspora)[1] appeared quietly in the nascent Chinese book market.[2] Though it is but one of a host of trends in this vibrant new arena, literature of the diaspora is linked to other cultural media and phenomena. Consequently it forms an important chapter in the story of the globalizing Chinese cultural scene of the nineties.

This literary phenomenon appeared suddenly in the cultural arena during the transitional period of the eighties and nineties. It arrived in the form of works such as *Beijingren zai Niuyue* (*Beijinger in New York*), *Riben liuxue yiqianri* (*One Thousand Days of Study in Japan*), *Yue shi guxiang ming – zhongguo guniang zai dongjing* (*The Moon Is Brighter at Home – A Chinese Woman in Tokyo*), and so on.[3] These books rapidly flooded bookstalls,[4] where they were jumbled together with popular books on taboo subjects and ideological tomes. A phenomenon similar to diasporic trends in popular culture also began appearing in the realm of so-called high culture at about the same time. For instance, a new work by "highbrow" director Xie Jin, *Zuihou de guizu* (*The Last of the Nobility*), which hit theaters in 1990, clearly emerged from the social and cultural context of the late eighties;[5] one of its main selling points was the image of New York and the experience of the Chinese diaspora depicted as "America" on Chinese movie screens. Plays that reflected Chinese people's experience overseas made up the majority of those staged in Shanghai's vibrant experimental theaters, such as the Heihezi juchang (Blackbox Theater): *Liushou nüshi* (*The Woman Who Remained*); *Meiguo laide qizi*

(*Wife from America*); *Dongjing de yueliang* (*Tokyo Moon*); *Xifuhui* (*Joy Luck Club*). Similar plays were performed repeatedly and enthusiastically received. In 1992, a young film director, Hu Xueyang, adapted *The Woman Who Remained*. Though a disaster at the box office, the film is considered one of the works that thrust the "Sixth Generation" film-makers (*diliu dai*) into the spotlight, as *The Woman Who Remained* won an award at the International Film Festival in Egypt.

But what really created a sensation and set the trend was author Zhou Li's novel, written in the "documentary literature" style (*jishi wenxue*),[6] *Manhadun de zhongguo nüren* (*A Chinese Woman in Manhattan*).[7] The novel was eventually published by Beijing Press, but the first chapter, "Ups and Downs of the New York Markets," initially appeared in the January 1992 issue of the well-known literary magazine *Shiyue* (*October*). Almost immediately after hitting the newsstands, the July and August issues virtually took the whole country by storm. By January 1993 it had gone through four reprints and demand still far exceeded supply: sales topped 500,000 copies. Floods of pirated versions, in quantities virtually impossible to measure, had already appeared in places such as Beijing, Shanghai, and Shenyang. According to some reports, when the pirated versions are included, sales of this book surpassed one million copies just in 1993.[8] The sensational impact of *A Chinese Woman in Manhattan* makes it comparable to the earlier furore that had accompanied the TV airing of China's first large-scale proto–soap opera, "Kewang" ("Yearning").[9] As a result of the runaway success of *A Chinese Woman in Manhattan* not only did previously published books on similar subjects regain popular attention, but the event came to herald a new consumer demand that persists to the present and has necessitated the incessant publication of books on the same subject (some of which have also become best sellers). Other popular titles included: Zhang Xiaowu's *Wo zai meiguo dang lüshi* (*I Am a Lawyer in America*); Chen Yanni's *Gaosu ni yige zhen meiguo* (*I Will Tell You about a Real America*) and *Chen Yanni: Niuyue yishi – ta zai dayang bi'an* (*Chen Yanni: New York Consciousness – She's on the Other Side of the Great Ocean*); Yan Li's *Niuyue bushi tiantang* (*New York Is not a Paradise*); Cao Guilin's *Niuyue shangkong de yeiying* (*Night Orioles over New York Skies*) and *Toudu ke* (*The Stowaway*); and Tang Ying's novelistic *Wife from America*.[10] In 1996, among the eye-catching books appearing in bookstores and bookstalls were Qian Ning's *Liuxue*

Meiguo – yige shidai de gushi (*Studying Abroad in America – Stories of an Age*) and Chen Yanni's new work, *Zaoyu Meiguo – Chen Yanni caifang lu: wushige Zhongguoren de Meiguo jingli* (*Experience in America – Chen Yanni's Interviews: Fifty Chinese People's American Experience*).[11]

In late 1992, several of the Wang Shuo cohort, including big names in the film world like Feng Xiaogang and Zheng Xiaolong, adopted Cao Guilin's *Beijinger in New York* for a TV series under the same title. China Central Television (CCTV) funded the series through loans (to be repaid in the form of television commercials) from the Bank of China, and the production crew journeyed to the United States to film it.[12] This was an unprecedented move and, along with its creators' star status, made the production a hot topic in media reports from its inception. The series's chosen subject and meticulous production – unprecedented for television series at the time – created an immediate national sensation on airing. In its wake, TV series of inferior quality on similar topics, such as "Xin dalu" ("The New World") (1995) and "Shanghairen zai Dongjing" ("Shanghainese in Tokyo") (1996), appeared in a rapid succession. Interestingly, at the very moment when the thematic repertory of the historical struggles of the "new immigrants" – their "chronicles of blood and tears" – had played itself out, works like *Wo zai Meiguo dang mama* (*I Am a Mother in America*) and *Wo zai Meiguo de xinxi gaosu gonglu shang* (*I Am on America's Information Superhighway*)[13] replaced them as the classical mode of social narration or metanarrative, and served as the new favorite entry point for publishers' commercial maneuverings.[14] It was certainly not the attractiveness of the topics of "mothering" children or the Internet that established the market position of these books. Rather, their success must be traced to the alluring double identity of the subject-narrator, an "I" who is both Chinese and a member of the diaspora in America. The complex sociocultural symptoms lying behind the public's reception, selection, and consumption of these cultural products provide an ideal object of inquiry for cultural studies.[15]

Global Imaginary and China

Without a doubt, the success of *A Chinese Woman in Manhattan* and the trendy best sellers that followed it is linked to the Chinese dream of "going global" and to popular longing for the occident, a historical complex that asserted itself in the 1980s.

If it is true that in the transitional period of the seventies and eighties, national ecstasy at redemption from the Cultural Revolution era ebbed and Chinese people began the historical process of encountering and confronting the world, then, to a certain extent, this reencounter and confrontation was deeply shocking and traumatic. What constituted this common experience was not China's sudden exposure to the Western world's material civilization, but the sudden discovery, amidst a deep sense of loss, that China was not "the center of the world revolution" or "the heart of redness," and that Chinese people were not the chosen ones "shouldering the historical mission of liberating two-thirds of the world's suffering masses." Its status as a "Third World country" turned out to mean something more nuanced than had China's earlier view that it was leading the resistance many countries and peoples had waged against the "two superpowers." If the psychological experience of the Chinese (especially the intellectuals) during the seventies and eighties tells the story of China's skid from an imagined place at the center of the world to an anonymous one, then the mainstream discourse of the eighties reconstitutes China's centrality by looking toward the West (more specifically, toward the US) as the center and advocating a great Chinese march toward it (called "going global" and "knocking on the century's door").

This newly conceived world imaginary, while figuring the West as a marvelous golden shore lying just beyond the horizon, also gave rise to Chinese people's desire for the West, especially America. The cultural importation projects of the 1980s accomplished a great deal through their large-scale translations of Western works, which introduced the achievements of Western knowledge in all fields. I have mentioned elsewhere that in terms of cultural experience, 1980s China seemed as though it was wandering through an aquarium.[16] Even if the viewing subjects met eye to eye within and outside of the glass box, only the Chinese observer would continue to turn a desiring gaze on the fascinating piscine world, on the colorful and strange "foreign objects" that would continue nonchalantly swimming about, heedless of the anxious attention being focused on them from the other side of the glass. Despite grand terms like "cultural dialogue," "vision of humankind" and "sharing the wealth of human civilization," the Chinese cultural imaginary of the 1980s demonstrated a one-sided desire, transmitting a deep sense of anxiety about a national identity in crisis. Only hybrid subject positions, such as a Chinese woman living in America – a familiar figure found in the nineties' literature of the diaspora and the new immigrants' documentary literature[17] – could assuage, however vicariously, and gratify the Chinese desire for America; they also provided a new advertising icon called "the diamond combination" because of its many facets.[18]

To a certain extent, the unexpected selling point of these autobiographies, eyewitness accounts, and testimonials is the figure of the compatriot who bravely enters the West, the US, or another foreign country as a guide and provides an inside look at a marvelous world previously only visible from afar. The attraction of these works no doubt comes from the spatial position that the narrator occupies. That the narrator is in the West (America) means that he or she can obtain, or at least share, the space's cultural superiority, which bestows on the narrator a special discursive power. It is highly significant therefore that even though a small minority of the Chinese population joined the wave of outgoing migrants spreading across the world once the "nation's gates" opened in the early 1980s, what is now referred to as the literature of the diaspora was written exclusively by those traveling or residing in Europe, America, and Japan. Only in 1996 did the sole work *Jia dao hei feizhou* (*Married to Black Africa*) appear on the book market.[19]

Leaving aside narrative contents for the moment, the secret attractions of these works are legible through their cover designs. The skyscapes of Manhattan appear on the front and back covers of *A Chinese Woman in Manhattan*, despite the fact that a "Chinese woman" – Zhou Li, a first-person narrator – is the speaking subject, and the narrative continually magnifies the "I," reflecting it through multiple mirror images. Antithetically, though *Married to Black Africa* has "Black Africa" as its subject, a Chinese woman in native African dress and adornment appears on its cover. Even though both books are categorized as autobiography, the selling point of the former is Manhattan (America) and the latter, the individual. In other words, it is due to our desire, our longing for America that we read the story of

Manhattan: in contrast, the attraction of *Married to Black Africa* lies in the daring exploits of a woman who travels from the "civilized world" to the "uncivilized tribal village," a plot line redolent of San Mao's Sahara story.[20]

The market obviously played an extremely important role in the making of cultural phenomena like *A Chinese Woman in Manhattan* and the literature of the diaspora (in America). But I would not attribute the novel's successful sales to the publishers' conscious marketing efforts. It is perhaps more appropriate to say that the trend in best sellers configured the burgeoning Chinese popular culture and book market in a certain direction. The choice to publish such works was certainly due to market considerations. But there was little planning involved in the initial sales pitch. *A Chinese Woman in Manhattan* achieved its popularity in three phases: first, its publication and impact as an unexpected sensation; second, the media's participation in the promotion of the book, providing absolutely free advertisement for its publisher; and third, the contribution made by well-known literary critics, some awarding hymns of praise, others condemnation. But in their high-mindedness, they all engaged a work wholly incommensurate to the classical metadiscourse to which their own critical exercises necessarily resorted. This peculiar asymmetry created an advertising effect of its own. Most surprisingly, then, the third phase unfolded with a battle of words and lawsuits. Starting with a New York Chinese businessman's castigation of Zhou Li for "fabrication" and "slander," and Zhou Li's "denunciation" of the Chinese media, and culminating in trans-Pacific, newsworthy turmoil, these events pushed the consumer sales frenzy to a climax. Thereafter, similar promotional tactics served as a basic model for book marketing in the nineties.[21] Other milestones of the nineties publishing industry, such as *Feidu* (*Decadent City*, 1993) and the American best seller *The Bridges of Madison County* (translated as *Langqiao yimeng*, 1994–95) followed the same fortuitous path on their way to popularity.[22] Haphazard measures constituted an effective model that was continually reproduced artificially.

The sensational impact of the literature of the Chinese diaspora in America provides an insight into Chinese culture in transition during the eighties and nineties. A characteristic move in this regard has been the emergence of a mature popular culture, reproducing elite cultural texts and discourses but in distorted form, successfully transforming them into an ideology of everyday "common sense." Popular culture gradually overwhelmed elite culture in the 1980s, becoming an active agent in the construction of a new social imaginary. *A Chinese Woman in Manhattan*, for instance, seems actually to have validated the discursive yearning of the eighties elite for a global imaginary. Never mind that the novel and its generic ilk are nothing more than caricatures of the Chinese soliloquy, no more than faint and distorted echoes of the tenacious monologue so prevalent in the eighties. Chinese audiences seemed to find in these "voices from the Western world" the semblance of cultural "exchange," a long-awaited "response" to their indefatigable beckoning to the West. Extremely successful examples of contemporary popular culture such as *A Chinese Woman in Manhattan* and the television series *Beijinger in New York* certainly rewrote and reinforced the Chinese complex; more importantly they also succeeded in integrating this complex into the very structures of the imaginary and its common knowledge. In a seminar I organized on Chinese popular culture in 1996 my students presented an interesting object for scrutiny: a brand of chewing gum called Five Pagoda, which is a traditional commoners' snack. On the two-tone gum wrapper, adjacent to an image of a young woman (shot in the style of the Western portraits of the early 1900s) is an advertising caption that reads: "When I am in Manhattan, I never forget the flowing creek of the Five Pagoda bridge. Perhaps this fragrant chewing gum will remain with me throughout coy maidenhood."[23] Leaving aside the tone of this little advertisement, its message is clear: in China, Manhattan is now the ultimate symbol of America and the West, themselves symbols of wealth and success. And everyone of all ages and both sexes knows it.

Yet the yearning to "go global," the "desire for the West," even the "America complex" cannot adequately lay bare the full range of sociocultural symptoms these best sellers display for us. In reality, the severe tremors that rippled through Chinese society at the close of the 1980s abruptly proclaimed the bankruptcy of the social policies that the elite intellectual world had helped construct. The expected great advance of the marginal towards the center consequently suffered great setbacks. The new trauma meant that the torn imaginary map of

China's relation to the world now required mending. Disheartened, in an anxious state, the masses sought a tempered, comforting image for reaffirming "China" and the Chinese imaginary in a global context. At this level, *A Chinese Woman in Manhattan, Beijinger in New York* (both the original novel and its TV adaptation), and similar works owed their popularity not merely to their display of the marvels of America, but more importantly to their efficiency in establishing, constructing, and confirming the Chinese people's and even China's world image within the ideology of the everyday life. Recounting the success stories of Chinese immigrants in America effectively created a new China-centric imaginary refracted through the image of Chinese people actually making it in the West. This new vision authorizes Zhou Li to dedicate her "autobiography" to "my fatherland and the people who find their own self-worth in times of adversity." "When my American customers addressed me as 'Manhattan's Chinese lady,'" she writes in her defensive, poignant text, "what interested me most was the part about China." Zhou repeatedly insists that she writes "for the patriotic spirit of noble struggle and passion." This is a clear allusion to a certain elite intellectual's witticism in which "a Chinese woman in Manhattan is, in a critical mode à la Cultural Revolution, 'busy' planting the Red flag on Manhattan."[24] The sensational TV series "Beijinger in New York" thus opens with the scintillating night scenery of Manhattan and ends with the protagonist Wang Qiming sitting in a luxury car, raising his middle finger towards the world out there – America.

In a preface Zhou Li wrote for *A Chinese Woman in Manhattan*, Zhou draws on highly emotional language (which I find nauseating) to explain her initial motives for writing this autobiography: she describes herself walking on Park Avenue,

> the symbol of American style and luxury, the generosity and majesty of the golden empire. A question that had often crossed my mind appeared again. Why is it that young women, whom the gods favored with seductive beauty, their necks draped in gold, visages set with haughty disdain, women born and raised here, why is it that in their country, America, these women can only find low-paying jobs as secretaries, answering phones, or working as salesladies, running errands?

Then Zhou Li employs a transitional phrase typical of her writing:

> But I: but I, on the other hand, a girl from a foreign country hustled into America in the summer of 1985 as a self-supporting overseas student, despite having no relatives, having to work as a nanny for an American family and wait on tables in a Chinese restaurant, was within the short span of four years able to achieve the success that even the angelic American women envy. I created my own company. I am managing import-export trade to the tune of tens of millions of dollars. I have my own apartment right near Central Park, and can take a vacation to Europe without a second thought.

Zhou does not limit herself to these examples, but continues:

> Who would have thought that one day I would sit in the oval office of City Hall, a building in the style of an eighteenth-century European palace, chatting with the mayor of New York? Or that I would be mingling with the socialites and wealthy businessmen at a festive Christmas banquet? Is it luck or fate, or some other force, that enables a foreign woman to stand her ground in this competitive country, America?[25]

After reading the whole book, the answer seems obvious: it is Zhou Li's own tenacious will power and extraordinary talents. Yet China itself, the China of Zhou's girlhood, and even the suffering people of China have created "superwomen" such as Zhou Li and made them what they are.

An interesting and unacknowledged symptom of all this is Zhou Li's failure to question the "racial superiority" of blond, blue-eyed people. Egregiously, she characterizes these "white-skinned, blue-eyed" individuals – or "those who seem to speak a precisely enunciated American English from birth" – as "those whom the gods have favored with all kinds of superior qualities." She makes equally clear her disdain for a certain kind of compatriot (Chinese in America). But her hardest sell concerns how "they" (Americans), the "angelic" ones, people who may be "graced with silver hair" or "wearing Western dress and shoes," are "looking at me with smiles and expectations." "They, because they are my American subordinates, do whatever I tell them to do, treat me respectfully, and listen carefully to everything I say, lest they lose their

jobs."[26] Though of a race that is now out of favor with a blond and
blue-eyed god, a person who could so thoroughly have conquered
must have been superior even to the superior race. This is a dubious
but nevertheless resounding theory of China's superiority and the victory of the Chinese.

In the television series "Beijinger in New York," a perhaps even
more complex, interesting symptom is manifested in one of the story's
recurring scenes. The male protagonist starts off in a basement apartment in Manhattan, then moves to the poor section of New York's
Chinatown. He finally winds up in a luxurious villa in a wealthy area of
Long Island. Interspersed with the story, forming part of the narrative
rhythm, there is a scene in which Wang Qiming gazes at a black street
drummer; come winter or summer, the drummer is unchanged. It
seems to be a typical New York street scene, as it rematerializes at turning points in the plot. But as a static spatial image, it serves as a
contrast to the protagonist's unwavering march toward success, a path
strewn with painful and distressing experiences from which he will
emerge victorious.[27] This scene has subtle racial implications: on the
hierarchical, progressively descending staircase of a "rationalized"
racial ranking, the Chinese are positioned between the American masters – the whites – and those on the social margin in white America –
the blacks.

In the early nineties, official youth and women's publications, which
served as effective media of mainstream ideology, kicked off a swift
and successful process of commercialization. Two types of editorials –
regular columns and occasional features – began to appear in these
publications, supplementing one another. The former bore titles such
as "Huangqiu huaren" ("Chinese around the World") and "Yuwai
huaren" ("Chinese on Alien Terrain"); the latter, titles like "Waiguoren
zai Zhongguo" ("Foreigners in China"). The columns reporting on the
Chinese overseas are full of Zhou Li–style miraculous success stories;
the accounts of foreigners in China happily recount stories about how
foreigners, especially Europeans and Americans, are transported by
Chinese culture, settle in China, and passionately love it. If we take
these two kinds of columns as two battlefields, then China wins on
both fronts. An article that made my blood run cold described the
reaction of an ordinary female worker who, seeing an Indian guard,

"said emotionally: 'finally, for once, the foreigners can serve us!'"[28] Here not only do we see ignorance about history, since, Indian guards, condescendingly referred to as *hongtou ahsan* (red-headed idiots), were often employed in Asian colonies and old Shanghai; but also the sort of racial prejudice commonly harbored. At the same time, as if serving as a balance or supplement to *A Chinese Woman in Manhattan* or *Beijinger in New York*, special reports and television series such as "Yangniu zai Beijing" ("Western Woman in Beijing"), "Zhongguo de yang nüxu" ("China's Western Son-in-law"), and "Miyue xinniang" ("Honeymoon Bride") also appeared on the Central and Beijing television stations. With the help of the market and the media, the Sinocentric imagination is again being gradually established as a part of the ideology of everyday life. This, no doubt, is but one of the indispensable strategies of the nativization of national culture in the process of globalization.

Transformation and the Cultural Floating Bridge

If we consider as a turning point Deng Xiaoping's speeches during his visit to South China in 1992 and 1993, Chinese society has indeed realized a cultural transformation that has many implications at every social level. The result is well known: popular culture has surmounted high culture and infiltrated mainstream social culture. It is the process of this transformation that interests me, as it reveals the important supporting and constructive roles that popular culture is playing in the formation of a new mainstream culture.

A pressing sociocultural demand for new and effective means of consoling a public on the rebound from the historical trauma of 1989 was visible beginning in the early 1990s. As early as 1991, undercurrents had already silently appeared in what became known as the secularization of culture (*wenhua shisuhua*) or the popularization of culture (*pingminhua*). Secularization involved things like "eschewing all [. . .] ideals (of any kind)," "discounting loftiness," as well as "affirming and embracing a this-worldly vision of 'today'" and the market. Rather than interpreting these cultural undercurrents in the light of postmodern culture's grand act of bridging the gap between high (*ya*) culture and popular (*su*) culture, or looking upon their appearance as testimony of a thorough purge of elite culture, it is more accurate to say that besides forming a necessary component of the commercialization of culture, popular culture was a choice (for lack of better alternatives) that a contemporary society (including its elite intellectuals) made in the face of the traumatic end of the eighties. We needed more than one parachute to bring people down off the heights where the 1980s hot-air balloon of optimism had taken them and land them safely on the ground level of reality. The best sellers and television series of the literature of the diaspora in America emerged as important supporting actresses right in the midst of this drama. It is evident that under the big proscenium arch of diasporic literature various modes of writing exist through which diverse cultural wishes are articulated. At this level, what Zhou Li did is not typical.

To some degree, the main theme of the literature of the diaspora of the nineties is "I'll tell you about the real America." And the real content of this message is that "New York (or America) is not a paradise." Cao Guilin's *Beijinger in New York* begins with the narrator's accounting of the "internal injuries" (*neishang*) he has suffered in the American dreamland. He gives a forced smile when friends back in China address him as a "foreign businessman" and envy his success. What he wants to recount are precisely those internal bitter feelings.[29] And so, coincidentally, echoing the cooling down of the emigration trends in the early nineties, the literature of the diaspora writes not only about the history of the new immigrant's struggle, but also about blood and tears, sadness and bitterness.[30] As a necessary step in the cultural parachutes' safe landing – their recognition that "America is not a paradise" – Chinese people may also come to understand that "China is not hell." It does provide an ethnocentric, China-centric view of the "real America" as a harsh reality that the new immigrants must face. By comparison it also provides a sense of relief and comfort to those who have not reached the distant golden shore and who lead lives that are far from ideal. Needless to say, though the narrator of *Beijinger in New York* felt hardship and adversity and suffered "internal injuries," China itself acquires the glory and honor attached to his success. This is compounded by the idea that, in New York, the nameless masses struggle and plummet to the bottom of American society. The individual who achieves abrupt fame and sudden wealth there is thus a person with a name, who has a story deserving detailed narration. Thus, this tale of the "real America" is clearly not the real America of the Americans, but the real condition of the new mainland immigrants. If the literature of the diaspora in America is a functional parachute, providing an escape route from the Chinese American dream, it also helps confirm its existence. Because, in narrating the cost and sacrifices paid for this dream, the story acknowledges the philosophy that resounded throughout the nineties, a philosophy of the powerful: "Survive in competition and natural selection, this is the survival of the fittest."

In making and participating in the logic of the cultural transformation at the turn of the 1990s, this repertory of best sellers, especially *A Chinese Woman in Manhattan*, unexpectedly served as a cultural floating bridge suturing a broken age. Yet even within the genre called documentary literature, the author uses a formula: the first chapter of *A Chinese Woman in Manhattan*, "Business Scenes in New York," leads to a linear progression that moves from "Childhood" to "Young Woman's First Love," "A Small Hut in the Northern Wilderness," "Studying Overseas in America – Meeting a Blue-eyed European Guy," and finally "Manhattan's Chinese Lady." This is a stock autobiographic device: a reexamination of the past from the pinnacle of one's career. The use of this device, however, consciously or unconsciously enacts a highly effective status-building strategy. In the beginning of this autobiographical novel, Zhou Li appears as a successful achiever whose stature has been established and substantiated quantitatively by money. If an important part of the social transformation of the nineties lies in the economic resurgence's programmatic replacement of political and cultural salvation, and if the accompanying social disorder further reinforces "money as truth", which in turn intensifies the popular worship of Mammon, then no doubt Zhou Li's case is quite typical. She achieves status and discursive power because she has panned the biggest gold nugget. What interests me is that while Zhou Li uses America as a mirror to reflect her successful and "golden" image, she also uses her newly acquired power to generate yet another image: she mirrors the elite intellectual who occupied the mainstream position in eighties culture, a height that otherwise Zhou Li could never have reached. Her consequently elevated position grants her the right to comment on the lives and deeds of other Chinese immigrants in America.

The three chapters "Childhood," "First Love," and "Northern Wilderness" are a melange of various nineteenth-century European and American, literary archetypes; they can also be seen as a narcissistic replication of the "literature of the wounded" and educated youth literature, literary genres popular in the early and mid 1980s. But if this form of expression has been inflated by a transaction common to the nineties, in which money buys cultural status, then Zhou Li's narrative has reversed the means and the end. For Zhou Li's superhuman character was actually fostered by her childhood, her youth, the hardships, losses, and deprivation she suffered in China. In her narrative, therefore, not only does she repair the disjuncture of the eighties and nineties, she also attempts the even more difficult task of establishing "outer-space linkages." By that I mean she is using her "autobiography" to suture the discourses of the worship of lucre to the elite culture's passionate idealism, patriotism, and revolutionary heroism.[31] In Zhou Li's account her years in China gave her spiritual wealth. What she is accomplishing now is nothing but a conversion of spiritual wealth into money. This is a recycled truism any Chinese reader or, perhaps more accurately, any middle-aged reader knows intimately: we are poor but wealthy people, because we possess a spiritual gold mine; moreover, we can transform spiritual into material wealth. If one agrees that *A Chinese Woman in Manhattan* attracts, even "misguides,"[32] its young readers with its captivating dreams of America, these mature and intimate narrative methods are what mesmerize and move middle-aged and older readers. They strike a chord particularly with those who are floundering in the money-grabbing frenzy, the rampant commercialization that descended abruptly on Chinese society. According to Zhou Li's logic, rather than displaying individual success, one should testify to the intellectual and spiritual wealth of Chinese contemporaries.

Obviously, Zhou Li does not materialize before us because she possesses intellectual and spiritual wealth; her emergence on the cultural horizon of China in the nineties should be seen as a timely response to a historic opportunity. Her chaotic, hybrid discourse creates a cultural floating bridge, which, while comforting those who are panic-stricken at the sudden, rapid cultural transformation, also brings them, in an act of imagination, safely across the chasms to the other shore. This reconfirms my point. What emerges from an epochal and cultural cataclysm is not a completely new structure, but an ugly cultural ruin which is occasionally haunted by a crippled ghost from the past.

The "American" Dream, Race, and Class

Similar narratives in the early nineties show us a hall of mirrors. Though all the discourses and images in this hall reflect one another and all seem alluring, in the end (at least on the level of social reception) each of them was produced to reflect back the image of what Eugene O'Neill calls that "demi-god of materialism – the successful person." Images and discourses from various periods, different contexts, all are mustered out to adorn the "golden saint." The parachute of popular culture brings us down to the plane of reality. But this floating cultural bridge edges us toward a materialistic, money-grabbing, commercial society. To a degree, then, the epochal project of the popular literature of the diaspora in America and related television series is nothing other than the legitimation of a new ideology. It provides both a means of articulating our national identity and a personal, imaginary solution to the onslaught of globalization and systemic transformation in what feels like an abrupt and commercial social transformation.

At the height of *A Chinese Woman in Manhattan*'s popularity, some critics had already started calling it the salesman of the American dream.[33] Indeed this is the old American dream. Backing the miraculous success of the prospector for gold is that imaginary "American" logic which holds that opportunity belongs to each and every person with a vision and the ability to struggle: if there's a will, there's a way. The dedication of *A Chinese Woman in Manhattan* to "those who find their self-worth in times of adversity" is an inelegant version of the discourse of humanism and, at the same time, an old Hollywood formula. The critic Yang Ping also referred to the "dream of an epoch," an identification which has yet to be elaborated, but which points, perhaps, to an even more crucial interpretation. In reality the conditions of the "new immigrants" on the American continent actually magnify while at the same time displace the real circumstances of the Chinese public in the nineties: the identity anxieties resulting from globalization and social transformation; the difficulty of survival in the face of commercialization; the inflation of desire; and the compression of material space. "America" – the America of Chinese popular imagination – has been transplanted, creating an appropriate space that provides an imaginary solution to the Chinese dilemma. This America is a thoroughly capitalist world in hot pursuit of money and material comfort; its myths are not supposed to resonate with any particular ideological implications. However, a different American dream does appear in the eighties' epochal discourse: in this dream, America possesses a healthy and rational system; in this America, everyone is equal and there is fair competition. This tale not only supports the successful, it unsympathetically banishes those who did not make it. In the midst of such equal and fair competition, in America, the land of the "new continent," there is no historical or social recourse; one must take full responsibility for one's own failure.

Although these sorts of narratives about the American dream could be read as the specific discursive construction of certain "individuals," in the contemporary Chinese context they are returned, without a doubt, to a discourse about class. The successful get money. On the wings of money the successful ascend to the upper reaches of society, while those who have failed tortuously spiral downward into the lower echelons. To a China facing the increasing disparity between rich and poor, the reconstruction of the discourse of class and the discussion of the legitimacy of the existence of class have become important and thorny sociocultural issues in the nineties. If the "individual" is the appropriate medium for establishing new class narratives, "race" appears to be an even more effective medium of popular culture. But to what purpose and for whose benefit? Employing the discourse of race to cover up or to underscore the reality of class constitutes a major thematic of culture in the nineties, as playing the race card is a basic strategy the media and popular culture have inadvertently adopted. Zhou Li's preface, which I discussed earlier, propagates not the idea of racial victory, but rather, and in an unabashed manner, the issue of class superiority.

Beijinger in New York displayed a similar symptom in an even richer and more complex form. The reasons for this complexity may lie in the scriptwriters' and directors' nativist identity and experience; the on-site production process – in itself a novel American experience – and the fact that the producers were more intimately familiar with Chinese popular culture may also have been factors. One of the more amusing scenes in the series finds the protagonist Wang Qiming looking into his sweater factory's empty production room and giving his imaginary employees a lecture on "justified exploitation." This activity certainly exposes the real intent of such work; it also satirically highlights the great disparity between the two types of ideological consciousness alive in China, rendering comedic the inner sense of bewilderment, discontentment, and insecurity endured by the Chinese public. Thus when his daughter, enthralled by American youth culture, turns her back on Wang Qiming and calls him a "stinking capitalist," the audience is delighted and amused.

Beijinger in New York is a more typical "rich man, poor man" story than *A Chinese Woman in Manhattan*. We follow Wang Qiming's fulfillment of the American dream. But we also see, and not without a twinge of self-satisfaction, that the same man who lives in the wealthy suburb of Long Island also winds up very much alone, his family shattered. We are allowed to share in this daydream, this American dream, despite Wang Qiming's ups-and-downs, and with this sharing we begin to accept and approve the new social reality in China, the new Chinese order.

A perhaps even more profound example of this ideological maneuver appeared in 1996 "amid the fervent voices of China saying 'No.'"[34] First came media reports of Chinese worker Sun Tianshuai's refusal to kneel in front of his female Korean boss (all media reports make clear the boss's nationality and sex) and his resolute resignation. In the language of the initial media narratives, Sun Tianshuai appeared to play the character of a national hero; subsequent reports amused readers with the information that an exception had been made for Sun Tianshuai at Zhengzhou University, where he had been subsequently accepted as an undergraduate majoring in international business and management.[35] This is transparently an example of class conflict, which is packaged as a racial confrontation in nothing less than an ideological strategy adopted by official government channels. One of the most interesting symptoms of the Chinese public's cultural receptivity in the nineties, despite or in spite of its increasing anxiety over real, emergent gaps separating the rich and the poor, is its refusal to consider anything related to the topic of class. The familiar discourse of class would certainly lead them back into memories of the not-too-distant past, which might signal a "regression" they would refuse without a second thought. Racial narratives and discourses must bear the burden of the public's willingness to make manifest a preference to hide, question, or legitimize a classed society. Thus the repackaged American dream, as a national fantasy, forms the indispensable core of Chinese reality.

A final description of culture. In the midst of *A Chinese Woman in Manhattan*'s popularity, some critics were decrying the "absence of criticism."[36] To my way of thinking, what has been absented is not literary criticism of popular culture, but the actions of intellectuals themselves from the arena of social critique. Facing the captivating scenery of globalization and the hall of mirrors that forms popular culture's representations, we find that nativization, cultural resistance and submission, the ending and strengthening of ideology, the crisis and affirmation of national identity may all occur on different levels and develop in various directions. In the midst of all this, the basic premise of the intellectual's cultural practice must be the preservation and maintenance of an enlightened and not totally simple critical posture.

Notes

1 The Chinese term *liuxuesheng wenxue* literally translated means "overseas students' literature." "Overseas students" is a blanket term covering everyone of an ambiguously mainland Chinese identity who goes abroad: students, visitors, business people, even illegal stowaways. They are named "overseas students" because this used to be the only legal status for the Chinese leaving the country and entering the United States. The English term *diaspora* is truly a more appropriate translation for this broad category.—TRANS.

2 This is very different from the earlier samples of the literature of the diaspora that began in the eighties. In the eighties, this term referred to works such as Zha

Jianying's *Dao Meiguo qu* (Going to America) and *Conglin xiade binghe* (The cold river in the forest) and the overseas writings of Liu Suola, You You, Yan Geling, and Hong Ying. These novels, which are set in Europe and America are more often than not written in Chinese – I have not included works published in English, which in my opinion belong to the realm of Asian American literature. They were published simultaneously in China and overseas, and became a branch of contemporary Chinese literature. Because a majority of these authors are women, they have also become an important branch of contemporary Chinese women's literature. Though the theme of the "marvels of the West" was also integral to these works, they were written and read primarily as literary works. In contrast, later works that make up the nineties trend of best sellers of the literature of the diaspora genre emphasize their "documentary" or nonfictional nature as a major selling point. Readers do not read them as literature. That is, the genre called literature points to the ambiguous category and position of publications which lie between fiction and nonfiction. Yet these works, especially the best sellers among them, all appear in the form of autobiography or personal testimonies and have made a major appeal to the reading public. Because of the ambiguity attached to the truth value of their alleged nonfictional status, however, the literature of the diaspora is often classified as literature.

3 Cao Guilin, *Beijingren zai Niuyue* (Beijinger in New York) (Beijing: Wenlian chuban gongsi, 1991); Xiao Cao, *Riben liuxue yiqianri* (One thousand days of study in Japan) (Beijing: Shijie zhishi chubanshe, 1987); and Li Huixin, *Yue shi guxiang ming – Zhongguo guniang zai dongjing* (The moon is brighter at home) (Beijing: Beijing chubanshe, 1989).

4 Bookstalls are a non-standard but vibrant method of popular bookselling that appeared after the mid eighties. They began in small and medium-sized cities, and gradually spread throughout the whole country. Similar, independently managed bookstalls gradually came under the control of independent book merchants who possessed substantial capital and became a huge, countrywide network of book distributors. In the nineties, this "secondary channel" of book distribution almost took over the "main channel" system controlled by the national Xinhua bookstores. According to distributors, the appearance of a book in the bookstalls of the large and mid-sized cities implies that it has at least an initial print run of 30,000 and the potential to gain even wider circulation later.

5 Adapted from the Taiwanese writer Bai Xianyong's short story, "Zhe xianren." Xie Jin, *Zuihou de guizu* (The last of the nobility), 1989.

6 The term *documentary literature* also points to the ambiguous positions of similar works. Like the reportage fiction that reached the height of its popularity in the eighties, the main attraction of documentary literature lies between reality (documentary, reportage) and literature (novel, fiction). The qualifier *documentary* meant that the materials in these works were based for the most part on real people, real events, while the term *literature* implied that their narrative and linguistic styles were no different from those of fictional works. For example, *A Chinese Woman in Manhattan* has been read as Zhou Li's autobiography: "nobody had ever

doubted its reality." See Xiao Yin's "'Kua yang' caifang zhaji" (Interviews across the ocean), in Xiao Yin et al., eds, *Kuayue dayangde gong'an – Manhadun de Zhongguo nüren zhengyi shilu* (Beijing: Guangming ribao chubanshe, 1993), p. 17. But once its nonfictional status is questioned, "literature" becomes its line of defense. Interestingly, this book has also been read as a collection of lies rather than as fiction.

7 Zhou Li, *Manhadun de Zhongguo nüren* (A Chinese woman in Manhattan) (Beijing: Beijing chubanshe, 1992).

8 Regarding the sales of this book in the beginning of 1993, different media reported different numbers: some said over 300,000; others, over 400,000 and 500,000. Of these numbers, 500,000 comes up the most often, but is perhaps somewhat exaggerated. But what can be verified is that this book had the largest sales and orders in the nation's fifth-largest book market; it was also first in the category of the ten books most beloved by readers (literature and the arts). Pirated versions appeared in many parts of the country. See Xiao Yin et al., eds, *Kuayue dayangde gong'an – Manhadun de Zhongguo nüren zhengyi shilu*. The estimate of one million, including pirated versions, came from the Words of the Editor section of this book.

9 Engineered by Wang Shuo, Zheng Wanlong, et al., China's first "large-scale indoor play" (*daxing shineiju*), a proto–soap opera, was shown on the Beijing Television station and created an unprecedented sensation, which was called "the 'Yearning' wave" by the media.

10 Zhang Xiaowu, *Wo zai Meiguo dang lüshi* (I am a lawyer in America) (Beijing: Beijing chubanshe, 1994); Chen Yanni, *Chen Yanni: Niuyue yishi – ta zai dayang bi'an* (Chen Yanni: New York consciousness – she's on the other side of the great ocean) (Beijing: Zhongguo shehui chubanshe, 1995) and *Gaosu ni yige zhen Meiguo* (I will tell you about a real America) (Beijing: Huaxia chubanshe, 1994); Yan Li, *Niuyue bushi tiantang* (New York is not a paradise) (Beijing: Huayi chubanshe, 1993); Cao Guilin, *Niuyue shang kong de yeying* (Night orioles over New York skies) (Beijing: Xinshidai chubanshe, 1994); Tang Ying, *Meiguo laide qizi* (Wife from America) (Shanghai: Shanghai yuandong chubanshe, 1995).

11 Qian Ning, *Liuxue Meiguo – yige shidai de gushi* (Studying abroad in America – stories of an age) (Nanjing: Jiangsu wenyi chubanshe, 1996); Chen Yanni, *Zaoyu Meiguo – Chen Yanni caifanglu; wushige zhongguoren de meiguo jingli*, parts one and two (Beijing: Zhongguo shehui kexue chubanshe, 1997).

12 Textual meaning aside, the method of production of the television series *Beijinger in New York* indicates Chinese television series's important step towards commercialization. With regard to the process of filming in America, see Ren Wen's reportage literature, *Zai Niuyue de Beijinren* (The Beijing people in New York) (Zhongguo guangbo dianshi chubanshe, 1993).

13 Xiao Lian, *An'an, guai – wo zai Meiguo dang mama* (I am a mother in America) (Beijing: Zhongyang bianyi chubanshe, September 1996); Yi Shui, *Wo zai Meiguo de xinxi gaosu gonglu shang*.

14 Other books still on sale in the 1996–97 book market included Zhang

Saizhou's *Yige zhongguo lao jizhe fumei tanqinji* (An old reporter's record of visiting relatives in America) (Datong: Beiyue wenyi chubanshe, 1991); Maizi, *Meiguo fengqinglu* (A record of the American condition) (Guangzhou: Guangdong lüyou chubanshe, 1994). The preface to the collection *Haiwai liaowang wencong* states that it asked "the Chinese who reside and journey overseas to write reflective essays": they include Lu Shuchao's "Huaren zai Meiguo" (Chinese in America); Sun Xiaoping's "Manyou meilijian," (Wandering in America) and "Hongduandai – aizibing baitai lu" (The red ribbon, the many faces of AIDS); Yang Fangfang's "Meiguo de yueliang" (The moon of America); Yi shu, *Haiwai liaowang wencong* (A collection of interviews from across the ocean) (Hefei: Anhui renmin chubanshe, 1996); Zha Kexin, *Zhongguo nühai kan Meiguo – yige Zhongguo nühai zai Meiguo ji qita xifang guojia de zhenshi jingli* (Chinese girl in America – a Chinese girl's real experience in America and other western countries) (Tianjin: Tianjin renmin chubanshe, 1996); Su Hang, ed., *A Chinese Child in America*, (Beijing: Kexue jiaoyu chubanshe, 1996); and other titles too numerous to list. Besides these "Chinese people's American stories," there were also a handful of works on "Chinese people's European (French, to be more accurate) stories," such as Xu Chi's *Meng bali* (Dreaming of Paris) (Beijing: Wenlian chuban gongsi, 1993); Zheng Bixian's "*Xingzhe de meng – guangguai luli de bali huaren*" (Waking dreams: strange Chinese Parisians) (Beijing: Zhongguo huaqiao chubanshe, 1996).

    15 In reality, what is called the literature of the Chinese diaspora in the nineties includes such diverse groups as those who studied in America or Japan, those who traveled in Europe, and so on. The literature by those who studied in America and Japan is especially prominent, forming two distinct strands in this genre. Although the values and orientation of the works about America were diverse, in general they either confirm or rewrite the American Dream. The literature of those studying in Japan, however, is different. To cite a few examples, the television series that were broadcast by the Central Television station and filmed with the assistance and sponsorship of Chinese students studying in Japan, "*Yinghua meng*" (Dream of cherry), "*Yue shi guxiang ming*" (The moon is brighter at home), "*Riben liuxue yiqianri*" (One thousand days of study in Japan), and also Peng Yi's novel *Yu Youling Chajian erguo* (Passing the ghost) (Beijing: Zuojia chubanshe, 1996), written in the style of *youling xiaoshuo* (ghost fiction). All these works without exception write about the traumatic experience of Chinese people in Japan and express a tormented yet distorted identification with Chinese ethnicity in the midst of harsh suffering, feelings of shame, and failure. This is no doubt linked to either the Chinese people's memory of World War II or to the reality of the difficult survival of the Chinese diaspora in Japan; but in China's native popular culture, those books clearly are linked to larger and more diverse contexts, discourses, and social realities. The animosity displayed in the results of the social survey entitled "The Image of Japan in the Mind of Chinese Youths," conducted in the January 1997 issue of *China Youth Daily*, sheds light upon the complexity and deeper meanings behind these problems. Though the literature of the Chinese diaspora in Japan may serve as an important reflection of and contrast to the literature of the

Chinese diaspora in America, due to the fact that it in itself constitutes a complex research topic, I will leave it aside for another essay. The literature of the diaspora discussed in this chapter focuses specifically on those works written by overseas Chinese Americans.

16 See the chapter, "Jieyu: jingcheng tuwei" (Conclusion: breaking out of the city of mirrors) of my *Jingcheng tuwei – nüxing, dianying, wenxue* (Surrounded by a city of mirrors – woman, film, literature) (Beijing: Zuojia chubanshe, 1995).

17 In books about experiences in a foreign country, gender is a topic deserving further attention. Rich cultural symptoms also lie behind what is called "the story of a Chinese woman in popular works published in Europe and America about the Chinese experience" – such as Nien Cheng, *Life and Death in Shanghai* (New York: Grove Press, 1986), and Jung Chang, *Wild Swans: Three Daughters of China* (New York: Simon and Schuster, 1991) – and works about Western experiences published in China. I am limiting the scope of this paper and will take up these issues elsewhere.

18 In the second chapter of *Da zhuang xing: hou xin shiqi wenhua yanjiu* (The great transition: research topics in the post–New Era culture) (Harbin: Heilongjiang jiaoyu chubanshe, 1995), pp. 46–7, Xie Mian and Zhang Yiwu do an interesting reading of the opening lyrics to the theme song to "Beijinger in New York," analyzing this "soliloquy" phenomenon. The lyrics are:

> Thousands, ten thousands of miles I call out for you, but you don't care; in my dream you are my one and only. *Once, once again, I ask me*, ask myself if I love you, ask myself if I can leave you. In this life I am fated to walk alone, my passion has been exhausted by you. I am no longer myself, but you are still you. *Once, once again, I ask me*, ask if I hate you, ask myself what is so good about you?"

The authors of this book take the "I" and "you" as "metaphors of the China/West relationship," a very keen insight. They further note that

> the sense of confusion reflected in the series of questions in the song arose from a nation which went through a hundred years of vicissitudes and found herself entangled in deep and never-ending ties with the West. . . . (T)his song ruthlessly exposes the shattering of old dreams and hopes and provides a very good expression of the experience of "China" in the post–Cold War new world order. Through this ruthless questioning, it leads us to reevaluate the journey that we have taken.

I do not, however, agree completely with the authors' conclusion. I believe a song that became popular thanks to a television series should not be read out of context (the text of the television series) or it will be very difficult to find its meanings beyond its sense as a love song. And the combination of the song with the picture on the screen is very powerful. As the theme song that comes at the beginning of the show, it is accompanied by the scintillating Manhattan night scene; when the song comes to an end, the camera descends upon the Brooklyn Bridge, and the song's refrain changes into the prelude of the American national anthem. When linked to this picture on the screen and to the series's narration of the American dream, we can only read this kind of metaphoric relationship between China and America as one of frustration and disappointment rather than as a form of "ruthless questioning" and "reevalua(tion)."

19 Qiu Cuiling, *Jia dao hei feizhou* (Married to Black Africa), (Beijing: Huaqiao chubanshe, 1996).

20 In the early and mid 1980s, Taiwanese fiction writer San Mao was very popular on the mainland. She exerted great influence on young students throughout the 1980s. A popular figure in 1970s Taiwan, she wrote anecdotal prose describing her adventures and life in Europe and Africa. When news of her suicide arrived in China, university students in Beijing held mourning ceremonies. With candles in their hands and tears in their eyes, they sang the popular Taiwanese campus song "Olive Tree," a song for which San Mao wrote the lyrics. The niche San Mao carved for herself in popular mainland culture is built not only on her unique personality and her symbolic value as "a free individual," but also on the image of her as a world traveler in eternal search of the "olive tree in her dreams." Young Chinese students found in San Mao their own dreams about the wondrous world outside of China. Her aura persists even though after her death many inquiries were held in Taiwan into the truth of her works.

21 See Xiao Yin et al., eds, *Kuayue dayangde gong'an – Manhadun de Zhongguo nüren zhengyi shilu.*

22 Jia Pingwa's novel *Feidu* (Decadent city) (Beijing: Beijing chubanshe, 1993) was a best seller and the subject of much debate in 1993. The American best seller *Bridges of Madison County* also sold quickly in China between 1994 and 1995; including pirated versions, its estimated sales reached over one million. The novel created another wave of interest in 1996, when the Hollywood movie based on it was shown in China.

23 This is the Five Pagoda Chewing Gum package that was produced by the Yangzhou Number One Food Company. This product was provided to me by Tian Yu, a master's student in world literature at Peking University in my popular-culture seminar.

24 See the speech given by Zhou Li, "Wo kongsu, cengjing canghai nanwei shui, wo haishi wo," (I protest, through all the changes, I am still I myself), in the press conference "Kongsu Beijing guangbo dianshibao" (Denouncing Beijing Television report) on 7 January 1993, p. 74. Xiao Yin, in *Kua yang caifang zhaji*, also quotes Zhou Li's speech given at the press conference held for the publication of *Mengdong de Zhongguo nüren* (The rash Chinese woman) see Xiao Yin et al., eds, *Kuayue dayangde gong'an – Manhadun de Zhongguo nüren zhengyi shilu*, p. 29.

25 See the preface to Zhou Li, *Manhadun de Zhongguo nüren*, pp. 1–2.

26 Ibid, p. 2.

27 I discuss this viewpoint in the four-person seminar "*Xin 'shi pipan shu'*" (The new "ten criticisms"), coauthored with Chen Xiaoming, Zhang Yiwu, and Zhu Wei (*Zhongshan*, vol. 1, 1994).

28 Quoted from "Qingnian qikan diaocha baogao" (An investigative report on youth journals), paper submitted by Ma Xiaodong (master's student in com-

parative literature and cultural studies at Peking University) in my seminar course on popular culture.

29 Cao Guilin, *Beijingren zai Niuyue*, p. 3.

30 The literature of the Chinese diaspora in Japan no doubt provides an even richer and more meaningful illustration of this point.

31 The writer Ah Cheng, who resides in America, talks about the hybridization of discourses in *A Chinese Woman in Manhattan*: "After I read *A Chinese Woman in Manhattan*, I felt that it was worthwhile material. There is a certain reality – unintended as it is – to it. The author captures the chaotic superficialities that constituted post-1949 mainland culture, a bit of European romanticism, a bit of the literature of Russia and the Soviet Union, proletarian literature, and a bit of the semi-commercial culture and popular vanity witnessed in recent years. . . . *A Chinese Woman in Manhattan* can also be seen as a rare unofficial history which supplements the real history of new mainland Chinese culture. It is quite honest, and perhaps should be placed in the category of reference books, to be flipped through anytime. Someone who avoids the reality of his own experience does not count as a true man (*nanzi han*)." *Xianhua xianshuo – Zhongguo shisu yu zhongguo xiaoshuo* (Random words randomly told – Chinese morals and Chinese fiction) (Taipei: Taiwan shibao chubanshe, 1994).

32 You Zunming, who journeyed in America, used *A Chinese Woman in Manhattan* as an example in a letter he wrote to a friend, "Qianwan buyao wudao dalu qingnian" (Please don't misguide mainland youths). Quoted in Xiao Yin et al., eds, *Kuayue dayangde gong'an: Manhadun de Zhongguo nüren zhengyi shilu*, pp. 78–9.

33 See reporter Yang Ping's "Meiguomeng de tuixiaoshang – *Manhadun de Zhongguo nüren*" (The salesman of the American dream – a Chinese woman in Manhattan), *Beijing qingnianbao*, 19 December 1992.

34 Song Qiang, Zhang Zangzang, Qiao Bian et al., *Zhongguo keyi shuobu – hou lengzhan shidai de zhengzhi yu qinggan jueze* (China can say no – political and emotional decisions in the post–Cold War era) (Beijing: Zhongguo gongshang lianhe chubanshe, 1996). This book started the nationalist trend in popular publications, gaining great attention in China and overseas.

35 *Gongshang shibao* (Industry and commerce weekly) reported this news, which was then later reported in all kinds of popular periodicals; *Beijing wanbao* also published Xie Tian'en's "Sun Tianshuai bei zhengzhou daxue luqu" (Sun Tianshuai accepted by Zhengzhou University), which was originally published in *Zhongguo shangbao* (Chinese commerce newspaper).

36 During the hot sales of *A Chinese Woman in Manhattan*, the well-known literary critic Wu Liang wrote "Piping de quexi" (The absence of criticism), *Shanghai wenyi yishubao* (Shanghai arts and culture news), 20 October 1992.

Translated by Eileen Cheng and Shu-mei Shih

8

Invisible Writing:
The Politics of Mass Culture
in the 1990s

Although it is still difficult for scholars like us to grasp the significance and intricacy of a changing China in the nineties, perhaps we can get an approximation of its complexity by way of analyzing the meaning of the term *guangchang* (a Chinese translation of the word *plaza*). In the term *guangchang* we see a new marketplace rhetoric intermingled with memories of the revolution. The development of such a rhetoric in literature, media, and street language reflects the dissonance between apparent economic prosperity and the increasingly widening gap between rich and poor.

From Square to Market

In Beijing and other big Chinese cities, though new buildings arise in postmodern style, one sees increasing numbers of giant malls, shopping centers, specialty stores, chain stores, and warehouse stores. The crowds of humanity surging in and out of these places form a striking spectacle. The plaza – a place combining assorted retail stores, supermarkets, fast-food restaurants, health clubs, hotels, and offices – is a good example of the globalization of Chinese urban areas. Along with the momentous issues facing a late-modernizing country, a smaller problem is finding names for such novel spaces, in this case, for a space that signals a new way of life.

Between 1995 and 1996, this new type of space gained a new name. *Guangchang* (literally, broad place) superseded the more familiar names for shopping areas, *dasha* (mansion) and *zhongxin* (center).

214 CINEMA AND DESIRE

Suddenly the word *guangchang* appeared everywhere at the new construction sites. Shops and medium-sized specialty stores started calling themselves *guangchang*, as for instance *Dianqi guangchang* (Electronics Plaza) and *Shizhuang guangchang* (Fashion Place). The weekend editions of newspapers, evening papers, and many of the entertainment dailies that mushroomed in the early nineties also used the term *guangchang* for special columns on fashion or shopping.

The English term *plaza* is a recent loan word from Spanish, where it refers to a large open space constituting the center of the city's public life, and increasingly its cultural and commercial life as well. On public signs in Hong Kong today, the English word *plaza* is commonly paired with its equivalent, the Chinese *guangchang*. So *guangchang*, meaning shopping center, traces its linguistic history from Europe to America, and from the US to developed parts of Asia, particularly Hong Kong. *Guangchang* is not a traditional Chinese term for a structure. Nor has the word traditionally named any sort of space. As has often been the case in modern Chinese culture, however, a new name promises excitement and new hope. Fenglian Guangchang just sounds more attractive than, say, Yansha Shopping Center. And, of course, because the term *guangchang* has had a very different usage in modern China, designating shopping centers this way is a representational phenomenon particularly symptomatic of Chinese culture in the nineties.

As an item in the memory inventory of Chinese intellectuals, *guangchang* not only refers to a modern space, it is also closely linked to the remembrance of modernity and revolution, leading ideas in the great political and cultural movements of the twentieth century. Its most salient use is in Tiananmen Square – in Chinese, Tiananmen Guangchang – where the May Fourth Movement began in 1919, marking the beginning of modern China and modern Chinese culture and inaugurating that open area of the city as a place of special meaning. Since then, Tiananmen Guangchang has been an important political stage associated with modern student movements and demonstrations. In the popular mind, it signifies revolution, progress, reform, passion, youth, blood, and more particularly the role and historical mission of Chinese intellectuals. As the place where Mao Zedong dramatically announced the founding of the People's Republic, and where the founding is commemorated each year, Tiananmen Guangchang is the symbol of New China and the socialist government. The phrase *Tiananmen Guangchang* signifies a mighty authoritarian state power and *the people*, that great homogeneous mass without classes or individuality.

Mao Zedong reviewed the Red Guard on eight occasions during 1966 and 1967 at Tiananmen Guangchang, adding to the significance of the place a heightened sense of tension between authoritarianism and revolution, worship and the collapse of order. And yet, though the Cultural Revolution was originally cast as a student movement, that is not how it is remembered in China today. The main connection linking the Cultural Revolution and the protest history of Tiananmen Guangchang, rather, is Beijing residents' decision to mourn there following the death of Premier Zhou Enlai, on 5 April 1976, which heralded the Cultural Revolution's finale and the downfall of the Gang of Four. Using the socialist model of mass movements, the people of Beijing restored the modern democratizing tradition of holding peaceful demonstrations at the Tiananmen Guangchang. The new practice of peaceful demonstration reached its exaggerated and glorious apex during the months of April to June 1989, at which time the Chinese finally came face to face with the secret of the modern governing order – peaceful demonstrations crushed by tanks and troops.

If the French Revolution provided modern France's revolutionary model of the urban mass rebelling on the barricades, then the 1919 May Fourth Movement supplied modern China's particular revolutionary script: young students leading the way to demonstrations at the Tiananmen Guangchang and eventually mobilizing other elements of society (particularly workers in Shanghai) to join the mass movement. As a special signifier in the Chinese political context, the *guangchang* is thus firmly associated with the memory of revolution and the politics of various historical eras. The *guangchang* itself is an important component of the Chinese discourse on modernity. It records the practices and processes of Chinese modernization.

In short, the mention of Tiananmen or *guangchang* almost always evokes complicated emotions because it has special significance in the Chinese political and cultural context. To attach the name *guangchang* to a plaza – a commercial business center – is a political transgression, signifying to the nation the gradual metamorphosis from socialism to a capitalist market economy.

The Commercial Displaces the Political

It is therefore possible to say that a kind of *guangchang* complex has existed in contemporary Chinese culture, particularly in the immediate post-Mao period. Yet starting in the late 1980s the complex has in a way been usurped, displaced. During 1987 and 1988, the sacred taboos surrounding the *guangchang* and socialist revolution became the subject of parody and playful games. Dangerous symbols were consumed, digested into commodity form. The successful commercial film *Yaogun qingnian* (*Rock'n'Roll Youth*), by Fifth Generation director Tian Zhuangzhuang, featured rock and roll music and dancing under the red walls of Tiananmen. In what people have dubbed "Wang Shuo year," 1988, four films were made from Wang's stories and half of them showed protagonists playing pranks at Tiananmen Guangchang. At Central Television Station's New Celebration in 1989, popular comedian Jiang Kun bantered about a rumor going around that "Tiananmen Guangchang's going to be turned into a farmers' market." The audience found the idea hilariously incongruous, and for a while some considered his comic "rumor" as an interesting social, political prophecy.[1]

In a complex outburst of political emotions, the very end of the 1980s saw several waves of political nostalgia, such as Mao Zedong fever, Cultural Revolution fever, and the like.[2] These movements were anything but supportive of the government. Along with such nostalgic movements in the first half of the 1990s, the *guangchang* complex became a kind of cultural bridge, turning the memory of old taboo into new cultural fashion. Together they "consumed" the sacred ideological symbols of the past, in both senses of destroying and employing them. Using the term *guangchang* for a commercial center, then, is a transgression because it appropriates an important symbol and uses it in nearly the opposite sense of its established signification. Tiananmen Guangchang had figured in the sinocentric imagination as the "red heart" of world revolution throughout the history of socialist China. Now the superhighways, chain stores, skyscrapers, giant shopping malls, and the flow of happy consumers form a picture of the generic, homogeneous world metropolis, a spectacle of globalization, featuring the "landscape of fast-food restaurants along the highway."

China encountered the world once again at the end of the Cultural Revolution in the late 1970s. The encounter smashed the image of socialist China as the center of world revolution. In hopes of achieving legitimacy, China apparently accepted the reality of its "backwardness" and acknowledged its peripheral position in the world (where the West is the center). Nonetheless, throughout the 1980s, the most powerful, effective mainstream ideological expressions – from official political strategists with their eyes fixed pragmatically on global economics to elite intellectuals propelled by their historical vision – are found encapsulated in maxims like "reform and open-door policy," "walking toward the world," "the triumph of historical progress over historical cycles," "modern civilization conquering Eastern backwardness," "moving toward the blue (maritime mercantile) civilization," and "the relationship between the global village and China's membership in the global village." Such mainstream discourse defines China's peripheralized position in terms of a grand march toward the center of the world, with the aim of eventually breaking into, indeed of becoming, the center.

True, the end of the eighties saw a profound setback for Chinese intellectuals. But this situation began to change again in 1992 when Deng Xiaoping "inspected the South" and made a speech calling for continued reform. The socialist market economy – or globalization and commercialization, or (to speak plainly) capitalist development – quickly mushroomed. Virtually overnight, Chinese social life went from stagnation and silence to robust, vital growth. The logical extension of this change is that plazas and shopping centers have come to serve as a substitute for what people used to call *guangchang*. Though in the Republican period it referred to modern space, the *guangchang* today signals postmodernity in China.

In a certain way, the contemporary usage of *guangchang*, a term that once had such special significance, exposes the passing of the revolutionary era and the arrival of the age of consumerism. We have experienced, if not a postmodern society, a post-revolutionary era. The following are two intriguing examples.

In a classic demonstration of official political education (in actual fact just another case of "consuming" past taboos of revolutionary ideology and memory), the government held a large-scale exhibition in 1996 entitled Red Crag. The display concerned a dark scene in Chinese modern history: atrocities were committed in the 1940s at Baigongguan and Zhazidong, two infamous political prisons run jointly by the American CIA and the Guomindang's intelligence bureau under the appellation "Sino-American Cooperation." Several hundred Communists and other political dissidents were cruelly tortured and murdered at these two prisons. Memoirs of prison survivors appeared in the 1960s, along with a novel entitled *Hongyan* (*Red Crag*) based on these memoirs and, subsequently, a film called *Liehuo zhong yongsheng* (*Live through the Flames*).[3] These works were considered revolutionary masterpieces. They represented the great and lofty communist spirit and the invincible faith, the unbreakable will power of Communists. Deeply imprinted in the memory of many Chinese, *Red Crag* became, for two decades or even longer, a most poignant and attractive image of revolutionary heroism.

Political pop artists therefore also made it an object of mimicry and ridicule in the late 1980s. Then, in the nineties, the government reauthorized the novel *Red Crag* as "patriotic reading material" for primary and secondary school students. The film *Live through the Flames* appeared among the officially selected One Hundred Patriotic Movies. Yet while the majestic Red Crag exhibition of 1996 seemed to have been a government effort at reinforcing revolutionary ideology, in actual fact what it most prominently projected were the advertisements of its commercial sponsor, *Fugui huakai gongsi* (Flowering Wealth & Status, Inc.). Their unforgettable advertising slogan at the exhibition was *Rang lieshi de xianxue jiaoguan fugui huakai* (Let the blood of the martyrs nurture the flowering of wealth and status!). Needless to say, there is an enormous gap between the aspirations of the common people as articulated by the marketing company and the grand Communist ideals for which revolutionary martyrs sacrificed their lives. Unlike political pop art, which intentionally mimics official ideological discourse so as to reveal its opposite, this exhibition is an act of displacement and suture with revolutionary ideology. The spectacle of globalization, the prospect of a prosperous future and a new life of wealth and comfort in *xianshi* (the world of the present) displaces the Communist ideal and socialist practice.

The new life is capitalist and consumer-oriented. As was the case in the 1950s and 1960s, when the slogan *Jianku fendou qinjian jianguo* (Live a plain life and wage a hard struggle to build our country) appeared in public places, in the 1990s commercial advertisements are ubiquitous in cities, against the backdrop of skyscrapers and clover-leaf intersections. The Chinese branch of the Coca-Cola Company even modeled its management system on the Chinese reward structure of the fifties and sixties, giving outstanding employees the title of *laodong mofan* (model workers) and designing its own reward logos.

The second example is probably even more vivid. During 1996 and 1997 a huge billboard stood on the central median of Chang'an Road, a Beijing boulevard that runs across the top of Tiananmen Guangchang. Its main panel consisted of three ads scrolling successively into view. One had a vermilion background and white Chinese characters stating, *Shenhua gaige jianshe you Zhongguo tese de shehui zhuyi* (Deepen the reforms and build a socialism with Chinese characteristics). Each of the other two panels had a distinct, colorful design advertising a well-known Western brand of liquor, Hennessy X.O.[4] We can view this billboard as a space signifying cultural conflicts in the nineties. The public interest–oriented announcement takes the traditional shape of socialist propaganda and forwards the implicit message that contemporary China is the last stronghold of socialism left in the world. The Hennessy X.O. ad, reflecting multinational capitalist and commercial influences, shows a modern, Western life of luxury.

The billboard appears engaged in its own internal ideological warfare, what Fredric Jameson might call a "life-and-death struggle" between the cultures of the so-called Third World nation-state and imperialism. Yet, in reality, it is a rather typical phenomenon in which Chinese socialism and Western capitalism occupy *gongyong kongjian* (shared space), and it is showing not conflict but cooperation. In the Chinese cultural discourse of the nineties, the spaces such advertisements create can be considered as strange and yet coherent cultural symbols.

The June 1989 Incident and movements in popular culture during the following years indicate both the collapse of socialist ideology and the consequent ending of hope for imminent political reform or political democracy. The result is that economic deliverance, the only pathway toward the future, has replaced socialist or democratic salvation. Commercialization, a by-product of globalization's progress, has become in the nineties the single most powerful contributor to the social, cultural tableau. The particular *guangchang* where the student demonstration was crushed in 1989 has become a deeply complex taboo: it symbolizes the socialist system but also the toppling of that system. So to name a commercial plaza a *guangchang*, to change the political meaning of *guangchang*, or at the very least to mask the significance of political mass movements with a happy shoppers' heaven, is a transformation that is by no means innocent.

It does not have the same resonances in every city, however. In Shanghai (the preeminent Chinese industrial city, before 1949 the premier seaport in East Asia, famous for its "ten miles of foreign commerce," and known at the time as a "paradise for Western adventurers"), the People's Guangchang has already merged into the vast sea of commercial advertisement. But since Beijing is the center of Chinese political culture, *guangchang* there still operates on two or more ideological and social levels. Though innumerable shops and shopping centers with generic names like Commercial City (*shangcheng*), Commercial Building (*shangsha*), Merchandise Center (*gouwu zhongxin*), Chain Store (*liansuo dian*), and Specialty Shop (*zhuanmai dian*) absorb the flowing urban crowds every day, Tiananmen Guangchang stills serves as the site of the National Day celebration.

On the evening of Hong Kong's return to China on 31 July 1997, the Chinese government organized large-scale, all-night celebrations in Tiananmen Square. In Guangzhou, southern China's premier city, a commercial center has been designated a "youth cultural *guangchang*" and is used for "constructing socialist civilization," that is, for arts performances and other organized activities for young people. These redefinitions of the term *guangchang* simultaneously expose and conceal the extremely complex ideological reality of China's transitional era, the massive infiltration of multinational capital behind the new economic prosperity. The more important fact that has been obscured by the fascinating commercialism of the nineties is the cruel, grim reality of the widening class divisions in Chinese society, the result of rapid marketization.

Silence on the Widening Gaps between the Classes

Countless shopping centers have materialized in Chinese cities during the nineties. McDonald's and Pizza Hut, European interior decorating companies, flower shops, bakeries, coffee shops, bars, and dance clubs have surged into the cities. To tempt the New Rich, expensive special residential areas and private houses and apartments have names like Noble Residence (*Gaoshang zhuzhai*), Otherworld Utopias (*Yi fang shiwai taoyuan*), European-style Private Villa (*Oushi sijia bieshu*), Contemporary Classics (*Shidai jingdian*), Modern Romance (*Xiandai chuanqi*), and Artistic World (*Yishu dadi*). Metaphors and ideals hotly debated among elite intellectuals in the eighties – encapsulated in slogans such as "marching towards the world," "China's global membership," and "knocking at the door of the twenty-first century" – are in the nineties easily attainable objects. Take for instance, an advertisement for the International Commercial Internet Company that says: "How far away is the information superhighway? 1500 meters north of right here." Or the coffee shop on Chang'an Road called Mayflower (readily recognized as the name of the Pilgrims' ship). A restaurant owned by the Institute of Geological Science has the name Global Village.

This is a really profound displacement and transformation: no more mass movements and political rallies (either for the government or against it), and no more leadership by the elite culture or elite intellectuals. Rather, leisure, shopping, and consuming serve the important function of mobilizing and organizing Chinese society. The shopping arena has become the space where social order is reorganized and reconstructed. The image of happy consumers in the plaza has replaced that of angry citizens at Tiananmen Guangchang. The postmodern capitalist phenomenon of obscuring the differences among classes through commercial consumption has replaced the faraway communist ideal of social equality, material abundance, and "to each according to his (or her) needs." Material consumption has now become heaven on earth in China.

Since 1994, the explosively expanding mass media – TV stations, cable, weekend editions of many newspapers, weekly journals, slick magazines for leisure reading, and other publications with successful marketing designs – not only have enriched and embellished Chinese life in the process of globalization, but also have disguised an increasingly complex and grim social reality. Amidst the layered reality of the nineties, the emergence of the New Rich class is a conspicuous fact. What the cultural discourse of the nineties calls for is the creation of a Chinese middle class. Indeed, elite and popular cultures both now dote on this middle class. Earlier, during the cultural debate of the eighties, Chinese intellectuals had cited instances of postwar economic success throughout the Pacific Rim, noting that the coalescence of a large mainstream middle class signified economic takeoff, indicated a means for escaping Third World status, and implied the advent of gradual nonrevolutionary transformation to social democracy. What such discussions and the analogous debates in the nineties ignore, however, is that China and its billion people have been presented with a global market pie that has already been divided into sections, and that China's historical process comes with baggage already attached.

Another interesting fact is that popular culture and the mass media in the nineties (at least, from 1993 through 1995) defined marketing targets in terms of allegedly middle-class taste and consumption levels. It is a matter of cultural imagination rather than actual need. Reversing the law of supply and demand, the Chinese media is attempting to sustain a middle-class community. Local editions of magazines such as the French fashion journal *Elle*, which aim to stimulate consumption, are available in the Chinese market now. Yet, according to the state's published statistics on urban poverty, each copy of these expensive magazines would cost between 5 and 10 percent of the monthly income of an average family.[5]

More affordable and consequently more successful commercial newspapers and magazines are aimed at ordinary city dwellers. They often sport titles like *Jingpin gouwu zhinan* (*Best Buys*), *Gouwu daobao*

(*Buyer's Guide*), and *Wei nin fuwu bao* (*At Your Service*). These publications teach their readers how to acquire "good taste" and thus how to "qualify" as members of the middle class. In one 1995 issue of *Best Buys* there is an article giving detailed instructions on what merchandise to buy to live up to any given income level. For instance, a person on a monthly income of 5000 yuan should wear a specific kind of clothes, belt, leather shoes, bag, and watch. A separate list of items was given for persons with monthly incomes of 4000, 3000, and so on.[6] More to the point, a housing advertisement just states, "*Wei mingliu bianxie shenfen de jianzhu*" (For those who have high status).

Commercial culture has entered public discourse with an unambiguous class bias. Soap operas fill prime-time television. China's first hundred-episode dramatic series, "Jingdu jishi" ("Beijing Events"), portrayed "commercial wars" and the lovely daily life of the New Rich. Television series in the eighties had previously skated on the surface, content to show off the glamour of middle-class life: grand hotels, shopping malls, luxury houses and apartments, fashionable clothes. By the mid-nineties popular series such as "Guo ba yin" ("Have Fun") and "Dongbian richu xibian yu" ("Sunshine in the East and Rain in the West") better captured middle-class morality and values. Out of the popular cultural trend that novelist Wang Shuo exemplifies (as late as the beginning of the nineties, thought to be a subversive political force), the active creation of a middle-class mass culture began in 1994 and 1995. Yet by the mid-nineties the politically subversive elements of that trend had been absorbed and transformed.[7] Contemporary literary critics promoting "Chinese postmodernism" also solicit "writing for the middle class." In the mid-nineties, unanimously, public discourse was celebrating the formation of the newly risen middle class. Amid the egregious social-class division in China, however, discourse on such negative reality is almost invisible.

Some people claim that Deng Xiaoping's state policy of "letting a few people get rich first" has made possible the emergence of a stable, wealthy, middle-class community. The truth of the matter is more troubling. During the transition from state to local collective and private ownership, while a self-satisfied class of New Rich did coalesce, vast numbers of others lost their jobs and now live below the poverty line. As China's rapid urbanization proceeded, rural farmers arrived in the cities to form a *dagong zu* (laboring class). Between 1993 and 1995 the most threatening social fact was this polarization of rich and poor. Compared with the sixties and seventies, Chinese living standards and general consumption levels are indisputably higher. But the social discourse celebrating the miracles of high consumption has overshadowed the fact of a widening gap between rich and poor.

In November 1996, the newspaper *Beijing qingnian bao* (*Beijing Youth Daily*) carried a report entitled "One Advertisement from Zhejiang Has Enraged the Masses," concerning whether certain kinds of advertising were appropriate or not.[8] According to the article, to establish its professional image, a clothing company in Zhejiang had published an ad for its Haideshen brand of men's suits that asked the following question: "How many Haideshen suits can 500,000 yuan buy?" The advertisement provided the answer: ten. Haideshen brand suits are made of imported cloth, with jacket buttons of gold and diamonds. Three lines of the company's suits sold respectively for 68,000, 48,000, and 20,000 yuan per unit. *Beijing Youth Daily* reported that the advertisement had angered many people. The paper cited one letter particularly, from a young worker in a steel factory. "I have been working," he wrote, "for five years alongside a blast furnace. You cannot imagine how I sweat and how frequently I've been injured on the job. My work should be my pride and honor. But I actually feel sorrow now, because after five years everything I've earned for my labor does not amount to enough to buy me even one single suit."

Realizing its blunder, the clothing company apologized to the public. "We neglected the possible negative effects of our advertising," they wrote. "Our ad could mislead consumers and increase high-end consumption. It is not good for socialist spiritual construction." At the same time, however, the newspaper report also mentioned that the company had either sold or had on order nine of the advertised suits. The buyers were mostly businessmen and real-estate dealers. The report discussed the rules of the game of commercial society but, wittingly or not, it also revealed the increasingly sharp division of classes. Fashionable suits and dresses costing more than 10,000 yuan are indeed a common sight in many specialty stores and *guangchang*. And they sell out quickly. Automobiles, the extremely expensive as well as the more moderate kinds, have become popular in urban areas. High-priced private apartments and private villas are sold every day.

Except in this sort of display, in disguised form shall we say, the reality of the division of classes is rarely mentioned. And, when it is, the term *class* is never used (except in the compound *middle class*), nor is the chasm between classes discussed. In fact, this obscurity is perhaps the most typical practice of ideological legitimization or cultural hegemony, to borrow Gramsci's concepts. On the one hand, there is the government's intentional cover-up: we cannot acknowledge the widening gaps among classes because ours is a "socialist system." On the other, intellectuals seem to be united in bidding adieu to the Revolution, after enduring the cultural fever and de-ideologized ideological constructions of the 1980s. They also sign off on discussions of class and equality, intent on avoiding the very concepts. Intellectuals equate the ideals and the practices of revolution and social equality with lies, catastrophes, and bad memories of the Cultural Revolution. Consequently, except for vacuous official essays, Marxist theory and social critical positions are absent in Chinese intellectual circles; indeed they are held in open or unstated contempt there. Discussions of "economic laws," "fair competition," "appeals for strong men," and "social progress" have replaced class analysis. The outbursts of material fetishism and the unquenchable desire for material comfort during the mid-nineties not only reflected anxiety about living standards and identity, but also expressed a kind of nameless hostility and hatred toward the chaotic pursuit of desire and the pressures of life.

In my view, the real object of discontent, then and now, is the unequal social distribution of wealth, along with the corruption of the bureaucratic class and the increasing social division between the rich and poor. The Chinese people have a vivid memory of socialism.

A kind of common knowledge or tacit agreement even more powerful than the political taboos of the present day, however, makes people unwilling to acknowledge or discuss the reality that they face: the existence of different classes. They appear to think that if you acknowledge class and discuss the question of equality, then you must reject reforms, the open-door policy, and democracy; you would have to call for historical "reversion" and oppose "freedom." Even the most innocent expressions of social concern are being denied or rewritten.

An advertisement for a housing sale in Beijing, for instance, rewrote the poet Du Fu's lyrical line, "*An de guangsha qianwan jian, da bi tianxia hanshi ju huanyan*" (If one could only find a million stately homes to shelter the shivering scholars and bring them joy!) as the slogan, "*Donghuan guangsha qianwan jian, da bi tianxia renjie ju huanyan*" (A million stately homes at the East Circle, to shelter the outstanding men of the world and bring them joy!).

Class is now a pervasive and conspicuous feature of Chinese life. But intellectuals choose to ignore it. I do not claim that they are happy with the situation; they actually seem to feel a huge and nameless hostility and hatred. But intellectuals prefer to find another name for their discontent, some other target – an external enemy, perhaps, but never, ever an internal threat. The rapid rise of nationalism in 1996 accompanying the publication of *China Can Say No* has many complex political, economical, historical, and cultural roots. Underlying them all is a profound need to transfer the "nameless hatred" afoot in Chinese society to an external enemy. After 1996, reports about the mistreatment of workers and exploitation by the managerial class are invariably about "foreign businessmen" who bully Chinese workers. (These "foreign businessmen" are mostly from the developed Asian countries and regions; they are businessmen from Japan, South Korea, Taiwan, and Hong Kong, or people of Chinese descent working for European or American companies.) In reports about capitalists who bully workers, the class conflicts are successfully transposed into conflicts among nations or regions.

Representation of Class Divisions

By 1996, however, the plaza phenomenon had begun to lose its power to conceal the widening gaps between the classes. For instance, that summer a record heat wave hit Beijing. At first, the unrelenting heat – over 100 degrees – induced people to buy cooling devices like electric fans and air conditioners. Soon supplies were exhausted. No electric fans or air conditioners were to be found. The city's overloaded electric power system failed, and blackouts became a common phenomenon. At the giant commercial *guangchang*s a strange spectacle unfolded: in the evening after seven, the *guangchang*s filled to capacity. "Families and residents from the neighborhood, wearing pajamas and slippers, carrying paper fans and folding chairs, swarmed into the plaza."[9] And they were not there to shop: they could not afford air conditioners and had come to share the cool air generated by the central air-conditioning system. This both created a chaotic situation and presented a striking contrast between the urban poor and the wealthy middle-class shoppers, as though someone had pushed the wrong button and suddenly the audience saw revealed the unpresentable backstage.

Commercialism is the most powerful political expression of the nineties. Superficially it has eliminated all class distinctions: anyone is welcome to the shops. Consumers are gods, the slogan says. On the other hand, the different levels and forms of consumption have divided the space of activities for people by class. The poor cannot afford to shop in the expensive plaza stores, so they rarely go there; absent from the *guangchang*, they do not share its material prosperity. That is not to say that the poor are nowhere to be seen, since people carrying heavy bags walking or taking public buses are a common sight in the big cities. Among ordinary city people the cut-price warehouses and other small discount stores in the residential areas are more popular than the plaza *guangchang*. Everyone knows these discount stores often sell counterfeits and items of inferior quality, but their cheap prices still attract many shoppers.

To complicate the situation further, as Chinese economic reforms move ahead vigorously the number of unemployed workers is increasing at an alarming rate. Most state-owned factories have closed down; many workers and low-level managers have lost their jobs. There is almost no existing welfare system or social security, and many unemployed workers are on the verge of starvation. These people who grew up with the socialist "iron rice bowl" are unprepared for the psychological trauma associated with the cruel fact of joblessness. Unemployment is consequently the most severe problem of the nineties and the most likely source of potential social unrest.

This grim social reality has begun appearing, albeit confusedly, in public media besotted with images of luxurious lifestyles and refined tastes. Alongside a discussion about the alarming phenomenon of college students' over-consumption habits, one sees a report calling for

financial aid to support college students who do not even have enough
to eat or wear.[10] The same journal reporting that "the new Asian generation is growing up in wealth," and whose language of rebellion is
phrased in such terms as "They seem to think I'm at the age for eating
McDonald's, but the fact is that I'm old enough to eat at Pizza Hut!,"
carries heart-wrenching reports about an educational relief program,
Project Hope, and children who cannot afford basic schooling.[11] On a
single page of another newspaper run parallel articles, "City
Consumers' Confidence Rising" and "Why Is It So Difficult for
Unemployed Women Workers to Find New Jobs?"[12]

Chinese intellectuals are keeping silent about these gross class divisions. Up to now, very few – the exceptions being some scholars in the
humanities and social sciences – have offered class analyses of the current situation or spoken openly on behalf of unemployed workers. It
is not so much that intellectuals are afraid of political taboos or
making mistakes; rather they have consciously chosen to take the position that the Revolution is over. Academics' refusal to use class analysis
to describe the current class divide leaves that task to official organs
and the state media. The suffering of the poor in the eighties was officially described as "temporary pain" during economic reform,
"historic sacrifice," part of the "process of progress." But these concepts are no longer sufficient to mask the increasingly prominent
social dilemma, and the new explanation for class division in the
nineties is even colder and more brutal.

After 1996 the media have focused on unemployed workers, interpreting their difficulties finding work as due to "lack of skills," "lack of
training," and "lack of flexibility." Discussions like this ignore the fact
that contemporary problems are rooted in the previous system (its lack
of a social welfare system or unemployment insurance, for instance)
and in the wrenching psychological disruption caused when the working class rapidly fell from being Chinese society's "leading class" to
being at the very bottom of all social, economic, cultural strata. Such
deliberations also ignore the fact that open age and gender discrimination characterizes the present labor market. They legitimize the
current government policy of viewing the unemployed workers as "naturally eliminated through fair competition" and attributing their
unsuccessful attempts at finding work to faults of their own.

Unemployed workers ensure a cheap labor force for the New Rich and multinational capital. Yet no one argues that it is unjust for workers to perform low-wage, high-intensity labor, unjust that they lack the protection of rights and benefits. New employers no longer want the unemployed over-forties. Sometimes you can even overhear arguments to the effect that unemployment is good because it enables people to find new occupations and to get rich fast. Reported success stories make unemployment sound like an opportunity sent from heaven.[13]

If such rhetoric is ineffective in the end, the return of realism in many television shows and literary works strikes a deeper chord. Realist works are beginning to find ways of addressing the reality of class division. Beginning in the waning months of 1995, stories about white-collar life and commercial wars began to disappear, replaced by family dramas, frequently in the genre of tragedy. Stories about the poor displaced stories about the New Rich. The crowded Beijing courtyard compounds and old worker apartment blocks rotated back to center stage, supplanting the plaza. Among the new TV series, two tragedies, "Zan ba zan ma" ("Our Dad and Mom," 1996) and "Ernü qingchang" ("Love between Man and Woman," 1997), became the most widely watched and hotly discussed shows of the era. They have similar plots: an old worker father is suddenly bed-ridden with an incurable disease. The factory where several generations of his family have all worked cannot afford to pay for his medical treatment. As the tragic drama unfolds, a loving family is on display, with kind parents and lots of filial sons and daughters. Scenes in hospitals and low-income apartments reveal the life of the poor, bereft of the socialist system's protections. Among the issues touched on are problems of aging, workers' living conditions, the high cost of medical treatment, the impediments faced by unemployed female workers, and class discrimination, both open and disguised. But at the end of the day, these programs do not offer a realistic exposé of the current situation, so much as a dramatic presentation that acts to conceal it.

In both TV series, the reality of class division and the suffering of working people are transformed into traditional Chinese family ethical themes. The problems of unemployed workers from state factories and the collapse of the socialist welfare system no longer appear as social issues, but as a special opportunity for exhibiting the unique power of family ties and restoring traditional filial piety. In these tele-vision shows it is not the nuclear family but a multigenerational extended family that surfaces again to serve as the boat ferrying the people through the "bitter sea." In Shanghai Television Station's "Love between Man and Woman," the old worker father, who is dealing with a serious cerebral hemorrhage, and the mother, who is in the advanced stages of cancer, are bravely fighting to prolong their lives so they can maintain the family's membership numbers and thereby garner more apartment space for their children when new public housing is assigned. (Here again the working people's hopes for sal-vation still rely on a state project aimed at realizing the Four Modernizations.)

The love of the aged and ailing parents for their children finally wins those spacious new apartments, but the real solution to the family's plight comes as a man from the New Rich class does them a good turn. The rich man falls in love with the family's oldest daughter, who happens to be a single mother. Having experienced the ups and downs of commercial business, sex games, and the changeability of human relations, the rich man realizes that what he really wants is a plain, kind-hearted "good wife and virtuous mother" of his own age. The old worker's unemployed middle-aged daughter, who was this rich man's high-school classmate, becomes the lucky woman. The old worker's family problems are solved by generous financial assistance from the rich man: their youngest son is able to get rid of his greedy, shameless, unchaste wife and remarry happily; another son can hold onto his bookstall; the unemployed elder daughter teams up with her brother's new wife, who previously worked as a lowly janitor, and the two women become the owners of a flower shop on a busy commercial street. The bad ex-wife of the youngest son marries a Hong Kong busi-nessman and moves to Hong Kong, indicating deplorable decadence and the seductiveness of money. The rich man's marriage to the old daughter signifies a return to virtue and the triumph of traditional values over money. Of course, it is no longer society or class, but family blood relations that constitute the fundamental social reality, the place to which people eventually return and belong. But in the end what really saves the poor is nothing less than a generous infusion of cash donations from the rich.

Another approach to dissolving the realities of class division has come with the appearance of what the critics call a "wave of realism in literature." This is particularly the case in prose fiction such as Liu Xinglong's "Fenxiang jiannan" ("Sharing Hardships"), Tan Ge's "Da chang" ("A Big Factory"), Guan Renshan's "Da xue wu xiang" ("Snow Has No Home"), He Shen's "Nian qian nian hou" ("Before and After the New Year"), Zhou Meisen's "Renjian zhengdao" ("The Main Path in the World"), Lu Tianming's *Cangtian zai shang* (*Heaven Above*), and Zhang Hongsen's *Chejian zhuren* (*Workshop Director*).[14] These and works like them have reinforced government propaganda, creating a new, special site for the merger of official ideology and mass culture. The reason for calling these works "realist" is that they boldly consider the "dark side" of society, which used to be nameless and unrepresentable: the difficulties facing state-owned enterprises; the hardships workers suffer; the corruption of the bureaucracy; and the exploitation of the peasantry. Yet at the same time, these novels are well within the mainstream of socialist literature, the literature of the workers, peasants, and soldiers.

The distinctive feature of these works is the commercial twist they add to their material. Thus they contain certain elements of the tragic drama; but instead of being confined to the family circle, the works tell tales about a large factory, a city, a town or a whole village. Disasters do not descend on a single individual but rather on entire communities. There is a prominent theme of suffering and salvation, although while the community's suffering is directly and concretely described, representations of the sources of its salvation are ambiguous. These books do not succeed in outlining any effective method of solving social problems, but they at least have incorporated into ideological discourse, through discussions of the imaginary scene, a fragmented and conflict-ridden social reality. The reality of classes and class conflict gets narrated in terms of good guys and bad guys, rich and poor. Only two kinds of characters are associated with the word *class*: economic criminals, who are eventually caught and punished, and the Wang Shuo types, who are young, carefree, flippant, and quick-witted, but do not claim any sense of social responsibility. So when the economic criminals use a capitalist vocabulary and abusive language to oppress the underdogs, their behavior is clearly wrong and cannot be held up as exemplary. When the Wang Shuo characters use funny expressions to talk about class, readers usually have a good laugh and dismiss them.

Wang Shuo himself has been one of the leaders of Chinese popular culture during the nineties. At the end of the eighties and the beginning of the nineties, his writing played a special double role of subverting and reconstructing socialist ideology. By using hackneyed political language in unbecoming situations, he subverted the significance of these sacred slogans. Yet dialogue in the Wang Shuo style, all about "capitalists," "oppressors," "bosses," "poor workers," "the sufferers," and "the running dogs of the capitalists," is not full of meaningless clichés but rather contains a recognition of the new social reality under construction. Of course, Wang Shuo's linguistic style has undermined the subversiveness of his discourse. And consequently his works, like others of their kind, still do not confront head-on the reality of class divisions. That reality remains unnamed and unanalyzed.

Protagonists in the "wave of realism in literature" mode are often not even those suffering most directly under the reforms. They are not ordinary workers or peasants, but officials at middle and low levels of the nomenklatura: factory managers, town mayors, village heads, and workshop directors. These intermediate people operate as bridges or links among the various sectors of the society – the government, the New Rich, agents of the multinational corporations, and ordinary people. In literary representations, they are helpless scapegoats and accomplices of evil. They have to fire workers because that is their job, but their guilty consciences trouble them greatly. These mid-level and low-level officials win the readers' sympathy. When readers identify with and feel sympathy for the officials, of course, they also accept the cruelty and helplessness of the new reality of class conflict, a reality which, though imperfect, is now the only legitimate reality.

In all the stories about large factories there is one necessary protagonist, and that is the old worker who used to be a model worker. He was a hardworking man, lived a plain life, and never complained. Yet his tale does not actually constitute a retelling of the story of the spirit of the working class of the past; rather it reconstructs a new professional ethic and class identity: the well-behaved worker who has no complaints and offers no resistance to harsh treatment. The theme of sharing hardships means that workers and peasants should share hardships with the state; or, more precisely, the state expects the worker to share its hardships. At the moment when the market economy, fair competition, the successful pursuit of profits, and self-fulfillment are mainstream goals, to call for the spirit of self-sacrifice characteristic of socialist times is a clear attempt to consolidate the reality of class division.

Popular culture plays the leading role on the Chinese cultural stage in the 1990s. Behind the glamorous commercial prosperity of the new *guangchang* displays lie the far more profound, disturbing, and yet invisible issues of division between the classes, and between the working class and the government. The politics of popular literature and culture legitimates the new ideological transformation, and this new legitimation process has not yet met any real cultural or intellectual resistance. The socialist legacy has either been abandoned or subverted. The presence of a public, critical social conscience is absent in our time.

Notes

1 The four films based on Wang Shuo's stories are Xia Gang, *Yiban shi huoyan, yiban shi haishui* (One half is flame and the other half is seawater), 1988; Mi Jiashan, *Wangzhu* (Masters of mischief), 1988; Huang Jianxin, *Lunhui* (Reincarnation), 1988; and Ye Daying, *Da chuanqi* (Heavy breathing). Both *Reincarnation* and *masters of Mischief* have scenes in which guards at Tiananmen Guangchang are ridiculed.

2 See my "Redemption and Consumption," *positions: east asia cultures critique*, vol. 4, no. 1, 1996, pp. 127–43. (Chapter 6 of this volume.—EDS.)

3 Luo Guangbin and Yang Yiyan, *Hongyan* (Red crag) (Beijing: Chinese Youth Press, 1961). Translation published as *Red Crag* (Peking: Foreign Languages Press, 1978). The film is Shui Hua's *Liehuo zhong yongsheng* (Live through the flames), 1965.

4 This interesting advertisement was the continuous background in a scene in one of Wang Shuo's films, *Baba* (Dad). In October 1997 the advertisement was changed: the two panels of Hennessy X.O. remained the same, but the political slogan became "Develop physical training and improve our people's health," a quotation from Mao Zedong.

5 See "Quanguo bufen chengshi zuidi shenghuo baozhang biaozhun" (The

lowest living safeguards for some cities in China), *Zhongguo zichan xinwen bao* (Chinese business news), no. 76, 28 February 1997.

6 *Jingpin gouwu zhinan* (Best buy), 7 June 1995.

7 Wang Shuo and his friends were also popular media producers. They produced the television series "Kewang" ("Yearning"), which captured the hearts of many viewers. From 1990 to 1995, their Haima chuangzuo zhongxin (Seahorse creative writing center) produced many important films and television programs.

8 *Beijing qingnian bao* (Beijing youth daily), 20 November 1996.

9 "*Jingcheng baixing naliang you fang*" (Capital residents find ways of cooling down), *Beijing qingnian bao* (Beijing youth daily), 15 July 1997.

10 Gao Bo, "Daxuesheng xiaofei: you ren huanxi you ren chou" (University students' consumption: some are pleased, others worried), *Zhongguo zichan xinwen bao* (Chinese business news), 11 April 1997.

11 *Sanlian shenghuo zhoukan* (Sanlian's life weekly), no. 7, 1997.

12 *Beijing qingnian bao* (Beijing youth daily), 20 November 1996.

13 Stories about "rechannelling" unemployed workers are prominent in the daily reports of all television stations and newspapers.

14 Liu Xinglong, "Fenxiang jiannan" ("Sharing hardships"), in *Shanghai wenxue* (Shanghai literature), no.1, 1996; Tan Ge, "Da chang" (A big factory), in *Renmin wenxue* (People's Literature), no.1, 1996; Guan Renshan, "Da xue wu xiang" (Snow has no home), in *Zhongguo zuojia* (Chinese writers), no. 2, 1996; He Shen, "Nian qian nian hou" (Before and after the new year), in *Renmin wenxue* (People's literature), no. 6, 1995; Zhou Meisen, "Renjian zhengdao" (The main path in the world), in *Dangdai* (The contemporary), no. 1, 1996; Lu Tianming, *Cangtian zai shang* (Heaven above) (Shanghai: Shanghai wenyi chubanshe, 1996); and Zhang Hongsen's *Chejian zhuren* (Workshop director) (Jinan: Shandong wenyi chubanshe, 1997).

Translated by Jingyuan Zhang

Rethinking the Cultural History of Chinese Film

Disciplinary Turn and Cultural Thinking

Zhou Yaqin: As some of the students and I understand it, over the last few years you have been engaged, actually you have really excelled, in studying contemporary and modern women's literature, mass culture of the eighties and nineties, and post-1949 Chinese film, paying particular attention to the period after 1978, the New Era. Lately, you've undertaken studies into the cultural history of Chinese film, particularly its pre-1949 roots. How do you account for this turn in your thinking?

Dai Jinhua: It may be more a question of extending my academic territory than any particular disciplinary turn. In fact, the study of women's literature and mass culture is an expansion of my film work. Women's studies used to be a sideline love for me. The more deeply I got involved in it, the less of a sideline it became, however. Generally speaking my work consists of three parts, each complementing the others: Chinese film, women's literature, and mass culture.

I began academic life working in film theory and criticism. Throughout the eighties I was primarily concerned with Chinese film studies, focusing on contemporary films, mostly of the New Era. Chinese film history grew out of a convergence of my reflections on and use of Western theories, my "ambition" to challenge these theories on the basis of complex film practices in China, and my wish to position contemporary Chinese film on a historical horizon.

Over the course of the nineties, I've reconfirmed my sense that films cannot be explained exclusively on their own terms. Since its inception at the end of the nineteenth century, film has always been situated at nodal points in modern society. A young art, the invention of science and technology, film entered the social circuit and was rapidly made an industry and a characteristic commodity. There is no disputing that film is one of the twentieth century's premier art forms. Yet at the end of the century it is already in decline. Since film becomes a unique, charming commodity available in any cultural market, inevitably it is linked to society, politics, ideology, fashion, consumption, all sorts of mass culture and urban culture and tendencies in the humanities and arts.

During the eighties I placed enormous faith in my belief that film is one of the great art forms – in its own way, an art as pure as anything ancient. I haven't abandoned this belief. But I find it too limiting now to accept, as a truly efficacious explanation, aesthetic, artistic criteria as sole issues in the study of film, particularly Chinese film. That is why I have begun extending my research into cultural studies and why I feel so strongly now that film work requires this emphasis. When I look back I see that in the past I was not exclusively in film studies, either. I always seem to have been trying to bring historical and cultural perspectives to bear. What I'd like to do is open up a larger platform for film studies, drawing on cultural studies and studies of the cultural history of film.

I love both literature and film, and women's literature had always been my sideline pursuit. Since I am a woman I'd initially been inclined toward women writers in a simple intuitive way. In leisure reading, however, I began encountering more and more representations that I did not or could not identify with; that is to say, I discovered the complexity of women's literary writing. In the process, my feminist positioning and conceptualizations surfaced, partly in response to my reflection on my own gendered experience, and partly from the film theory that I was studying and teaching.

So-called Western film theory coalesced at the turn of the sixties and in the seventies, a time of climax, the beginning of the end of the last revolution of the twentieth century in Europe. Film theory is revolutionary; it is theory that, at least in some US and European universities in the seventies and eighties, was inherently critical and leftist. In the course of my study of film theory I received my primary theoretical training. Of course, as a special cultural industry, film is deeply implicated in gender processes and gendered order. My theoretical position as a feminist took shape in the course of studying film.

Besides film theory I have read quite widely in feminist literary, sociological, and other theories. This links up naturally to my sideline pursuit in women's literature and hence the work of women writers spills over into what I do. My heightened concern with women's writing is also connected to the opportunities that the 1995 United Nations Fourth World Conference on Women opened up. Still, commitment to any study has to be total; for me, film is what I am devoted to body and soul and literature must consequently remain a side interest.

Zhou: What specific historical, cultural, and critical insights do you feel you have gained into Chinese film?

Dai: Chinese film's emergence, development, and change all present to researchers a challenging and enriching cultural syndrome. Certainly much of what happens in the field of Chinese film can be considered specific, but in some senses it represents larger Chinese cultural developments. I think that film studies should be able to offer insights into Chinese cultural studies generally. Let me take for example a general trend at work in cinematics throughout the New Era, which I call truncated periodization fever (*duandaire*) and retrogressive naming syndrome (*nituifa*). The eighties were a period of elated, forward-looking enthusiasm. Speaking more ironically, it was an era of abundant Great Leap Forward deployments, and I was one of those mouthing the line. People were chronically enthused with truncated periodization fever during this era of epoch-making discourses of innovation and breakthroughs, and they were pronouncing the emergence of new trends, new phenomena, new epochs, new generations, and so on, and so on. And it is quite true that such discursive strategies did indeed testify to the reality of the eighties, which had its own distinctive features in the areas of literature, arts, and the humanities. Three generations of intellectuals erupted onto the scene simultaneously as everything was reviving again with great fanfare at the conclusion of the Cultural Revolution.

Looking back now, truncated periodization fever was a very special, interesting cultural event. In the film arena, at least, it involved a retrogressive – as opposed to purely chronological – historical narrative. It was only when a cohort of young directors (now-familiar names like Chen Kaige and Zhang Yimou) graduated from the film academy in 1983 that the term *Fifth Generation* suddenly emerged. In the face of a new Fifth Generation, directors who had started their careers around 1979, less than five years earlier, a group still considered as "young directors" at the time, these people were retrogressively anointed as the Fourth Generation. Directors who were key figures in Chinese film after 1949, like Xie Jin, were consequently retrogressively named as the Third Generation.

For a long time no one seemed particularly concerned about who the First and Second Generations of Chinese film directors were. Nor did anyone ever ask whether generational lines were being drawn on the basis of a logic of periodization specific to the history of film art, the history of political culture, or to some other field. Nobody seemed concerned with such matters because we all seemed to be situated in the same context, and to share a certain consensus or tacit understanding of contemporary history. I realized that the end of an epoch is pronounced only after the beginning of a new epoch has been declared. We allude to death only through the metaphor of a new birth, and, to put it crudely, the whole duration of the eighties was imbued with cheap optimism. Or should I say that the era was saturated with discourses of passion and a longing optimism that pervaded humanists' studies of culture. Not to mention the dangers of this kind of thinking, it has surely disregarded or obscured the rich dimensions history can reveal to us. In a rush toward endless tomorrows we overlooked the continuousness of history.

Rethinking the Eighties

Zhou: The eighties were a truly significant epoch. Many of us experienced, in some way, the intensity of its landmark events, and participated in making its epochal narratives. Reflecting on the cultural memory and intellectual resources that the eighties served up, your generation of scholars must have developed important insights. Would you care to offer your personal reflections?
Dai: Among all the visible and invisible themes of the eighties, one I find particularly significant is the question of history. I'm thinking, for instance, about movements for historical and cultural reflection, or cultural thoughts and movements like the one to rewrite literary

history. A theme running through humanist thinking in the eighties, history emerged as a giant, invisible term sprawling beyond the phenomena of thought and movement, overwriting virtually everything. As I remember it, everyone was in some sense speaking to history, or speaking in the name of history. To describe it a bit simplistically, eighties culture was an attempt to rewrite history. Which is to say, history experienced reconstruction.

The reconstruction consisted of two major elements, in my view. One was what I would call recovery from history, or supplement to history. It proffered for reevaluation historical facts shrouded in specific political taboos. The other, I would term subversion of the existing canonical order, a rethinking and renaming of the canon, especially in art and cultural history. We all know that history writing is itself rather typically the operation of a discourse of power. "History," as Walter Benjamin says, "is the victor's inventory." Hence, the so-called supplement to history is not really a matter of writing into history's blank crevices. Except in extraordinary circumstances, historical writing never leaves a blank space or an obvious gap the way that Nationalist censors did in newspapers before 1949. So-called recovery or supplement does not actually fill up blanks to reveal a full historical picture. It is, on the contrary, a surfacing of factors formerly consigned to oblivion, a surfacing that contributes to altering the whole picture. The canonical rearticulation in the eighties, like the foregrounding of Shen Congwen and Zhang Ailing, even the extraordinary decision to substitute Jin Yong for Mao Dun, illustrates a de-ideologizing of culture and art, a reordering of canons, that is, with reference to transcendental aesthetic values.[1]

In terms of my own engagement with Chinese film history in the eighties and my praxis then, I have two further observations. First, unlike other fields in the humanities, the arena of film during the eighties did witness tumultuous events, the advent of new talents, and a series of climactic incidents, but there never was an effort undertaken to rewrite film history. And this in spite of the fact that important papers on shadow plays did get written; the director Fei Mu was rediscovered; the film *Shennü* (*The Goddess*) was unearthed. This latter is quite impressive in and of itself, for although Chinese film was born in 1905, making it older than New Literature, even in the eighties it had not become a subject of study, reconsideration, or reflection. That belated task has consequently fallen to me.

I do not, however, intend to rewrite film history the way the history of literature was rewritten in the 1980s. This is of course due to the distance separating the media of literature and film from the specific cultural role each has played in modern China. If in the realm of literature one can regard practices of aesthetic judgement or criticism of pure literature as significant in themselves, establishing such coherent criteria would be difficult in the context of Chinese film history. As I said before, inasmuch as film is an art of modern industrial civilization, whatever remains – once we remove all "impurities" – as pure art may be so insignificant that we wouldn't be able to amass sufficient material for writing a history. It is really quite important, moreover, that people working on catching up maintain a sober, reflective mind.

Underlying the so-called revision of history in the eighties and the conceptualization of a twentieth-century China, I would argue, were efforts to establish continuity on the one hand and transcendence on the other, as if we could eliminate, by means of new interpretation and ellipsis, the internal disruptions of twentieth-century Chinese history. Rewriting history illuminates facts and truths that had been thrown into oblivion. It casts new shades and shadows. Today, we can more easily see, with the benefit of hindsight, that history is not a roll of film that can be freely montaged.

On my part, having endured rather painful changes in the transition from the eighties to the nineties, I have been able to clarify my own cultural position and have determined that I will not adopt methods into my historical film studies that subscribe to so-called transcendental objectivity and value. I adhere to the notion, now a cliché, that all histories are contemporary histories. The historian is not motivated by the will to return to the past. Similarly, despite people's expectations to the contrary, history writing is not motivated by the wish to make visible in its true colors that which has vanished forever. We all write history quite definitively for our living present. The anticipated reader is always a contemporary. It is the present we speak to when we are writing history.

Ruptured History and the Return of the Original Picture

Zhou: A hot topic since the nineties began has been the question of cultural transition, which assumes that big differences separate the eighties from the nineties. How do you relate your experience of the nineties to your idea about rewriting history?

Dai: On the cusp of the nineties, I experienced the phenomenon of the "return of the original picture" quite strongly. The nineties have indeed registered another cultural transition, but one that is in fact a variation on the passion and optimism of the eighties. Then people were once again periodizing, naming, applauding the emergence of ever more "new" trends one after another. Many observers have pointed out totally new cultural configurations, or a totally new attitude toward life, a new way of living. It really only takes a little basic historical understanding to discover that such things are not new at all, indeed they may have persisted within the great transformation in Chinese culture and history from late Qing to modern republic times. When history begins to repeat itself in some astounding way, an observer or a witness should remain vigilant. I see the act of uncovering the repetitive nature of the "new" as the beginning of genuine reflection. Yet while experiencing shocking similarities in history, we should also beware the trap of simplifying history. For history never, in any real sense, repeats itself. Recurring phenomena are always related to the specific context of past history.

This "return of the original picture" syndrome takes me back to the time of Chinese film's birth at the beginning of the twentieth century. In my view, tracing the tortuous transformations from the late Qing period (*jindai*) to modern times in the first half of the twentieth century (*xiandai*)[2] is actually a thoroughly contemporary topic, a way of reviewing and assessing modern Chinese history now, at the end of the twentieth century. My scholarly concern never exceeds my concern for the cultural reality of the China in which I live. All my scholarly research inevitably revolves around my concern for contemporary China, contemporary Chinese people, and contemporary Chinese intellectuals. Perhaps this is what I am good at as an intellectual and where, at the same time, I might possibly flounder as a scholar. The changes in China's society and culture in the eighties and the nineties have determined my decision to go further back to earlier periods in my choice of research topics. It is not a personal choice.

In addition I have taken on the task of reviewing the eighties from the perspective of the nineties. It is not a "revolutionary critique" sort of review, but more a self-reflection. And it has been a difficult and painful process. For me it is in fact an autocritique, even to a large extent a self-negation. I do not know how much I have accomplished, but this is what I have been doing. And what I've discovered is that when we spoke, in the eighties, we were speaking to the history of the Cultural Revolution, or the history that formed a breeding ground for the Cultural Revolution. At that time, our horizon was blocked and confined within the dividing line of political history. Familiar eighties narratives are extremely interesting in the sense that they actually mask singularities and differences in the history of modern China from the mid nineteenth century to 1979, and consequently give little thought to how modernization processes have unfolded over the century as a whole – amidst much suffering and in a peculiar way – and how, in this history, the discourse of modernity has emerged in multifarious forms.

For instance, a consensus about history in the eighties held that the Cultural Revolution was feudal, fascist, and autocratic in nature and thus a kind of ultrastable structure of Chinese history. It was as if feudal autocratic history essentially continued unchanged up until 1976 (1979 was portrayed as inaugurating a new era); at that time, we entered the epoch of modernization. This transformed the entire discourse of the eighties into an enlightenment discourse: we were compelled to address an obscurantist, feudal, ultrastable, immutable, indestructible iron house, which had to be blown up before the process of modernization could be reinitiated.

This discourse of enlightenment was actually quite legitimate then, since it is itself an effective ideological strategy for de-ideologization. However, it eventually turned into a mainstream intellectual discourse. Looking at it now, we should reveal what such an enlightenment discourse so grossly conceals. We should reinvestigate the process of the transformation of modern China, beginning at the mid nineteenth century and extending to the May Fourth Movement and beyond, and then reexamine the history and meaning of contemporary China. Undoubtedly, socialism is an integral part of modern Chinese history.

It is an extension, rather than a rupture, of the historical mission of modernization, since its only distinction lies in its attempt to use non-capitalist means to modernize China.

Zhou: The periodization approach to history, which is still quite popular, sees history as a linear temporal flow of incessant transcendence and progression. Are you suggesting that we should take an approach that stresses disruption, discontinuity, or cyclical change in understanding historical development?

Dai: Regarding the development of academic scholarship in the eighties, running parallel to notions of periodization is the idea of rupture, as if Chinese history were divided by a series of splits into essentially different historical phases that have no relation to each other. This "othering" approach views history as consisting of disparate sections and never takes account of continuity, particularly in relation to the lengthy process of the construction of the discourse of modernity, the project of modernization in China.

On a whole other register is the transcendence-cum-continuity approach. This posture assumes that history is some sort of homogeneous medium and that, like a film director, a historian can produce a montage, cut and mix. In theory we could lightly dismiss or transcend an old era, old habits. Such rewriting of history performs precisely the same violence that is targeted for critique by those engaged in the rewriting of history.

For me, both linear and cyclical approaches to history are specific discursive constructions, rather than truths. In the attempt to rethink and comprehend questions of historical writing, I have sought to abandon two approaches. The first tries to articulate historical continuity on the basis of a presumed transcendent point extrinsic to history as a means of claiming an allegedly pure objectivity. The second is the idea of history as rupture. Ruptures have indeed frequently occurred in modern and contemporary China. But, like some futile attempt to divert the flow of a river using a knife, ruptures actually manifest themselves as the extension of history in another form. At each historical rupture distinct forkings or diversions appear, but these also uncover historical fault lines where layers of historical sediment that had been previously concealed are now exposed. Where fault lines appear, the original picture returns and the specters of history reemerge.

The *Jindai* China Fever in Academic Circles

Zhou: In fact, an important starting point for many scholars concerned with the study of transition is the cultural reality of the nineties. They have come to advocate different views of history through their different assessments of how the nineties relate to the past. In the last few years, research into cultural transition has been trendy. Are there more complex factors feeding into this theme that we should reconsider?

Dai: Every historical epoch is engaged in the construction of a peculiar version of breaks and connectedness out of its contemporary needs. This challenge has arisen in my academic research. I am aware that it may appear to a suspicious eye that my shift to considering changes in China at the turn of the last century is just falling into line behind a trend.

During the nineties the reconsideration of China's transition in the eighties and nineties yielded what I call the *jindai* fever and the Shanghai fever. These are hot research topics undertaken by overseas Chinese scholars and by eminent scholars in China. Two things account for this academic trend among China studies scholars in the States. One is specific to American academia, which has its own logic: its attempt at self-renewal and subversion gave rise to specific theoretical concerns like postcolonialism, orientalism, cultural studies, cultural criticism, reflections on or critiques of Eurocentrism, and the review of the discourse of modernity. In the context of such theoretical concerns, modern China was rediscovered as a site that offers myriad possibilities for studying how a resourceful, enclosed oriental empire was sucked into the global capitalist process, how the transformation took place. And how the richness, heterogeneity, contingency, and multiplicity of history have manifested themselves.

The other factor is the issue of contemporaneity. Changes in Chinese society in the eighties and nineties and our frontal reencounter with the world cannot but compel us to reexamine the past. Specifically in Chinese academic circles, some eminent scholars have chosen to return to academic research at the end of the 1980s. Accompanying their return was an advocacy for academic norms and serious reflection on these norms. Discussion invariably had to begin with the historical moment when the modern disciplines were born in China. Or shall we say that a sorting out and establishing of the academic history of each discipline invariably accompanied those debates. Besides, each scholar has his or her own specific cultural or academic reason for choosing which specific path to take.

I have mentioned my own route and motivations. An academic friend once questioned my research, suggesting that it deviated from Chinese academic topics and discourses. The subtext as I understood it was, Are you trying to ride a wave, to echo academic topics that are hot in the West? He may very well be right in that my present theoretical background and chosen topics may, in some respects, fail to tie in with some aspects of the domestic academic agenda and therefore may convey the impression that my research agenda is more closely linked to the West. Yet, on the other hand, I sense that my topics are immediately relevant to Chinese realities. I feel comfortable with that. And that is because I am propelled in my turn toward history by my concern for contemporary social and cultural problems and my urge to respond particularly to contemporary issues. I take this to be a meaningful challenge at both the personal and academic levels. So I am by no means abandoning the contemporary in favor of *jindai*. Rather I am pursuing the meaning of *jindai* along different lines.

Zhou: What does the word *cultural* mean when you talk about the cultural history of Chinese film?

Dai: You know as well as I do that works on Chinese film history are scarce. *Zhongguo dianying fazhanshi* (*A History of the Development of Chinese Film*), a volume that Cheng Jihua and his collaborators edited in 1963, brought the review of Chinese film up to the 1950s. It remains the most authoritative history available. Since 1979 several books have been published on Chinese film which, I feel, have not yet managed to surpass Cheng's officially authorized book in terms of historical material and critical perspective. Lately, *Zhongguo wusheng dianying shi* (*A History of Silent Film in China*) has come out and its materials are remarkably substantial, yet in terms of historical coverage it stops at the 1930s.[3]

Two considerations went into the title *Zhongguo dianying wenhua shi* (*The Cultural History of Chinese Film*), which I gave to the course I am now teaching and to my forthcoming book. I will not be able to surpass Cheng Jihua and his collaborators in terms of the richness of historical materials they considered for the era between 1905 and 1949. However, my genuine concern with film history is not really with film per se. In my view one cannot confine oneself to the film itself or to film auteurs when analyzing or writing film history, for this would never lead to an adequate explanation of film as a medium or a phenomenon. Such an approach cannot provide the outline of an adequate picture of Chinese film history, nor can it offer an adequate interpretation of the problems that such a history of film may present to us contemporaries.

I know it sounds funny, but I initiated my course on the cultural history of Chinese film for overseas students while I was at the film academy. Later, it took shape as an intensive summer course offered to young professors and doctoral candidates from American academies, at Ohio State University. This is the first time I have offered this attempt to incorporate cultural studies approaches into Chinese film history to Chinese students. Of course I'll put my training as a film specialist to good use. But here my emphasis is more on the rich cultural meanings I discern in film artists, works, and phenomena. I would like to show how film, as mass culture, commercial culture, popular culture, and high culture all at once manifests to us complicated cultural meanings in a complex and intertwining context. I hope to include in this study processes of production, distribution, and film screening, and to examine their relationship and multiple links to contiguous areas of cultural formations, such as the production and reception of other genres of mass culture. Through film history, I am hoping to draw a profile for Chinese contemporary cultural geography. This is what I mean when I refer to the cultural history of film. Frankly speaking, I doubt I can command sufficient academic resources to meet the incredible demands of such a task.

Zhou: Could you briefly compare *A History of the Development of Chinese Film* and *A History of Silent Film in China*?

Dai: Both are still very useful today for readers because they give the basics of Chinese film history. The problem with *Development* is that its emphasis on the political significance and social function of film prevents it from giving an adequate assessment of film aesthetics. But interestingly, opposing or different approaches still might not yield a different conclusion than the one the book reaches. If we examine the leftist film movement of the thirties, in terms of artistic achievement it constitutes a Chinese art film movement, though not in a pure sense. If we refrain from pruning history in obscurantist ways or fitting it into a homogeneous narrative coherent with one's own view, we may see that few commercial or "soft" films of the thirties are as artistically sophisticated as the leftist films. As for *Silent Film*, the data are very solid. Unlike the former volume's omniscient authoritative manner, this book was written in an academic, exploratory style and attempts to clarify historical issues. It is an interesting reading experience to compare the parts on silent film in each book.

Film Theory and Cultural Studies

Zhou: You mentioned that Western film theory developed in the sixties and seventies. What about Chinese film theory?

Dai: My sense is that, regrettably, Chinese film theory in the strict sense has yet to develop. As in many places in the world, in China film theory began in a fragmentary way when enthusiasts began writing impression pieces that weren't particularly systematic or academic. These could be film criticism, a simple film textbook, or an essay on how films are made. Such products do not constitute what we would call a discipline today. But, in some sense, this is "clean" theory because it is not institutionalized. What motivated such work was simple love of film rather than the need to get an academic degree or promotion. To this moment, Chinese film theory remains, on the one hand, ideas about scriptwriting and directing or studies of filmmakers, and, on the other, studies of cinematic technology. In the mid eighties some of us undertook some attempts at theorizing. In retrospect, I think we have only managed to introduce Western film theory into China in a systematic fashion and apply it to reading Chinese films. That does not constitute our own film theory.

Zhou: Earlier in this interview, you mentioned that cultural studies provides the indispensable theoretical framework for film studies. When you used the concept of "shadow play" (*yingxi*) in the study of film history, you resorted to Raymond Williams' method in *Keywords*.[4] I have gotten a lot out of this genealogy of concepts. What is cultural studies for you? A methodology? A position? Or what?

Dai: Maybe it is easier to see cultural studies as a series of changes in theoretical positions, perspectives, and horizons. To see it, that is, as an interdisciplinary field rather than a methodology. Cultural studies is a quasi-discipline. It is at the very least a popular element in the Euro-American academy. Cultural studies for me is first of all anchored at a theoretical position where the critic makes no attempt at concealing the self-critical stance, the political and ideological make-up of his or her own cultural positioning. One unequivocal aspect of my cultural studies position is also a return to Marxism. Not just Western Marxism, but rather a return to classic Marxism. I don't mean to say that this is a panacea; it is, rather, ammunition. I am also quite certain on another point, which is that in using a critical weapon one does not abandon the critique of the weapon itself. So my premise may not rest on any transcendental aesthetic judgement, but neither does it imply a radical abandonment of aesthetics.

My work has always delivered cultural criticism, even ideological judgements. And yet therein I confront a dilemma, which is how do I relate to questions that the art film presents? How will I be able to sustain the critical edge of an aesthetic judgement so that my concern, my recognition, that film is an art will not be lost? On the other hand, cultural studies also involves the shift of perspectives and horizons, beyond an exclusive concern with cinema in general, specific films, or specific filmmakers. Of course we need to avoid formulaic, simplistic political readings, but this does not mean that we introduce an omnipotent artistic judgement or make a cultural judgement based on a close reading of the text.

Though I am good at close reading, bringing in the perspective of cultural studies means breaking the self-containment and closure of the text, even extending the concept of the text to cover more objects. We need to contextualize the text. That is, we need to read texts in their specific contexts, as well as to textualize the context, which is to say that changes in the social context must also be taken as texts for close reading.

For instance, the text that requires close reading is both itself a film phenomenon and the specific social context in which the phenomenon as such arises. To read closely then requires studying the means of production of film and the changing modes of production, the establishment of film capital, box-office income, and even a history of the cinema – that is, sites and ways of screening, modes of watching a film, and audience stratification (for instance, were film audiences in early times stratified, and if so, how?). My Chinese film study cannot focus on only domestically produced films, either. I also need to find out whether at any specific period Chinese films ever dominated the Chinese market, or whether American or French films always did, and what the relative proportions were. These are all things I must include in my studies.

The bringing in of cultural studies also means a change of method. For instance, the genealogy of keywords you mentioned can help us ascertain whether certain concepts have recurred throughout the entire history of film and whether these remain constant or undergo changes over the course of time and, if the latter, what their determining contexts are. In light of poststructuralism, I do not think one can reproduce the truth of a certain period in a film history, though of course I hope I can uncover more historical materials, fill in some of the blank places. But I am actually more concerned with unveiling the multiplicity and diversity of culture and cultural discourses. So importing cultural studies does not mean bringing in a whole set of definite approaches or methodologies, but encountering the complexity of history, accepting the challenges it presents us, and allowing my scholarship to embrace them. I may not be able to achieve this entirely, but I am willing to give it a try.

Film History and the Discussion of Modernity

Zhou: You have been examining the theme of modernity in the last few years. What in Chinese film history do you connect to your modernity studies? Could you elaborate your views on modernity from the perspective of film history?

Dai: My concern with modernity is one major reason I have been looking back further into film history. As far as the problematic of the construction and expansion of the discourse of modernity in China is concerned, film history offers the best research material. Of course, this may just reflect my predilection for the subject of my study.

Once warships and cannons forced open the doors, China was thrown into a process of modernization in the face of imperialism's military, political oppression and economic infiltration, which is to say that modernity is no simple matter. Indeed, modernity is no simple matter in any country in any historical period. In China, too, modernity is beyond the ken of any one single discipline within the humanities, and its explanations can only be found at the very least in the course of interdisciplinary research.

So, in a sense, film has a natural advantage over other subjects of study. For not only is it both a commercial and an industrial system, it is also both a mass culture as well as a cultural field that elite, serious culture has chronically interpenetrated. Finally, film is a stage on which distinct, intense political struggles play themselves out. Confronting this subject of study is the very best possible situation for problematizing, inspecting, and even clarifying the discourse of modernity.

My concerns about modernity are related to a reconsideration that those bold steps taken in the eighties and the nineties commercial tide have forced me to make. Frankly, I have reservations about people's grand optimism and enthusiasm for modernization. Even if we grant that its benefits outweigh its demerits for today's China, I think we run many implicit risks for tomorrow. If today, in the midst of radical changes and reconstruction, we do not retain our sobriety about the modernization process and the expansion of the discourse of modernity, we are risking a lot. Maybe this sounds unduly alarmist. But the theme of modernity that is drawing increasingly more and more attention is still new, indeed as unfamiliar to many people as it is to me. In Western academic circles, this notion is already outmoded. Or, should I say, modernization is still important but its focus is differently placed. Modernity aroused general concern for some time in the West because of its centrality to Western intellectual thought and the academy. Soon people realized, however, that discussion of the question of modernity in itself does not really offer any solutions, since modernity turns out to be an all-embracing theme, a cultural reality any country that is voluntarily or involuntarily going through modernization will have to encounter.

The word itself accommodates too many varying realities. In each developing, modern state or nation, the construction and expansion of a modernist discourse will be different. So-called wholesale Westernization has always been a myth; it has never occurred in any country or region. Yet modernization is indeed Westernization or globalization, a process of enforced emulation of the West. The more important problematic then is how each different country has appropriated Western forms, and how it deals with its own tradition, culture, and national survival in the larger landscape of globalization. Of course, necessarily and as part of our effort to sort things out, we must undertake an archaeology of knowledge. Such an approach enables us to understand the production and development of the modernity discourse in Western academic history and in the history of Western intellectual thought. Though I shall try my best, this is truly beyond the reach of my capacities.

What concerns me more is the formation and rewriting of the discourse of modernity in China. At the beginning of Chinese film history, we can see how people borrow an imported form, an art form that is industrial, technological, scientific, and modern. With this art form they tried to incorporate the life experience and representation of different social groups in premodern China. For discussion's sake let's take a real classic, the first commercially successful, domestic production, *Gu'er jiuzu ji* (*The Story of the Orphan Saving the Grandparents*, 1923). Films like it fold premodern narratives and moral values into a modern narrative, reconstructing it so that it becomes an effective component of modern experience. The film is a typical story of the Qin Xianglian or Zhao Wuniang type: a woman is wronged and endures all sorts of suffering in order eventually to have the wrong redressed. A happy ending is transplanted into the perfectly representative space of the modern school: grandparent and grandchild are reunited in mutual recognition after a separation. The suffering daughter-in-law, who is consequently vindicated, donates half her property to run a school because she believes firmly that the family will survive its ordeal if it relies on education. Obviously, this is a classic enlightenment discourse in which education saves China in its entirety and each individual Chinese person as well. The film also raises issues such as the legal system of inheritance, the camera, and modern welfare. That makes it an appropriate subject for my reflections on the heterogeneity of modernity.

Theoretical Resources and Rethinking

Zhou: What is the relation of the theoretical approaches informing your scholarly work to such intellectual resources as poststructuralism, postcolonialism, and Western Marxism that were introduced into China in the eighties and nineties? What insights do you have in regard to your own reception of imported theory?

Dai: It is an embarrassing thing to discuss. I began establishing my epistemological and theoretical framework and deciding on the course my scholarship would eventually take in the eighties. My key resources were Western film theory and, in a natural extension, poststructuralism. For me the two most influential theories have been poststructuralism and Western Marxism. During the nineties, the influence of Marxism on my work, the importance I place on it, and its weight in my academic research have all become more prominent. Poststructuralism was my biggest influence in the eighties. Then I was mainly engaged in two tasks: learning to use Western theory and film; and participating in translating and introducing Western film theory. I benefitted greatly from that process.

My training in theory has been haphazard, but quite effective. I never received any rigorous academic or disciplinary training. My choice of theories has been governed by a pragmatic criterion: whether or not a theory was inspiring or useful. Consequently it has all been quite subjective. There was a lot of misreading in the process and some serious decontextualization. I neither knew nor particularly cared about how theories were generated in their own specific contexts or what scholarly or ideological purposes they were brought to serve. So I was also doing a lot of quoting out of context. The change at the turn of the eighties and in the nineties compelled me to rethink and critically reflect on Western theory and film theory. As I have frequently said, rethinking does not mean a rejection of theory or a return to a pretheoretical state. To this point, structuralism and poststructuralism have been important intellectual resources for me. In fact, in the West the discipline of cultural studies evolved out of the very process of reflecting on theory. What has struck me over the course of the nineties is a growing sense of a lack of continuity in contemporary Chinese scholarly tradition. Each generation thinks it is creating an original new world, unconcerned with what has previously been accomplished. I think this is what motivated eminent scholars at the beginning of the nineties to propose investigating the norms of academic practice, which means, on the one hand, sorting out the history of disciplinary practices and nurturing the consciousness of problematization and, on the other hand, understanding what scholars in and outside China in the same field may already have done, whether their work and ours intersect, and whether dialogues are a possibility. I think that with advancing modernization, more and more channels for dialogue are opening up and spatial distance is being continuously compressed. We are no longer wanting in terms of information resources and can establish relations of exchange, even challenge others in our fields in other places all over the world. So, at the very least, we can now avoid inventing calculus before modern mathematics, that is, we need not repeat the foundational work that has already been done.

Postcolonial theory had a powerful impact on me at the beginning of the nineties. As transnational capital entered China, intensifying the globalization and marketization of Chinese culture, China's Third World cultural status became more and more obvious. Sensitive intellectuals were aware of this. My partial grasp of postcolonial theories nonetheless did offer me a new perspective, new spaces. Now, with better understanding and more reconsideration over the years, it seems to me that we should not apply postcolonial theories in a simplistic way. One obvious reason is that China has not undergone a colonial history in the strict sense of the word. Hence "postcolonial culture" in China must be considered in relation to its formation, features, and implications. Each needs to be systematically examined and thought through. At the same time, strictly speaking, postcolonial theory is a leftist resistance theory generated by Third World scholars in the US academy. Our reception of this Western theory cannot proceed in a vacuum; rather, we must try to understand what the conditions generating the theory have been, what the theorists' speaking positions are, and who their audience is. Once decontextualized, postcolonialism tends to be essentialized, simplified, and objectified into truth. Postcolonial theories still concern me, but in a more prudent way now. In the broadest sense, orientalism and postcolonial theories belong in the same camp.

Feminism and the Writing of Film History

Zhou: How does your feminism figure in the study of the cultural history of Chinese film?

Dai: In a disciplinary sense, feminist theory and a feminist position are fundamental and imperative to film study. I have noted that where scholars totally reject feminism, as some eminent scholars do, they run the unnecessary risk of blind spots in their film analyses. Feminism is also a central component of cultural studies. And gender studies shares many spaces with cultural studies. The study of women per se – the study of women directors or women staff or the image of women in film – is only one part of what constitutes gender studies, and these issues are not the most important component in my work. Women's discourse and the study of discourse on women, that is, how gender as a discourse is effectively organized in the mainstream, peripheral, or resistance discourses, are more relevant. Are the worlds these discourses inhabit related to the worlds inhabited by women, and if so, how? These are some of my concerns.

Take for example, *The Story of the Orphan Saving the Grandparents*. Wang Hanlun, who played the film's woman protagonist, Yu Weiru, was the first prominent actress in the history of Chinese film, as well as its first film star of the tragic type. At the time Wang was called "Number One Tragic Female Role." Her experiences as a film star could serve as a subject for women's studies. But what also concerns me is how the director, Zheng Zhengqiu, modernized a premodern narrative and temporal experience by way of subjecting his female character to a series of tragic outcomes: she loses her husband, is slandered, gets banished from her husband's family, loses her father, and is impoverished. Fashioning a Chinese-style tragicomedy through the characterization of a suffering woman produced an effective mode of narration for Chinese filmmakers – and an archetypal tragic drama.

In other instances, the influence of enlightenment culture on early Chinese film culture was complex, its infiltration of gender concepts in many films quite chaotic. We could say that early film culture maintained what could be called an anti-feudal gesture in the best sense. There is indeed substantial premodern, feudalistic writing. But, on the other hand, there is sufficient sobriety and vigilance in the construction of gender imagery. Take as an example the subversive use of the idea of virginity in a very traditional story. During the silent film era, in the martial art film *Hong xia* (*Red Chivalrous Heroine*, 1929), much plotting concerns a villain's attempts to possess by force a lovely girl, and suspense is constructed around whether or not the girl loses her virginity. The villain eventually gets what he wants. But the story ends with the chivalrous heroine using her authority to marry the girl off to a good man, as though the girl's compromised virginity is a negligible matter. The narrative's two cultural logics are contradictory. These complex gender representations also characterize the diversity of the entire contemporary cultural construct, in which interweaving of the different representations of modern and premodern experiences coexist with crisscrossed popular and enlightenment discourse.

Another good example is the film *Nü xia bai meigui* (*White Rose, the Chivalrous Heroine*, 1929). As the film opens, we see a girl in a sports uniform performing in a modern space, the playground of a women's college. Upon winning the championship, her reward is a set of clothes decorated with the words "A manly heroine." In the next scene, she appears transformed into precisely this "manly heroine," like a Hua Mulan, and is drawing her bow to shoot an arrow. Her family is then overwhelmed by a crisis that is constructed in the genre of the the American Western: some villains forcibly seize the family "ranch." Just then White Rose's elder brother gets sick, so she dresses herself up as a man, all decked out like a cowboy, and sets out to resolve the family crisis. She straps on a Chinese sword that has a Western saber hilt, and she wields her sword in the style of a Western swordsman. When she arrives back at the ranch, the villains are Indians played by Chinese actors with faces smeared black. Villains and heroes enter into a life-and-death combat at close quarters. When she clothes herself as a woman again, White Rose appears in a low-cut, long Western dress. You can see how the woman's image traverses diverse discursive systems, as a sign that sutures a discursive system fraught with gaps and fissures, enabling the constitution of a modern Chinese narrative. Of course, the filmmakers at the time were not making a conscious effort to get this effect. Possibly they were only concerned with box-office returns and mass entertainment. Nonetheless, their film's gender discourse is truly interesting.

Since I became engaged in film study, feminism has been my basic position and research method, though this seems to have gone largely unnoticed. Only when I proclaimed myself to be a feminist and conducted research on women writers and female directors did I encounter loud applause and condemnation. I find this truly interesting. It is as if feminism cannot be recognized (or maliciously resisted) until it comes out on a banner. For me, feminism is an important position, an integral part of my theoretical position. More importantly, it is an experience and a way of life.

Zhou: Will your study of film history pay attention to the significance of art in the development of Chinese film? Also, do you intend to uncover previously unknown films and directors as part of the film history you are describing?

Dai: As a specific artistic genre with its own development, changes, and evolution, Chinese film has its own peculiar history, and within that history, aesthetic concepts and creative principles that change. I am skeptical of the authority of canons, at least from the point of view of my current position. I do realize, however, that I am vested with the power and the obligation to reiterate canons. Of course, revisiting the history of film again will certainly involve a reassessment of directors and works that have been previously neglected. Still I am not fully confident in this regard because the most difficult thing about working on a film history is access to film materials. And that depends on non-academic, non-cultural factors like money and power. I will try my best in this endeavor, of course. Reassessment of works and directors is an inevitable process, not an end in itself.

Film, Literature, and Personal Habit

Zhou: The relation of film and literature has been highly entangled, especially in the history of Chinese film. How do you approach this problem?

Dai: Except for the period from 1949 to 1979, film and literature have always poached on each other's preserves. They are neither as close nor as distant as many people imagine. If we take the view that there are seven great arts, then among them the relationship of film and literature is most intimate. Film is also closely related to art, music, and in a sense even to architecture and drama. Yet film and literature, and I mean fiction here, are both narrative modes generated in the modern context and inscribed with elements of mass culture. As widely received forms, their influences were mutual and direct.

We are all familiar with films adapted from great literary works. Not all of us are very familiar with the fact that many popular novels in the post-industrial era are written for films. Many best sellers are produced in order to promote the film. I just read a book review of *The Horse Whisperer* (*Mayuzhe*) that advised against spending twelve bucks for a badly written best seller, because eventually it will turn into a thrilling Hollywood film that one can enjoy for just a few dollars. You can find piles of paperbacks in American supermarkets with titles like *The Bridges of Madison County* (translated into Chinese under the title *Langqiao yimeng*) which generally speaking are written for Hollywood. Hence, in the twentieth century, film has to a large extent reversed the equation to exert an influence on literature – at least, on popular literature.

Regarding serious literature in the early twentieth century, the modernist literary movement as a reference point for film art, and under competitive pressure from it, could not avoid reflecting on its own medium in order to contemplate what it might accomplish on its own and in conjunction with film. Language experimentation had already emerged in serious literature for some time, making modern fiction closer to poetry than to more conventional narrative prose. As the sixties began, literature's unilateral impact on film ended. But in the seventies and eighties, when film theory became the cutting-edge theory in Europe, an adverse theoretical current occurred. Film theory began to impact literary theory. For example, Teresa de Lauretis, an eminent contemporary scholar and feminist from the United States, is a specialist working on film theory. But her book *Alice Doesn't* begins with film theory and then reviews the work of almost all structuralist and poststructuralist masters as well. It is a pioneer work for the humanities.

This relationship between literature and film has not yet drawn much attention in China. The historical situation of contemporary Chinese film is rather unique. The stress on film's social function and the demand that film be an instrument of socialist realism have resulted in a disproportionate emphasis on literature in the field of contemporary Chinese film. Indeed, the dominance of the script over the visual and the influence of literature on film in the fifties and sixties manifest themselves in two aspects: one is the literariness of film, and the other is the dramatic form film takes. These constitute the specific legacy passed on to us from a specific history. Yet ironically in the period when script and dramatic film enjoyed such unshakable status, Chinese film was most deficient in literary terms. Richness of narration and the complexity of characterization were far from adequately developed. So the alleged dramatic quality of these films completely squandered the artistic power of the drama as such – its self-reflexive quality and its capacity for cross-fertilization with other art forms. In this predicament, film art entered into a stage of total loss.

Over the eighties and nineties that old quest for literary film, dramatized film, the emphasis on the script have all fallen under multidirectional attacks from the Fourth and Fifth Generation filmmakers, whose portentous agenda became the purism of pure film, film as experimentation in film language. The sad thing for so many generations of modern Chinese people is that history leaves us transitional moments that are all too brief. We always seem to be in a state of longing for a period of stability, so we can find time to reflect, ponder, and explore as we are implicated in yet another portentous event.

The experimental period for Chinese art film and film language, and film language's self-conscious reflection on itself, was very brief. Commercialization began soon after. As if goaded by commercialization, many films took off again in uncritical pursuit or courtship of literature, seeking sensational plots, narrativity, and entertainment value. Adaptation from literary works became trendy again, ushering in another trend I would call literature for translation. This phenomenon, in which writers produce works for "translation" into film, has not been discussed much. The Zhang Yimou phenomenon strongly influenced the literary arena in the early nineties. It reached its extreme point in 1993, when it was said that the whole literary world had been roped into film and TV production, with the sole exceptions of Wang Anyi and Zhang Chengzhi. Soon after that, of course, Zhang himself adapted his own *Hei junma* (*Beautiful Black Horse*) and Wang

Anyi signed on as scriptwriter for *Fengyue* (*Romance*). So film captured everyone in the end.

This is not salubrious for either film or literature. It's the sad outcome of market pressure and the general cultural condition of being in the Third World. With the onset of the era of mass media, postindustrial media such as TV have transformed our lifestyle and marginalized film as well. Ideally, film should continue to survive like any other ancient genre of art. When it is no longer authoritative and all-encompassing, infiltrating the everyday life of every modern being, perhaps film will enact a new dialogue with literature as their destinies draw closer together.

Zhou: Would you please talk about how your reading and personal interests related to your academic research?

Dai: I remember when I graduated from university, I read a short essay by Xu Chi, which impressed me very strongly. He was advocating a reading campaign for the whole populace, under the slogan *Bolan quanshu, buqiu shenjie* (Reading Extensively without Depth). He wanted to see how much reading people could do in ten years, and he hoped it would have good effects. He inspired me. I was a teenager during the Cultural Revolution when there was not much around to read. So I allowed myself the privilege of believing that all books are good. Consequently, I read virtually anything I could lay my hands on without any discretion whatever and in a very promiscuous and disorganized fashion. Looking back, this is quite a spiritual treasure trove but also a deeply rooted bad habit that prevents me from making myself into a modern scholar who specializes in a discipline.

Xu Chi's advice and my choice were premised on a sort of elitist reverence for culture, a belief that all books are beneficial, so I read all sorts of books in the humanities and beyond. It was also possible to do this sort of thing because there weren't many books available at the time, and I was a fast reader. So I read a lot of mixed stuff. Now, with the boom in the book market and voluminous publications pouring off the press of a truly mixed quality, I wouldn't dare claim that reading any book is good. I remember in the mid eighties when China suddenly went on a cultural kick and everyone was reading something on the bus: martial arts, romance novels by Jin Yong, Gu Long, Qiong Yao, Yi Shu, Xi Juan, and so on. Popular reading does not resemble the sort of early eighties beneficial reading. It is cultural consumption, no different from buying fashionable clothes or eating an ice cream. Of course, I am not saying that Jin Yong and others have no worth. What I mean is that the modes of production and reception are recognized and confirmed in terms of consumption.

On the other hand, I myself have been forced to be more disposed to the disciplines. I cannot afford to read so extensively on different subjects anymore. Still, reading is the most important part of my life and the most enjoyable. My friends long ago nicknamed me "the book hedonist." Then I read a lot and wrote little. Now I write more and have little time for reading. Both are problematic. The dilemma that scholars in the humanities face is that society is more and more professionalized, and the disciplines, more and more specialized. I do not think this is good. Extensive reading is one possible way for a good scholar in the humanities to resist and escape being captured by her discipline and her profession. Every scholar in the humanities has his or her own taste, though we know after Bourdieu's critical work that "taste" is an indicator of class or caste.

I think what truly challenges thought is perhaps not only the latest developments in the discipline, but academic events of all sorts in related disciplines. I take up cultural studies because it is *inter*disciplinary. My sense is that in the twenty-first century what the humanities have to offer will derive from their professionalization, despite China's current problem of inadequate specialization and disciplinarity. In terms of the future directions for the humanities both in the domestic Chinese context and globally, interdisciplinary attempts will undoubtedly emerge to provide an alternative.

Zhou: Your textual analyses of novels and films are very thorough and delicate. How many times must you read a film text for such a task?

Dai: I don't dare open my mouth until I've watched a film at least three times; I see it at least five times before writing about it. The *Dianying yu shisu shenhua* (*Film and Popular Myth*) essays are based on films I saw at least twenty times. I often joke that I've destroyed two possible entertainments in life: novel reading and film watching. That is why I will never try my hand at music. Otherwise, I will be left with no pleasures at all.

I've gotten to the state where I cannot watch a movie or read a novel for fun. There is a big difference between the experience of watching a movie the first time around and then watching it again later. I agree wholeheartedly with a visiting American professor at the film academy who said as a critique of film theory that its reading of film is actually anti-filmic. That is truly the case in the sense that general audiences see a movie once, since so few films deserve or attract people for a second viewing. When I was at university, I encountered the latest Western literary theory, New Criticism, and learned that the best experience is close reading – a lesson I was actually learning myself from translating and reading on my own.

Zhou: Let's get to some personal questions. How do you work? Late at night?

Dai: That is difficult to answer. I used to pull all-nighters. I'd wake up at ten in the evening and start working. But as I enter middle age and have more social obligations, there is no way I could go to sleep at 5 A.M. and get up at 2 P.M. My lazy, sloppy lifestyle is no longer possible. Also, I recognize the need to be more disciplined, like requiring myself to write one or two thousand words a day. Otherwise I will never complete what I want to get done. With more projects but less energy than I used to have, I seem to have lost my capacity to rush deadlines. It may not just be capability. Facing more complex conditions, I have become more prudent, less willing to exhaust myself with one sensational event and miss out on others at any given moment. I want to be more cool and careful. Also, I am working on changing my florid and free-flowing writing style of the eighties. A plain, simple, and lucid style is more difficult to achieve.

Zhou: Do you rely much on the computer?

Dai: Absolutely. In 1992, I spent my entire fortune on a Stone word processor but, alas, it became totally obsolete very rapidly. My reason for using the computer is highly personal. In high school, I developed a special type of longhand that is not quite the same as anyone else's. My handwriting is consequently unintelligible to the workers at the presses. I cannot really change my handwriting at this stage, so I started using a computer and very rapidly became so dependent on it that I now basically cannot compose by hand. It is terrible. A true nightmare of modernism.

There is something symbolic here. Our lives are more and more deeply immersed in our modern urban milieu. There is no need to deny that we are, or at least I am, infatuated with the various conveniences of modern life. Recently I wrote in an essay that as Third World intellectuals we are confronted with a three-fold role: participate in and promote China's modernization; suffer the pain that without question accompanies modernization; and reflexively criticize China's modernization and discourses of modernity.

In the modern West and even post-democratized Taiwan the financial crisis that nearly devastated Southeast Asian countries this year keeps reminding us that a modernized future is no utopia. This is even more true for China, which is just entering globalization at an accelerated pace as the century turns. To exaggerate a bit, whether China, at this critical juncture and with its 1.4 billion people, can choose a better, more appropriate path is a matter of consequence for the China of tomorrow but for the world as well. We may offer a better alternative to Europe and particularly to the United States. On the other hand, we may also be a disaster for the world.

This is not, of course, the question of "who will feed China?" The question is more complex and serious than that. To identify China's future path and affirm our role as intellectuals, we need a frame of reference that not only acknowledges the recent historical experience but also incorporates China's modern experience. We cannot just caress the scars that history has left and daydream about some idyllic future. We must embrace a truly global perspective, a system of multiple references, a visionary mode of thinking and observation. I believe not just in promoting China's modernization today. We must also join in considering what kinds of intellectual resources we offer the China of tomorrow. This is intellectual work that each of us needs to engage in today. That will require formulating our agenda concretely and with keen insight.

Notes

The interview was conducted by Zhou Yaqin, Ph.D. candidate, Department of Chinese, Peking University, on 29 September 1997.

1 The novels of Jin Yong – martial arts fiction – were imported into mainland

China from Hong Kong in the early 1980s. They soon gained popularity and a huge readership that included elite intellectuals, college students, young workers, and peasants. So-called Jin Yong fever persists to this day. The Joint Publishing Co. brought out *The Complete Works of Jin Yong*, a best seller reprinted in serial editions, including pirate editions. Wang Yichuan, professor at Beijing Normal University, put Jin Yong into the twentieth-century Chinese literary canon, displacing Mao Dun.

2 Whereas the Chinese terms *jindai* and *xiandai* are customarily translated into English as "modern," they refer to two different periods. *Jindai* refers to the late Qing dynasty, from the Opium War in the 1940s to the setting up of the Republic in 1911. *Xiandai* refers basically to the first half of the twentieth century.

3 Cheng Jihua, Li Shaobai, Xing Zuwen, eds, *Zhongguo dianying fazhanshi* (A history of the development of Chinese film) (Beijing: Zhongguo dianying chubanshe, 1963); Li Suyuan and Hu Jubin, *Zhongguo wusheng dianying shi* (A history of silent film in China) (Beijing: Zhongguo dianying chubanshe, 1996).

4 "Shadow play" (*yingxi*) was the initial translation into Chinese of the term *movie*. In 1984 and 1985, writings and discussions on rewriting film history used "shadow play" as a keyword to critique the so-called errors or demerits in Chinese culture. It was argued that the introduction of movies into China was merely to record or rewrite traditional Chinese opera, hence a continuation, in both form and content, of the last vestiges of feudalism. When these writings were translated into English, the special term "shadow play" was used. Dai Jinhua used the term as an entry point to discussing the features and problems of the study of film history and the entire historical and cultural rethinking movement of the 1980s.—TRANS.

Translated by Lau Kin Chi

Dai Jinhua: A Short Biography

Dai Jinhua speaks passionately of her maternal grandmother. In tracing the sociohistorical origins of Dai's feminist consciousness, we should no doubt follow her lead and consider the fate of this unfortunate person, a member of the last generation of women raised under feudal conditions. Dai's grandmother married a man who spent his time in brothels, yet whose family she was compelled to serve with devotion. In spite of it all, the old woman was, in Dai's own words, proud and intelligent, possessing an exquisite memory and an obstinate determination to educate herself. Dai grew up at her grandmother's side in a rich storytelling culture. The older woman treated the little girl to folk legends, vernacular tales, Peking opera dramas, and classical novels, as well as to her own story of personal suffering. The grandmother was acutely conscious of her victimization and identified the institutions – marriage, the gender hierarchy, the system of the extended family – which were to blame for it. The dictum that she passed on to young Dai Jinhua, engraving it deeply into her mind, was *Yihou jiaoshu, bao dushen zhuyi* (Be a teacher when you grow up. Stay single.). Her own grandmother was Dai's original teacher and cracked open the door to feminist critique for her.

Born in Shandong in 1959, Dai grew up with a father who came from a peasant background, a loyal Party member who had a passion for literature even though social turbulence had denied both him and Dai's mother any chance at a college education. Dai herself entered Peking University in 1978, among the several post–Great Proletarian Cultural Revolution cohorts whose ranks included so many other profoundly intelligent, irrepressible intellectuals; this was the group that plunged headlong into the cultural reflection movements of the 1980s. After graduation, Dai Jinhua immediately started her teaching career at the Beijing Film Academy, where at around the same time she began translating European and American film theories. In 1987, Dai and a colleague established a major in film theory, China's first.

Dai Jinhua obtained and then, after some consideration, declined a scholarship to study for her doctorate at a US university in the immediate moments after the June 1989 Incident. Her decision to abandon the path of overseas graduate training was deliberate and it grew out of her reluctance to leave China. She stayed on, she says, to witness at first hand how the currents of history would continue to flow in the wake of this epochal moment. In 1993, the Institute of Comparative Literature and Comparative Culture at Peking University formally recruited her onto its faculty. There, she initiated a graduate major in cultural studies in 1995, as well as commencing her own project of developing a critical studies in Chinese popular culture. Between 1990 and the present Dai has visited New Delhi, Paris, Hong Kong, Taiwan, and Tokyo, where she gave lectures on Chinese cinema, cultural history, and women's films and literature. She has also traveled extensively in the United States where she has given seminars, classes, or presentations at Duke, Cornell, UC Santa Barbara, UCLA, Ohio State University, Pittsburgh, UC Berkeley, UC Irvine, Harvard, and Rutgers.

Dai and Jing Wang initiated a multi-year collaborative project in 1997 that centers on modern and contemporary Chinese popular culture. Wang, Dai, and their many collaborators come from a wide range of global locations and are developing an interinstitutional, international, and interdisciplinary Chinese popular cultural studies project. No doubt her grandmother would be more than satisfied that Dai Jinhua has become an influential, inventive, productive scholar. Perhaps she would be a little more than amazed to find her granddaughter happily married too. The fruit of all the older woman's struggle is certainly borne out in the ecstatic intellectual and rich personal life her granddaughter is privileged to live.

Select Bibliographies

Selected Works by Dai Jinhua

Books

Dianying lilun yu piping shouce (Film theory and handbook of criticism) (Beijing: Keji wenxian chubanshe, 1993).

Jingcheng tuwei: dianying, nüxing, wenxue (Break out of an encirclement in the mirror city: a collection of essays) (Beijing: Zuojia chubanshe, 1995).

Jing yu shisu shenhua: yingpian jingdu shiba lie (Mirror and secular myth: eighteen examples of film close reading) (Beijing: Zhongguo guangbo dianshi chubanshe, 1995).

Pintu youxi (Piece together: a collection of essays) (Jinan: Shandong Taishan chubanshe, 1999).

Youzai jingzhong: Dai Jinhua fangtan lu (Like in the mirror: interviews with Dai Jinhua) (Beijing: Zhishi chubanshe, 1999).

Jingcheng dixing tu: jiushi niandai Zhongguo wenhua yanjiu (The cultural typography of the mirror city: Chinese cultural studies of the 1990s) (Taipei: Taiwan Lianhe wenxue chubanshe, 1999).

Shedu zhi zhou: xin shiqi nüxing shuxie yu nüxing wenhua (The wading boat: female writings and cultures since 1979) (Xi'an: Shanxi jiaoyu chubanshe, 2000)

Yingxing shuxie: jiushi niandai Zhongguo wenhua yanjiu (Invisible writing: Chinese cultural studies of the 1990s) (Nanjing: Jiangsu renmin chubanshe, 1999).

Wu zhong fengjing: Zhongguo dianying wenhua 1978–1988 (Scenery in the fog: Chinese cinema culture 1978–1988) (Beijing: Peking University Press, 2000).

Dai Jinhua and Meng Yue, *Fuchu lishi dibiao* (Emerging on the horizon of history) (Zhengzhou: Henan renmin chubanshe, 1989).

Edited Volumes

Shiji zhi men: jiushi niandai nüxing wenxue zuopin xuan (The gate of a century: an anthology of mainland female writings of the 1990s) (Beijing: Zhongguo shehui kexue wenxian chubanshe, 1998).

Xiandai wenxue mingzuo: Lu Yin (Great works of modern literature series: Lu Yin) (Beijing: Renmin wenxue chubanshe, 1998).

Articles

"Dianying: Ya'nusi shidai sanren tan" (Film: Janus era dialogues), *Dianying yishu* (Film art), no. 9, 1998, pp. 3–14.

"Xieta: chongdu disi dai" (Slanting tower: rereading the Fourth Generation), *Dianying yishu* (Film art), no. 4, 1989, pp. 3–13. Also *Zhongguo dianying lilun wenxuan (1920–1980)* (Chinese film theory from 1920 to 1980: an anthology), edited by Luo Yijun, vol. 2, pp. 481–92 (Beijing: Wenhua yishu chubanshe).

"Liegu de ling yi cepan: chudu Yu Hua" (The other side of rift valley: a preliminary reading of Yuhua), *Beijing wenxue* (Bejing literature), no. 7, 1989, pp. 26–33. Also in *Zhongguo dangdai zuojia mianmian guan* (Aspects of Chinese contemporary writers), edited by Lin Jianfa and Wang Jingtao, pp. 682–98 (Changchun: Shidai wenyi chubanshe, 1991). Also in *Xunzhao de shidai* (The era of search), edited by Li Jiefei and Yang Jie, pp. 107–21 (Beijing: Beijing Normal University Press, 1992).

"You shehui xiangzheng dao zhengzhi shenhua: Cui Wei yishu shijie yiyu" (From social symbol to political myth: a corner of Cui Wei's art world), *Dianying yishu* (Film art), no. 8, 1989, pp. 15–20.

"Duanqiao: zi yidai de yishu" (Severed bridge: the art of the young generation), *Dianying yishu* (Film art), nos. 3, 4, 1990, pp. 135–47; 64–78.

"Xin Zhongguo dianying: disan shijie piping de biji" (The films of New China: notes of criticism on the Third World), *Dianying yishu* (Film art), no. 1, 1991, pp. 46–54. Also in *Yuwang yu huanxiang: dongfang yu xifang* (Desire and idol: east and west), edited by Yue Daiyun, pp. 218–23 (Nanchang: Jiangshi renmin chubanshe, 1991).

"Dazhong chuanbo meijie: yige wenhuaxue de sikao biji" (Mass media: a reflective note on cultural studies), *Shanghai wen lun* (Shanghai literature criticism), no. 6, 1991, pp. 12–16.

"Lishi xushi yu huayu: shiqi nian lishi ticai yingpian er ti" (Historical narrative and discourse: two subjects of the historical film in the seventeen years era), *Beijing dianying xueyuan xuebao* (Beijing Film Academy journal), no. 1, 1992, pp. 185–92.

"Lishi zhi zi: yingtan diwu dai" (The children of history: the Fifth Generation of Chinese cinema), *Meixue yu wenyi xue yanjiu* (Studies of aesthetics and literature), no. 1, 1993, pp. 113–22.

"Jingcheng zhi zhong: xifang nüxing zhuyi dianying lilun zongshu" (In the city of mirror: a summary of Western feminist film theory), *Shanghai wen lun* (Shanghai literature criticism), no. 4, 1992, pp. 17–22.

"Taotuo zhong de tuowang: Ling Zifeng daoyan yishu biji" (Falling prey while fleeing: notes on Ling Zifeng's directing art), *Dianying yishu* (Film art), no. 5, 1992, pp. 8–14.

"Ci'an: jiushi niandai dianying biji zhi yi" (This side of the bank: the first note on mainland films in the 1990s), *Beijing dianying xueyuan xuebao* (Beijing Film Academy journal), no. 2, 1992, pp. 97–106.

"Liegu: jiushi niandai dianying biji zhi er" (Rift valley: the second note on mainland films in the 1990s), *Yishu guangjiao* (Wide-angle art), no. 6, 1992, pp. 4–13.

"*Ren, gui, qing*: yige nüren de kunjing" (*Human, Woman, Demon*: The dilemma of a woman), *Shanghai wen lun* (Shanghai literature criticism), no. 1, 1992, pp. 59–64.

"'Xinxiang': wutai, chuantong yu fugui" (Aroma in heart: tradition and return), *Dangdai dianying* (Contemporary cinema), no. 4, 1992, pp. 20–25.

"'Qiu Ju da guansi': changren gushi" (Qiu Ju: the story of an ordinary person). *Zhongguo shibao* (China times), 12 March 1991. Also in *Qiu Ju da guansi* (Qiu Ju's lawsuit), edited by Jiao Xionping, pp. 66–71 (Taipei: Wanxiang tushu chuban gongsi, 1993).

"Bukejian de nuxing: xin Zhongguo dianying zhong de nüxing xingxiang yu nuxing de dianying (Invisible women: contemporary Chinese cinema and women's film), *Dangdai dianying* 6, 1994, pp. 37–45. Also in *positions: east asia cultures critique* 3, no. 1, 1995, pp. 255–80.

"Hongqi pu: yizuo yishi xingtai de fuqiao" (The chart of red banner: a floating bridge of ideology). *Dangdai dianying*, (Contemporary Cinema), no. 3, 1990, pp. 26–43. Also in *Re-Reading: Popular Culture and Ideology*, edited by Tang Xiaobing (Hong Kong: Oxford University Press, 1993).

"*Qingchun zhi ge*: lishi shiyu zhong de chongdu" (The song of youth: rereading the historical vision), in *Re-Reading Popular Culture and Ideology*, edited by Tang Xiaobing, pp. 166–83 (Hong Kong: Oxford University Press, 1993).

"Sisuo yu jianzheng: Huang Jianxin zuopin" (Thought and testimony: the works of Huang Jianxin), *Dangdai dianying* (Contemporary cinema), no 2, 1994, pp. 46–52.

"Benwen de celüe: dianying xushi yanjiu" (Strategy of the text: studies on film narrative), *Dianying yisho* (Film art), no. 1, 1994, pp. 58–63.

"Zhuiwen ziwo: nü daoyan Huang Shuqin" (A conversation with Huang Shuqin), *positions: east asia cultures critique*, vol. 3, no. 3, 1995, pp. 790–805.

"Miwang zhi lu: Zhou Xiaowen zuopin" (The journey of bewilderment: the works of Zhou Xiaowen), *Dangdai dianying* (Contemporary cinema), no. 5, 1994, pp. 37–44.

"Jing yu minzu yuyan: jiushi niandai wenhua biji zhi yi" (Mirror and national allegory: the first note on 1990s culture), *Shanghai wenhua* (Shanghai culture), no. 4, 1994, pp. 31–40.

"Shedu zhi zhou: jiushi niandai wenxue biji zhi'er" (Ferry boat: the second note on 1990s culture), *Shanghai wenhua* (Shanghai culture), no. 5, 1994, pp. 16–22.

"Meiyu shijie: dianying 1993" (Rainy season: mainland film in 1993), *Dangdai dianying* (Contemporary cinema), no. 5, 1994, pp. 12–19.

"Suilie yu chongjian de jingcheng" (The disintegrated and reconstructed city of mirrors), *Jinri xianfeng* (Avant-garde today), no. 1, 1994, pp. 113–19.

"*Bawang bieji*: lishi de jingpian" (*Farewell My Concubine*: the historical scene), *Dongfang* (Orient), no. 1, 1994, pp. 76–8.

"Jingcheng yiyu" (A corner in the city of mirrors), *Zhongshan* (Bell mountain), no. 5, 1994, pp. 120–26.

"'Shiji' de zhongjie: chongdu Zhang Jie'" (The end of "century": rereading Zhang Jie), *Wenyi zhengming* (Literature & art contend), no. 4, 1994, pp. 35–45.

"Tuwei biaoyan: jiushi niandai wenhua miaoshu zhi yi" (A performance of breaking out of a trap: a portrayal of the 1990s culture), *Zhongshan* (Bell mountain), no. 6, 1994, pp. 97–104.

"Jiushu yu xiaofei: jiushi niandai wenhua miaoshu zhi'er" (Redemption and consumption: a second portrayal of the 1990s culture), *Zhongshan* (Bell mountain), no. 2, 1995, pp. 194–200. Also titled "Redemption and Consumption: Depicting Culture in the 1990s", *positions: east asia cultures critique*, vol. 4, no. 1, 1996, pp. 127–43.

"Chi Li: shensheng de fannao rensheng" (Chi Li: a sacred distressful life), *Literary Review*, no. 6, 1995, pp. 50–61.

"Xu Kun: xixi zhushen" (Xu Kun: playing with gods and spirits), *Shanhua* (Pediment), no. 1, 1996, pp. 66–70.

"Wuzhong fengjing: chudu diliu dai dianying" (Five landscapes: a first reading of Sixth Generation Films), *Tianya* (Horizons), no. 1, 1996, pp. 32–47.

"Gerenhua xiezuo yu qingchun gushi" (Individualized writings and youth stories), *Dianying yishu* (Film art), no. 3, 1996, pp. 10–12.

"Yijiu jiuwu nian Zhongguo dianying beiwang" (Memorandum of Chinese film in 1995), *Zhongguo wenhua lanpi shu* (The blue papers of Chinese culture), pp. 255–79 (Guilin: Lijiang chubanshe, 1996).

"Qiyu yu tuwei: jiushi niandai nüxing xiezuo" (Adventures and breaking out of

270 CINEMA AND DESIRE

traps: female writings in the 1990s), *Literary Review*, no. 5, 1996, pp. 95–102. Also in *Xinhua wenzhai* (New China digest), no. 1, 1997, pp. 125–9.
"Xiangxiang de huaijiu" (Imaginary nostalgia), *Tianya* (Horizons), no. 1, 1997, pp. 3–12. Also in *Boundary 2* 24, no. 3, 1997, pp. 143–61.
"Wenhua dixing tu ji qita" (Cultural typography and miscellaneous notes), *Dushu* (Reading), no. 2, 1997, pp. 7–12.
"Pintu youxi: *Huacheng* 1996" (A puzzle game: *Flower City* 1996), *Huacheng* (Flower city), no. 3, 1997, pp. 199–208.
"Zhizhe xue: yuedu Wang Xiaobo" (Wiseman's jocosity: reading Wang Xiaobo), *Dangdai zuojia pinglun* (Contemporary writers review), no. 2, 1998, pp. 21–34.
"Fenxiang xiyue: yuedu *Choujiao dengchang*" (Sharing pleasure: reading *The Clown's Entry*), *Huacheng* (Flower city), no. 4, 1998, pp. 197–207.
"Jingxiang huilang zhong de minzu shenfen" (National identity in the corridor of mirrored images), *Guangzhou wenyi* (Guangzhou literature & art), no. 6, 1998, pp. 52–9.
"Ziwo chanrao de mihuan huayuan: yuedu Xu Xiaobin" (The illusory garden of self-entanglement: reading Xu Xiaobin), *Dangdai zuojia pinglun* (Contemporary writers review), no. 1, 1999, pp. 17–35.
"Jianzheng yu jianzheng ren" (Witness and eyewitness), *Dushu* (Reading), no. 3, 1999, pp. 10–17.
"Yinxing shuxie: jiushi niandai dazhong wenhua de zhengzhi xue" (Invisible writing : the politics of Chinese mass culture in the 1990s), *Tianya* (Horizons), no. 2, 1999, pp. 37–51. Also published as "Invisible Writing: The politics of Chinese Mass Culture in the 1990s", *Modern Chinese Literature and Culture* 11, no. 1, 1999, pp. 31–60.
"Binghai chenchuan: Zhongguo dianying 1998" (The sunken ship in ice sea: mainland film 1998), *Huacheng* (Flower city), no. 3, 1999, pp. 112–26. Also in *Dangdai Zhongguo dianying* (Contemporary Chinese cinema:1998), edited by Huang Wulan, pp. 235–51 (Taipei: Shibao chuban gongsi, 1999).

Translated by Wang Chang

Works used for this book

Bai Fengxi, "Fengyu guren lai" (An old friend), *Bai Fengxi juzuo xuan* (Selected plays of Bai Fengxi) (Beijing: Zhongguo xiju chubanshe, 1988), pp. 83–160.
Brontë, Charlotte, *Jane Eyre* (Edinburgh: J. Grant, 1924).

Cao Guilin, *Beijingren zai Niuyue* (Beijinger in New York) (Beijing: Wenlian chuban gongsi, 1991).

Cao Xueqin, *Hong lou meng* (Dream of the red chamber) (Beijing: Renmin wenxue chubanshe, 1957), pp. 331–2.

Chen Kaige, "Qin guoren" (The people of the kingdom of Qin), *Dangdai dianying* (Contemporary cinema), no. 4, 1985, pp. 101–7.

Chen Shunxin, Preface and "Nuxing zhuyi piping yu zhongguo dangdai wenxue yanjiu" (Feminist criticism and contemporary Chinese literary studies), *Zhongguo dangdai wenxuede xushi yu xingbie* (Narrative and gender in China's contemporary literature) (Beijing: Beijing daxue chubanshe, 1995), pp. 22; 87–8.

Dai Jinhua, "Wenhua dixingtu ji qita" (Cultural geography and miscellaneous notes), *Dushu* (Reading), no. 3, 1997, pp. 7–12.

—— "Redemption and Consumption", *positions: east asia cultures critique*, no. 1, vol. 4, 1996, pp. 127–43.

—— "Qingchun zhi ge: lishi shiyuzhong de chongdu" (Song of youth: an historicized rereading), *Dianying lilun yu piping shouce* (Film theory and handbook of criticism) (Beijing: Keji wenxian chubanshe, 1993), pp. 199–217.

—— "Xieta: chongdu disidai" (The slanted tower: rereading the Fourth Generation), *Dianying lilun yu piping shouce* (Film theory and handbook of criticism) (Beijing: Keji wenxian chubanshe, 1993), pp. 8–12.

—— "Invisible Writing: The Politics of Mass Culture in the 1990s", *Modern Chinese Literature* 11, no. 1, 1999, pp. 31–60.

Dai Jinhua, et al, "Xin shi pipan shu" (The ten new critiques), *Zhongshan* (Bell mountain), no. 2, 1994, pp. 185–203.

Gilbert, Sandra, M., and Susan Gubar, eds, *The Madwoman in the Attic: The Woman Writer and the Nineteenth Century Literary Imagination* (New Haven: Yale University Press, 1979); *Nuquan zhuyi wenxue lilun* (Feminist literary theory), trans. Hu Min, Chen Caixia and Lin Shuming (Changsha: Hunan renmin wenyi chubanshe, 1989).

Haiwai liaowang wencong (Overseas Watching Series), edited by Yi Shu (Hefei: Anhui renmin chubanshe, 1996).

Henderson, Brian, "The Searchers: An American Dilemma", *Movies and Methods: An Anthology*, edited by Bill Nichols (Berkeley: University of California Press, 1976), pp. 429–58, trans. Dai Jinhua, "Suosuozhe – yige meiguo de kunjing", *Dangdai dianying* (Contemporary film), no. 4, 1987, pp. 65–80.

Hong Juan, "Yi pingdeng de xintai shuxie xingbie: fang xuezhe Dai Jinhua" (Writing gender with a balanced mentality: interviews with Dai Jinhua), *Zhonghua dushu bao* (Chinese Readers' newspaper), February 1996, no. 2.

Hu Lancheng, *Jinsheng jinshi* (This life, this cycle), vol. 2 (Taipei: Sansan Books, 1990).

Kristeva, Julia, *About Chinese Women* (New York: Marion Boyars, 1974).

de Lauretis, Teresa, "Cong mengzhong nü tanqi" (Opening the discussion with women in a dream), trans. Wang Xiaowen, *Dangdai dianying* (Contemporary film), no. 6, 1988, pp. 13, 38–47.

Li Xiao, "Shanguang de jinshi: Weinisi dianying jie jian jie" (Shining golden lion: an introduction to the Venice Film Festival), *Film World*, no. 3, 1994, pp. 11–12.

Li Yiming, "After the Act of Patricide", *Dianying yishu* (Film art), no. 6, 1989, pp. 9–18.

Liu Kang, "Subjectivity, Marxism and Cultural Theory in China", *Politics, Ideology and Literary Discourse in Modern China*, edited by Liu Kang and Xiaobing Tang (Durham: Duke University Press, 1993), pp. 23–55.

Liu Xiaofeng, "Guanyu 'siwu' yidai de shehuixue sikao zhaji" (A collection of sociological thoughts on the May Fourth generation), *Dushu* (Reading), no. 5, 1989, pp. 35–43.

Long Yusheng, ed., *Tang Song mingjian cixuan* (Anthology of Tang and Song verses) (Shanghai: Shanghai guji chubanshe, 1980).

Ma Shutian, "Daojiao zhushen" (Daoist gods), *Huaxia zhushen* (Gods of China) (Beijing: Yanshan chubanshe, 1990), pp. 265–79.

Mao Zedong, "Lun lianhe zhengfu" (On the united government), *Mao Zedong xuanji disijuan* (Selected Works of Mao Zedong), 4th ed. (Beijing: Renmin chubanshe, 1960), pp. 1029–1100.

—— "Zai zhongguo gongchan dangquanguo xuanchuan gongzuo huiyi shang de jianghua" (A talk at the Chinese Communist Party Conference on National Propaganda), *Mao Zedong xuanji* (Selected works of Mao Zedong), 5th ed. (Beijing: Renmin chubanshe, 1977), pp. 406, 433–48.

—— *Mao Zedong sixiang shengli wansui* (Long live Mao Zedong thought) (Beijing: Renmin chubanshe, 1969).

—— "Datui zichan jieji youpei de changkuang jingong" (Beat back the attacks of the bourgeois rightists), edited by the Editorial Committee for Documentation of the Central Committee of CCP, *Mao Zedong xuanji* (Selected works of Mao Zedong), 5th ed. (Beijing: Renmin chubanshe, 1977), pp. 471–86.

—— "Jianding de xiangxin qunzhong de daduoshu" (Resolutely believing the masses), *Mao Zedong xuanji* (Selected works of Mao Zedong), 5th ed. (Beijing: Renmin chubanshe, 1977), pp. 487–550.

Meng Yue and Li Yijian, *Benwen de celue* (Textual strategies) (Guangzhou: Huacheng chubanshe, 1988).

Mo Yan, "Reflections on the film *Red Sorghum*", *Dangdai dianying* (Contemporary film), no. 2, 1988, pp. 53–4.

Mulvey, Laura, "Visual Pleasure and Narrative Cinema", *Narrative, Apparatus, Ideology: A Film Reader* (New York: Columbia University Press, 1986), pp. 198–209.

Ni Zhen, "Hou wudai de bufa" (The marching of the post–Fifth Generation), *Dazhong dianying* (Popular film), no. 4, 1988, p. 11.

Ning Dai, "*Beijing Bastards* Plot Briefing", *Dianying gushi* (Film story), no. 5, 1993, p. 9; color plates 2–3.

Rayns, Tony, "Future: Astounding!", supplement to *Sight and Sound*, 1992, pp. 10–11, trans. by Li Yuanyi, "Qianjing lingren Zhenjing!", *Dianying gushi*, (Cinema story), no. 4, 1993, p. 11.

Shen Deqian, ed., "Song of Mulan", *Gushi yuan* (Source of ancient verse) (Beijing: Zhonghua shuju, 1963), pp. 326–7.

Shen Fu, *Fusheng liu ji* (Six records of a floating life), edited by Yu Pingbo (Beijing: Renmin wenxue chubanshe, 1980), trans. Leonard Pratt and Chiang Su-hui (New York: Penguin, 1983).

Su Su, *Qian shi jin sheng* (Previous life, this life) (Shanghai: Shanghai wenyi chubanshe, 1997).

Wang Gan, "Shixing de fuhuo: lun xin zhuang tai" (Resurrection of the poetic: on the new human condition), *Zhongshan* (Bell mountain), no. 4, 1994, pp. 96–114; no. 5, 1994, pp. 179–88.

Wang, Jing, *High Culture Fever: Politics, Aesthetics, and Ideology in Deng's China* (Berkeley: University of California Press, 1996).

Wu Wenguang, "A Roundtable on New Urban Cinema", *Dangdai Dianying* (Contemporary cinema), no. 5, 1994.

—— *Longxie Shu* (Dragon blood tree) (Hong Kong: Tiandi Pub. Co., 1992).

Xiao Yin, "Kua yang caifang zhaji" (Random records of interviews abroad), *Kuayue dayangde gong'an – manhadun de zhongguo nüren zhengyi shi lu* (A case of crossing the Atlantic: the controversy of *The Chinese Lady in Manhattan*), edited by Xiao Yin, Yi Ren et al. (Beijing: Guangming ribao chubanshe, 1993), pp. 29, 8–9.

Xie Mian and Zhang Yiwu, "Entering New Space", *The Great Transition: Research Topics in the Post-New Era Culture* (Harbin: Heilongjiang jiaoyu chubanshe, 1995), pp. 46–7.

Xie Yuan, "Ta jiao Chen Kaige" (His name is Chen Kaige), *Dangdai Dianying* (Contemporary cinema), no. 1, 1993, pp. 84–90.

Xu Yuanzhong, *Song of the Immortals: An Anthology of Classical Chinese Poetry* (Beijing: Xinshi chubanshe, 1994).

Yang Ping, "A Director who wanted to change the audience: an interview with young director Tian Zhuangzhuang", *Dazhong dianying*, no. 9, 1986, p. 4.

You Zunming, "Qianwan buyao wudao dalu qingnian" (Please don't misguide mainland youths), *Kuayue dayangde gong'an: Manhadun de Zhongguo nüren zhengyi shi lu* (A case of crossing the Atlantic: the controversy of *The Chinese Lady in Manhattan*) (Beijing: Guangming ribao chubanshe, 1993), pp. 78–9.

Zhang Ling, "Waiguoren yanzhong de Zhang Yimou" (A foreign perspective of Zhang Yimou), *Dianying pinglun* (Film review), no. 3, 1993, pp. 9–10.

Zhang Xudong, "Cultural Discourse", *Chinese Modernism: In the Era of Reforms* (Durham: Duke University Press, 1997), pp. 35–99.

—— "Filic language and the Hiistorical Object: On the New Chinese Films", *Dianying yishu* (Film Art), no. 5, 1989.

Zhang Yiwu, "Xin zhuangtai de jueqi" (The rise of the new human condition), *Zhongshan* (Bell mountain), no. 5, 1994, pp. 114–19.

—— *Cong xiandaixing dao houxiandaixing* (From modernity to post-modernity) (Nanning: Guangxi jiaoyu chubanshe, 1997).

—— "Hou xinshiqi Zhongguo dianying: fen lie de tiaozhan" (Post–New Era Chinese film: the challenge of fragmentation), *Dangdai dianying* (Contemporary cinema), no. 5, 1994, pp. 4–11.

Zhao Yuan, *Di zhi zi: Xiangcun xiaoshuo yu nongmin wenhua* (The son of the earth: rural fiction and peasant culture) (Beijing: Shiyue wenyi chubanshe, 1993).

Zheng Dongtian, "Congqian you kuai hong tudi" (Once there was a piece of red earth), *Dangdai dianying* (Contemporary cinema), no. 1, 1988, pp. 69–72.

Zheng, Xianghong, "Duli yingren zai xingdong: suowei Beijing 'dixia dianying' zhenxiang", *Dianying gushi* (Cinema story), no. 5, 1993, pp. 4–7.

—— "Zhang Yuan fangtan lu" (Interview with Zhang Yuan), *Dianying gushi* (Cinema story), no. 5, 1994, pp. 8–9.

—— "Gangtie shi zheyang lianchengde: Tian zhuangzhuang tuichu diliudai daoyan" (How the steel is made: Tian Zhuangzhuang promoting the Sixth Generation directors), *Dianying gushi* (Cinema story), no. 5, 1995, pp. 16–18.

Zheng Yefu, *Daijia lun: yige shehuixue xin shijiao* (The cost of argument: a new sociological perspective) (Beijing: Sanlian shudian, 1995).

Zhou Li, "Wo kongsu, cengjing canghai nanwei shui, wo haishi wo" (I protest through all the changes, I am still I myself), *Kongsu Beijing guangbo dianshibao* (Denouncing Beijing Television Report), 7 Jan. 1993, p. 74.

Zhou Yaqin, Interview with Dai Jinhua, Beijing University, 29 Sept. 1997.

Zhu Jian, *Wumian yinghou Ruan Lingyu* (Ruan Lingyu, the crownless queen of actresses) (Lanzhou: Lanzhou daxue chubanshe, 1997).

Zhu Ma, ed., *Dianying shouce* (Notebooks on cinema) (Chengdu: Sichuan daxue zhongwen xi, 1980).

Zong Li and Liu Qun, *Zhongguo minjian zhushen* (Chinese folk gods) (Shijiazhuang: Hebei renmin chubanshe, 1986).

Notes on the Translators

Wang Chang is an undergraduate student at the Department of History of Arts, University of Illinois. His research interests include contemporary Chinese arts and film.

Eileen Cheng is a graduate student at the East Asian Languages and Cultures Department, University of California, Los Angeles. Her research is focused on the relationship between gender, fiction, and nationhood in the late Qing and modern China.

Lau Kin Chi at Lingnan University, Hong Kong, teaches comparative literature, gender, and cultural politics, and contemporary Chinese literature and society. She is also the Chairperson of the Executive Board of Asian Regional Exchange for New Alternatives (ARENA).

Kirk Denton is associate professor of Chinese literature at Ohio State University. He is the editor of the journal *Modern Chinese Literature and Culture*, the author of *The Problematic of Self in Modern Chinese Literature: Hu Feng and Lu Ling* (1998), and the editor of *Modern Chinese Literary Thought: Writings on Literature: 1893–1945* (1996).

Edward Gunn teaches Chinese literature and related topics at Cornell University. His most recent book is *Rewriting Chinese: Style and Innovation in Twentieth-Century Chinese Literature* (1991). He is currently studying the use of local languages in Chinese media.

Harry H. Kuoshu teaches at Cinema Studies Program in Northeastern University in Boston. He is the author of *Lightness of Being in China: Adaptation and Discursive Figuration in Cinema and Theater* (1999).

Jonathan Noble is a doctoral candidate in the Department of East Asian Languages and Literatures at the Ohio State University. His research interests include contemporary Chinese drama, fiction, and film.

Lisa Rofel is associate professor at the Department of Anthropology of the University of California at Santa Cruz. She teaches about contemporary China, gender studies, and cultural theory. She is the author of *Other Modernities: Gendered Yearnings in China after Socialism* (1999).

Shu-mei Shih teaches twentieth-century Chinese literature and cinema from Taiwan, China, and Hong Kong, Asian American literature, and literary theory at University of California, Los Angeles. She is the author of *The Lure of the Modern: Writing Modernism in Semicolonial China* (2000).

Hu Ying teaches Chinese literature at University of California, Irvine. She is the author of *Tales of Translation: Composing the New Woman in Late Qing China* (2000).

Yiman Wang is a Ph.D. candidate in the Program in Literature of Duke University. Her academic interests include comparative literature and Chinese film studies with special focus on the discursive, cinematic construction of women.

Jingyuan Zhang teaches modern Chinese literature and film in the Department of East Asian Languages and Cultures, as well as in Women's Studies and Comparative Literature at Georgetown University. She is the author of *Psychoanalysis in China: Literary Transformation, 1919–1949* (1992).

Index

Hua Mulan 8, 102, 104–6, 111, 134,
    152–60, 255
Huang Shuqin 8–9, 133, 142; *The
    Black Cannon Incident* 21; *Human,
    Woman, Demon* as feminist film 8,
    143, 153–68

Jianjun *see* He Jianjun

Lacan, Jacques, Lacanian analysis 3–4
Lao Gui, *Blood-Red Sunset* 181–3
Li Chunbo, "Xiaofang" 185–7
Li Shaohong 133; *Bloody Morning*
    136; *Blush* 137
Literature, and class division 231–2;
    diaspora 189, 193, 195; educated
    youth 179–83; reading 9, 257–8;
    see also film, culture
Liu Miaomiao 133
Lou Ye, *Bewitching Girl* 96–7; *Weekend
    Sweetheart* 75, 93, 95
Lu Xun, *Diary of a Madman* 15

Manhattan, as symbol of the West
    195–6
Mao Zedong 8, 15, 214–15;
    bestsellers on 174–8; era of
    120–22, 124, 134, 137; portrait of
    172, 173–4; sayings of 99, 176–8;
    veneration of 175, 178
Mao Zedong Fever 9, 172–8, 216
Marxism 1, 3, 225, 248, 252 *see also*
    feminism
May Fourth movement 15, 16, 51–2,
    99, 123, 214–15, 242
Meng Yue 2; and Dai Jinhua,
    Emerging on the Horizon of History 3
modernity 3, 71; and film history
    249–51
modernization in China, 49, 243 *see
    also* urbanization
MTV 81, 83, 95

nation, as patriarchal power 112

nationalism 226
New China 2, 99, 104, 175; film of
    101–2, 132
New Rich 221, 23, 229–30
nostalgia, for Cultural Revolution
    184–5, 216

orientalism 3, 90, 91, 253

Postcolonialism 4, 5–7, 92, 253
Postmodernism, Chinese 73, 221; of
    1990's culture 49, 71, 92, 199, 219
Poststructuralism 2, 249, 252

Qin Xianglian 102, 104
Qui Cuiling, *Married to Black Africa*
    193–4
Quan Yanchi, *Mao Zedong off the
    Altar* 174–6

race, racial prejudice 197–9, 204–6
Red Guards 15,17, 87, 215
Ruan Lingyu 109

Seventeen-Year Era 7; literature of
    113, 135
Shi Jian 86; *I've Graduated* 75, 87
Sixth Generation directors 4, 72,
    74–5, 80, 90–96, 190; avant-garde
    position of 84–5; critical
    discourses of 75–6; Dai Jinhua's
    denial of 77–8; and 90's culture
    93; reception of by European
    circuits 89–90
socialism, socialist ideology 225,
    232–3, 242
Sons, *see* Fathers and Sons
Sun Zhou, *Add a Little Sugar to the
    Coffee* 44–5, 82

taotuo zhong de tuowang ("fleeing
    from one trap while falling into
    another") 6, 22–3, 30, 50, 53, 59,
    65